Best Hikes Near
Breckenridge and Vail

HELP US KEEP THIS GUIDE UP TO DATE

Every effort has been made by the author and editors to make this guide as accurate and useful as possible. However, many things can change after a guide is published—trails are rerouted, regulations change, techniques evolve, facilities come under new management, and so on.

We would appreciate hearing from you concerning your experiences with this guide and how you feel it could be improved and kept up to date. While we may not be able to respond to all comments and suggestions, we'll take them to heart, and we'll also make certain to share them with the author. Please send your comments and suggestions to the following address:

GPP
Reader Response/Editorial Department
PO Box 480
Guilford, CT 06437

Or you may e-mail us at: editorial@globepequot.com

Thanks for your input, and happy trails!

Best Hikes Near
Breckenridge and Vail

MARYANN GAUG

FALCONGUIDES

GUILFORD, CONNECTICUT
HELENA, MONTANA

AN IMPRINT OF GLOBE PEQUOT PRESS

**This book is dedicated to Keith Brown, my best friend
for over forty years.**

FALCONGUIDES®

FalconGuides is an imprint of Globe Pequot Press.
Falcon, FalconGuides, and Outfit Your Mind are registered trademarks of Morris Book Publishing, LLC.

All photos by Maryann Gaug

Maps: DesignMaps Inc. © Morris Book Publishing, LLC
Text design: Sheryl P. Kober
Project editor: Julie Marsh
Layout: Melissa Evarts

   Library of Congress Cataloging-in-Publication Data
Gaug, Maryann.
  Best hikes near Breckenridge and Vail / Maryann Gaug. -- First edition.
    pages cm
  Includes index.
  ISBN 978-0-7627-8076-1
1. Hiking—Colorado—Breckenridge Region—Guidebooks. 2. Hiking—Colorado—Vail Region—Guidebooks. 3. Breckenridge Region (Colo.)—Guidebooks. 4. Vail Region (Colo.)—Guidebooks.
I. Title.
  GV199.42.C62B7434 2014
  796.5109788—dc23
                                                        2014014818
Printed in the United States of America

10 9 8 7 6 5 4 3 2 1

Contents

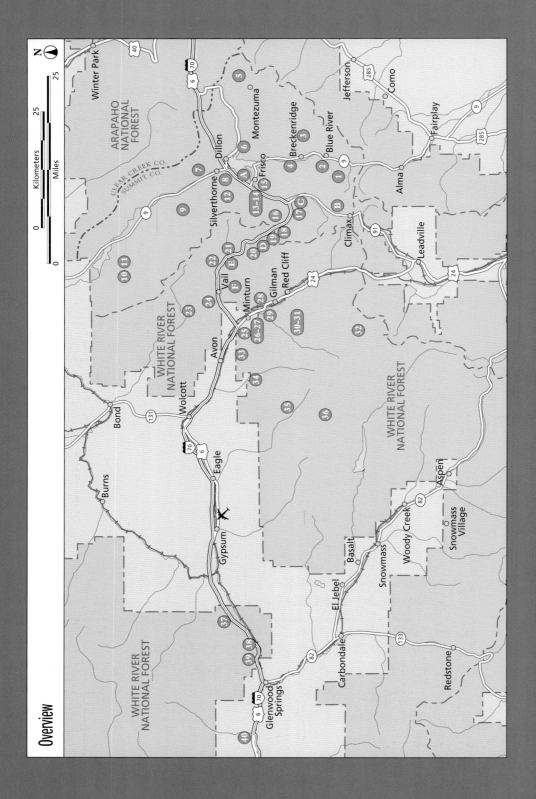

Overview

View of the Gore Range from the Lenawee Trail (hike 5)

Acknowledgments

Many thanks to all of my contacts in the USDA Forest Service, the Bureau of Land Management, and the Towns of Dillon, Breckenridge, Vail, and Glenwood Springs for working with me on which trails would be most appropriate for this book. Despite the "big brother" image that federal and public employees often have, these people love the backcountry and were eager to answer questions, review the chapters, and provide feedback. Thanks to Jaci Spuhler of the Eagle County Library for researching several of my questions. In the Colorado Historic Newspapers Collection, I found interesting information on the area in old newspaper articles written between 1859 and 1923 (www.coloradohistoricnewspapers.org). I researched the history of the Eagles Nest, Ptarmigan Peak, and Holy Cross Wildernesses in the Denver Public Library's Western History Collection (www.history.denverlibrary.org). Several people at the Summit Historical Society and Breckenridge Heritage Alliance answered various questions about Breckenridge's mining history.

Because I typically hike the trails by myself, thanks to my best friend, Keith Brown, who anxiously awaited my phone calls that I was safe and not lost in the woods.

Special gratitude to my mom and my dad, for encouraging me to do what I want to do and strive for peace and happiness.

Last but not least, thanks to you—readers and fellow hikers—for buying *Best Hikes Near Breckenridge and Vail.* I hope you find it useful and interesting, and may you enjoy many hours hiking the trails described between these covers.

Paintbrush and Shrine Ridge Trail (hike 19)

Introduction

Rugged peaks reflected in high mountain lakes, sparkling streams tumbling through flower-filled meadows, high ridges where the view is forever, and a rich mining history make the country around Breckenridge and Vail a hiking gem. Today's hiking trails may have started when Native Americans followed game trails for their summer hunts. Miners scoured the area hoping to strike it rich after gold was found in the region's creeks. Railroads followed to move ore and bring supplies. Settlers arrived and worked the land, living here year-round through beautiful summers and snowy, cold winters.

I love hiking through the various ecosystems of this area in which I live, from Gambel oak–filled canyons near Glenwood Springs to colorful meadows to clear lakes reflecting pointy peaks to the high alpine tundra with views of mountains

South Willow Creek Falls (hike 8)

as far as the eye can see. Hiking to a lake then relaxing along its shores while listening to a chorus of birds is a great way to spend a day or weekend! Along the way you may see pine squirrels busily caching cones for the sure-to-be-long winter, deer browsing in meadows, or elk sunning themselves while chewing their cud in a high valley. Ospreys and eagles soar in the clear blue Colorado sky. Along the trails a colorful carpet of wildflowers graces every nook and cranny, attracting bees and other pollinators during the short summer. Although seldom seen, black bears and mountain lions patrol the area, while moose munch on willows in wetlands. Little cascading rivulets born in high snowfields join together to create creeks that wind and tumble to the river in the valley below.

Some trails take me back to the mining boom days of the late 1800s. Only a few logs remain of cabins that once shared the happy times and sad tribulations of their owners. A mound of dirt and rocks by a hole in the ground is all that remains of a miner's dream.

Today the mining boom has gone bust, but Summit County (Breckenridge), Eagle County (Vail), and Garfield County (Glenwood Springs) are booming with recreation highlighted by seven ski areas, seven Nordic centers, several reservoirs, gold-medal trout streams, and hundreds of miles of trails in the White River National Forest and Bureau of Land Management (BLM) lands. For a more remote and primitive hiking experience, hikers can spend many hours exploring three congressionally designated wilderness areas: Eagles Nest, Ptarmigan Peak, and Holy Cross. The towns of Dillon, Breckenridge, and Vail own open-space parcels with hiking trails that lead to beautiful overlooks, back into mining history, or around special natural areas.

The forty hikes in this guidebook are within an hour's drive of either Breckenridge or Vail. Most lie within 30 miles of I-70. I chose these trails to take you on a hiking tour of the areas around Breckenridge, Vail, and down through Glenwood Springs. Several easier trails are listed in the Honorable Mentions.

Leave No Trace skills have become very important to the preservation of Colorado's wildlands and parks as the population grows and increasing numbers of visitors discover our magnificent state. We need to think about thousands of feet instead of just our own.

The trails described in this book are located at high elevation. The lowest trailhead is at 5,680 feet, and most hikes start at over 8,000 feet. The high point is the shelter at 13,077 feet on Notch Mountain. Hikes range from easy to strenuous, from a 2.4-mile loop around Lower Cataract Lake to overnight backpacks.

High elevation and winter snowpack means trails can be covered by snow into July. Hikers should check with the listed land management agency for current trail conditions.

Here are some guidelines as to approximate times when trails dry out (from the USDA Forest Service Dillon Ranger District).

Below 9,500 feet—mid-May

Between 9,500 and 10,000 feet—end of May

Between 10,000 and 10,500 feet—mid-June

Between 10,500 and 11,500 feet—July 1

11,500 feet and above—mid-July

Speaking of winter, when the snow flies, you can still continue to enjoy the backcountry on foot, snowshoes, or cross-country skis. Several trails are popular year-round and are often packed by many feet, so snowshoes are not necessary except after a large snowfall. I use Yaktrax on my boots for extra traction (www .yaktrax.com). These easy-to-slip-on coils provide great traction on firm snow and icy patches.

Hiking is a great way to explore your surroundings and use all five senses to enjoy your journey. While walking around our public lands, you may learn a lot about yourself. Away from the motorized, mechanized, and electronic world, you may discover more about what your body needs, how strong you are both mentally and physically, or how little you know about the world around you. Hiking provides each of us many opportunities to grow and become more alive.

If you enjoy hiking, consider volunteering for trail work at least one day each year. None of the land management agencies have huge budgets, so more and more they are relying on volunteers to help with basic trail work. A sampling of volunteer trail groups is listed in the back of the book. You'll meet some really great

Upper Piney River Falls (hike 23)

Flower field and Mount of the Holy Cross (hike 19)

folks and gain the satisfaction of a job well done at the end of the day. One friend commented how much fun she had showing people the bridge she helped build.

A word about the details in this book: Trail mileage is as much an art as a science, even for land managers. I used a Global Positioning System (GPS) to obtain the mileage. In some areas poor satellite reception may have provided less than accurate information. Please realize that trail locations and conditions, roads, and signage are subject to change over time. Even trailheads can move, and some trails are rerouted to prevent environmental damage. Finding accurate historical information also was sometimes interesting when different books contained conflicting information! I tried to find appropriate websites, only to discover URLs change rapidly.

Henry David Thoreau said, "In wildness is the preservation of the world." Aldo Leopold added years later: "When we see land as a community to which we belong, we may begin to use it with love and respect." My wish for you is to enjoy hiking and learn about yourself and the world around you, in which we all belong. Remember, only we can preserve wildlands for ourselves and for future generations.

As you hike around this beautiful region, capture part of nature's spirit and hold it close to your own, so that no matter where you travel or live, the peace and beauty of this wild country will remain with you forever.

Colorado Weather

Difficult to forecast and prone to change quickly, high country weather is a wonder in itself. Mountains often create their own weather. On the west slope of the Continental Divide where these hikes are located, weather may be entirely different than in the Denver metro area on the east side.

Hiking around Breckenridge and Vail is best from late June through early October. The trails near Glenwood Springs are great spring and fall hikes. I have noted trails that are hikable year-round or are popular for snowshoeing and cross-country skiing. Some trails disappear under winter's white mantle.

High country residents head to warmer climes during April and May for good reason—hiking is not very good! Snow still covers the trails, and you can sink in over your knees in the rotting snow even with snowshoes. When trails start to melt out, they can be quite muddy. If you do hike during "mud season," remember to get muddy—walk through the mud! Walking around muddy areas enlarges the size of the mess.

Summer attempts to begin in June, but winter's last gasp may still drop some snow. June is also the start of thunderstorm season. By July wildflowers bloom profusely. Be aware: Snowstorms do occur on the Fourth of July above 8,500 feet! Colorado experiences a monsoon season starting about mid-July and ending in early September. Afternoon thunderstorms are common. Two problems result from thunderstorm development. One is lightning, a killer from above; the second, more subtle, is rain. In Colorado rain tends to be cold, and unprepared hikers

Tenmile Range from the Ridge Trail (hike 6)

Trail through the boulder field and view of the Tenmile Range (hike 12)

can become hypothermic very quickly, even in midsummer. Monsoonal rains can last for several days in a row.

Fall can be the best time to hike, with "fall" meaning mid-August to mid-September above the trees and from September to about early October below treeline. Thunderstorms are less frequent, and the air is crisp and cool with dazzling blue skies. Aspen turn gold and red about the third week in September. By mid-October, snow tends to bring an end to most hiking in the high country.

Winter travel typically requires snowshoes or skis. If you travel on backcountry trails during winter, at a minimum take an avalanche awareness course. Colorado often leads the nation in avalanche deaths, with many occurring in Summit County! In spring and early summer, avalanches can still pose danger to hikers and climbers.

No matter the season, always bring layers of clothes and rain (or snow) gear. Check the local weather forecast before heading out. Weather changes quickly, and a temperature drop of 10°F to 20°F in one hour is not unheard of. Be prepared!

Flora and Fauna

The Breckenridge and Vail region contains the foothills (6,000 to 8,000 feet), montane (8,000 to 9,500 feet), subalpine (9,500 to 11,400 feet), and alpine (above 11,400 feet) life zones. Ecosystems, encompassing the physical environment and the organisms living within a given area, can vary within these zones.

Ecosystems include mountain shrublands, piñon-juniper woodlands, ponderosa pine and Douglas fir forests, mountain grasslands and meadows, mountain wetlands, lodgepole pine, aspen, Engelmann spruce and subalpine fir, limber and bristlecone pine, and alpine tundra. While hiking through these different environments, notice what plants and animals live where. For example, aspen grow in moist, protected areas. Bushes such as chokecherry, gooseberry, serviceberry, and snowberry provide browse for mule deer. Grasses and other plants offer good eats for elk, who also scrape the bark off aspen in winter. Black bears leave claw marks climbing their favorite aspen tree. Keep an ear open for the chick-a-dee-dee-dee song of the mountain or black-capped chickadee.

As you gain elevation, you can observe how animals and plants have adapted to shorter summers, less oxygen, wind, and colder temperatures. Above treeline you can't miss the little pikas scurrying around with mouthfuls of grasses and flowers or the lazy marmots sunning themselves on rocks. Chipmunks, ground squirrels, and marmots will almost attack you expecting a handout. Please don't feed them as they may not forage for themselves. Crows, magpies, blue Steller's jays with their black crowns, pesky Clark's nutcrackers, and gray jays (nicknamed "camp robbers") are easily spotted birds. Occasionally you might catch a glimpse of an eagle, osprey, or red-tailed hawk soaring above.

If normal or greater precipitation has occurred during summer, mushrooms pop out in August and early September. Many mushrooms are poisonous while others are incredibly delicious and edible. Don't eat any unless you know what you're doing!

Between the alpine tundra and spruce-fir or limber pine ecosystems, krummholz grow. These stunted trees, usually spruce, fir, or limber pine, form tree islands with a few flag trees sticking up. The deadwood on the windward side protects the rest of the tree organism, so please don't use it for firewood.

The most incredible plants grow above treeline: alpine forget-me-not, sky pilot, moss campion, old-man-of-the-mountain, alpine avens, and Parry's clover, to name a few. Each flower has its own particular niche, whether on windblown slopes or next to sheltering rocks. If you have a chance, learn about this incredible land above the trees and how you can protect it while hiking.

Black bears, mountain lions, and moose live in the area, and if surprised, they can get downright nasty. Even deer, elk, bighorn sheep, and mountain goats can pose problems, especially if they think their young are threatened. Remember, they've been here for many years, and we're treading on their territory.

Wilderness Restrictions/Regulations

Hikes featured in this book include trails in three wilderness areas: Eagles Nest, Ptarmigan Peak, and Holy Cross. If you plan to hike or backpack in one of these wildernesses, please contact the responsible USDA Forest Service office or www .fs.usda.gov/whiteriver (click on Special Places) for up-to-date information and regulations. Each chapter containing a wilderness hike lists some of the regulations for quick reference. For all three wildernesses, group size is limited to no more than fifteen people per group or a combination of twenty-five people and pack or saddle animals in any one group. All dogs must be on leash in the Eagles Nest and Ptarmigan Peak Wildernesses, while the Holy Cross Wilderness requires that all dogs be under control (i.e., uncontrolled dogs must be on leash). When backpacking in the Holy Cross Wilderness, one person in each party camping overnight must carry a valid wilderness use permit (free). Make sure to read regulations regarding campfires and camping, as each area has different rules and campfires are prohibited in some places.

Leave No Trace Principles

The member-driven Leave No Trace Center for Outdoor Ethics (LNT.org) teaches people how to enjoy the outdoors responsibly. This copyrighted information has been reprinted with the organization's permission.

Please understand and practice these principles on every hike and backpack.

- Plan Ahead and Prepare
- Travel and Camp on Durable Surfaces
- Dispose of Waste Properly
- Leave What You Find
- Minimize Campfire Impacts
- Respect Wildlife
- Be Considerate of Other Visitors

Leave No Weeds

Noxious weeds tend to outcompete (overtake) our native flora, which in turn affects animals and birds that depend on them for food. Noxious weeds can be harmful to wildlife. Just like birds and furry critters, humans can carry weed seed from one place to another. Here are a couple of things hikers can do to minimize the spread of noxious weeds: First, learn to identify noxious weeds and exotic species. The Colorado Weed Management Association (www.cwma .org) is a good source of information. Second, regularly clean your boots, tents, packs, hiking poles, and vehicles of mud and seeds. Brush your dog, horse, goat, or llama to remove any weed seed. Avoid camping and traveling in weed-infested areas.

Getting Around
Cell Phones and GPS Units
A word of caution: Cell phone coverage is lacking on many trails and even state highways in this book. On a few hikes, drainages are narrow and GPS units have trouble connecting with enough satellites for good readings.

Area Codes
Breckenridge, Vail, Glenwood Springs, and nearby towns use area code 970.

Roads
For current information on road conditions, construction, travel alerts, and current weather, contact the Colorado Department of Transportation (CDOT) at their toll-free hot line (877) 315-7623 or 511 on your cell phone (Colorado only). The same information can also be found by visiting CDOT's website at www.cotrip .org. You can download CDOT's mobile app.

Local Public Transportation
Generally speaking, you will need a vehicle to reach the trailheads. If bus service is available, it is noted in the Finding the trailhead section.

Summit County has a free bus system, the Summit Stage, PO Box 2179, Frisco 80443; (970) 668-0999; www.summitstage.com.

Storm King Mountain (hike 40)

The town of Breckenridge has a free bus system, Town of Breckenridge Free Ride Transit System, 1105 Airport Rd., Breckenridge; (970) 547-3140; www.breck freeride.com.

The town of Vail has a free bus system, Vail Transportation Center, 241 E. Meadow Dr., Vail; (970) 479-2178; www.vailgov.com.

Eagle County Regional Transportation (ECO Transit) provides bus service around Eagle County, 3289 Cooley Mesa Rd., Gypsum; (970) 328-3520; www .eaglecounty.us/Transit/.

By Air

Denver International Airport (DIA) is 23 miles northeast of downtown Denver. For more information, contact its website at www.flydenver.com or call (303) 342-2000 or (800) 247-2336.

Eagle County Regional Airport (EGE) lies between Vail and Glenwood Springs. Contact them at (970) 328-2680 or www.eaglecounty.us/airport/.

Aspen Airport is located just north of the town of Aspen, south of Glenwood Springs. For information, call (970) 920-5380 or check out its website at www .aspenairport.com.

By Rail

Amtrak's California Zephyr stops in Glenwood Springs. For more details, call (800) 872-7245 or visit www.amtrak.com.

By Bus

Greyhound stops in Frisco, Vail, and Glenwood Springs. Call Greyhound at (800) 231-2222 or visit www.greyhound.com for more information.

Rosy paintbrush (hike 19)

How to Use This Guide

Take a close enough look, and you'll find that this guide contains just about everything you'll ever need to choose, plan for, and enjoy a hike near Breckenridge and Vail. Stuffed with useful area information, *Best Hikes Near Breckenridge and Vail* features forty mapped and cued hikes. Here's an outline of the book's major components:

Each section begins with an introduction to the region, in which you're given a sweeping look at the lay of the land. Each hike then starts with a short summary of the hike's highlights. These quick overviews give you a taste of the hiking adventures to follow. You'll learn about the trail terrain and what surprises each route has to offer.

Following the overview you'll find the hike specs: quick, nitty-gritty details of the hike. Most are self-explanatory, but here are some details on others:

Distance: The total distance of the recommended route—one way for loop hikes, the round-trip on an out-and-back or lollipop hike, point to point for a shuttle. Options are additional.

Hiking time: The time range it will take to cover the route depending on whether you hike quickly or stop to smell the roses. It is based on the total distance, elevation gain, and condition and difficulty of the trail. Your fitness level will also affect your time.

Difficulty: Each hike has been assigned a level of difficulty. The rating system was developed from several sources and personal experience. These levels are meant to be a guideline only and may prove easier or harder for different people depending on ability and physical fitness. The level includes reasons for the rating, including the elevation gain.

Easy—4 miles or less total trip distance in one day; elevation gain less than 600 feet; paved or smooth-surfaced dirt trail; less than a 6-percent grade average.

Moderate—Up to 8 miles total trip distance in one day; elevation gain of 600 to 1,200 feet; a 6- to 8-percent grade average.

Difficult—Up to 12 miles total trip distance in one day; elevation gain of 1,200 to 2,500 feet; an 8- to 10-percent grade average.

Most Difficult—Up to 16 miles total trip distance in one day; elevation gain of 2,500 to 3,500 feet; trail not well defined in places; a 10- to 15-percent grade average.

Strenuous—Mainly reserved for steep climbs; greater than 15-percent grade average.

Trail surface: General information about what to expect underfoot.

Best season: General information on the best time of year to hike.

Other trail users: Such as equestrians, mountain bikers, etc.

Canine compatibility: Know the trail regulations before you take your dog hiking with you. Dogs are not allowed on some trails in this book.

Land status: National forest, county open space, national park, wilderness, etc.

Fees and permits: Whether you need to carry any money with you for entrance fees and permits. Some hikes require a free self-issued permit if you are backpacking and camping overnight.

Maps: A list of other maps to supplement the maps in this book. USGS maps are the best source for accurate topographical information, but not necessarily the current trail alignment—if the trail is even shown on the map. Other commercially available maps that show topographical information are also listed. The trail locations on these maps are often more accurate than on USGS maps. Use both.

Trail contact(s): This is the location, phone number, and website URL for the local land management agency(ies) in charge of all the trails within the selected hike. Get trail access information before you head out, or contact the land manager after your visit if you see problems with trail erosion, damage, or misuse.

Other: Other information that will enhance your hike.

Special considerations: This section calls your attention to specific trail hazards, like a lack of water or hunting seasons.

The **Finding the trailhead** section gives you dependable driving directions from the closest exit on I-70 to where you'll want to park.

The Hike is the meat of the chapter. Detailed and honest, it's a carefully researched impression of the trail. It also includes area history, both natural and human.

Destination kettle pond reflecting Gore Range (hike 9)

Under **Miles and Directions,** mileage cues identify all turns and trail name changes, as well as points of interest. On many hikes, options are also given to make your journey shorter or longer depending on the amount of time you have.

Please note that the GPS coordinates are WGS84 datum, which work well on electronic

Golden-mantled ground squirrel

maps such as Google, but do not work with paper USGS or other topo maps, which are based on NAD27 CONUS. A quick and reasonably accurate trick to convert between units is to subtract 0.03 from the decimal part of the WGS84 west (W) coordinate. For example, if you have W106 13.09′ in WGS84, the NAD27 coordinate would be approximately W106 13.06′. This conversion will get you very close!

The **Hike Information** section provides information on local events and attractions, hiking tours, and hiking organizations.

Two of the regional sections end with **Honorable Mentions,** detailing some shorter and easier hikes that weren't included in the forty hikes. Be sure to hike these trails for fun. One hike is accessible via the gondola at Vail and another from a chairlift at Copper Mountain.

Don't feel restricted to the routes and trails that are mapped here. Be adventurous and use this guide as a platform to discover new routes for yourself. For your own purposes you may wish to copy the route directions onto a small sheet of paper to help you while hiking, or photocopy the map and cue sheet to take with you. Otherwise, just slip the whole book in your pack and take it all with you. Enjoy your time in the outdoors, and remember to pack out what you pack in.

How to Use the Maps

Overview map: This map (see page vi) shows the location of each hike in the area by hike number.

Route map: This is your primary guide to each hike. It shows all of the accessible roads and trails, points of interest, water, landmarks, and geographical features. It also distinguishes trails from roads, and paved roads from unpaved roads. The selected route is highlighted, and directional arrows point the way.

Trail Finder

Hike No.	Hike Name	Best Hikes for Back-packers	Best Hikes for Waterfalls	Best Hikes for Geology Lovers	Best Hikes for Children	Best Hikes for Dogs	Best Hikes for Great Views	Best Hikes for Lake Lovers	Best Hikes for Canyons	Best Hikes for History Buffs
1	McCullough Gulch Trail		●			●		●		●
2	Mohawk Lakes		●			●		●		●
3	Minnie Mine Loop				●					●
4	Iowa Hill				●					●
5	Lenawee Trail						●			●
6	Dillon Nature Preserve				●		●			
7	Ptarmigan Peak						●			
8	South Willow Creek Falls		●							
9	Kettle Ponds			●						
10	Eaglesmere Lakes	●						●		
11	Lower Cataract Lake		●		●			●		
12	Buffalo Mountain						●			
13	Lily Pad Lake				●			●		

Trail Finder

Hike No.	Hike Name	Best Hikes for Backpackers	Best Hikes for Waterfalls	Best Hikes for Geology Lovers	Best Hikes for Children	Best Hikes for Dogs	Best Hikes for Great Views	Best Hikes for Lake Lovers	Best Hikes for Canyons	Best Hikes for History Buffs
14	Meadow Creek Trail						●			
15	Masontown/Mount Royal						●			●
16	Wheeler Lakes	●						●		
17	Guller Creek Trail	●				●				●
18	Wilder Gulch Trail				●	●				●
19	Shrine Ridge Trail			●			●			
20	Bowman's Shortcut Trail						●			
21	Gore Lake	●				●	●	●		●
22	Booth Lake	●	●	●			●	●		
23	Upper Piney River Falls		●							
24	North Trail					●	●			
25	Meadow Mountain					●	●			●
26	Grouse Lake	●						●		

Trail Finder

Hike No.	Hike Name	Best Hikes for Backpackers	Best Hikes for Waterfalls	Best Hikes for Geology Lovers	Best Hikes for Children	Best Hikes for Dogs	Best Hikes for Great Views	Best Hikes for Lake Lovers	Best Hikes for Canyons	Best Hikes for History Buffs
27	West Grouse Creek Trail					●				
28	Two Elk National Recreation Trail				●					
29	Cross Creek Trail	●		●						
30	Notch Mountain			●			●			●
31	Lake Constantine	●						●		
32	Missouri Lakes		●	●				●		
33	Beaver Lake							●		
34	East Lake Creek Trail	●				●				
35	Lake Charles					●	●	●		
36	Mount Thomas		●	●		●	●			
37	Hanging Lake			●				●	●	
38	Grizzly Creek Trail					●			●	
39	Jess Weaver Trail					●			●	
40	Storm King Memorial Trail									●

Trail Ratings

Easy
- 6 Dillon Nature Preserve
- 11 Lower Cataract Lake

Moderate
- 3 Minnie Mine Loop
- 4 Iowa Hill
- 8 South Willow Creek Falls
- 9 Kettle Ponds
- 13 Lily Pad Lake
- 15 Masontown only
- 17 Guller Creek Trail
- 18 Wilder Gulch Trail
- 19 Shrine Ridge Trail
- 20 Bowman's Shortcut Trail
- 23 Upper Piney River Falls
- 24 North Trail
- 29 Cross Creek Trail
- 31 Lake Constantine
- 34 East Lake Creek Trail

Difficult
- 1 McCullough Gulch Trail
- 2 Mohawk Lakes
- 5 Lenawee Trail
- 10 Eaglesmere Lakes
- 14 Meadow Creek Trail
- 16 Wheeler Lakes
- 25 Meadow Mountain
- 27 West Grouse Creek Trail
- 28 Two Elk National Recreation Trail
- 32 Missouri Lakes
- 33 Beaver Lake
- 35 Lake Charles
- 36 Mount Thomas
- 38 Grizzly Creek Trail
- 39 Jess Weaver Trail
- 40 Storm King Memorial Trail

Most Difficult
- 7 Ptarmigan Peak
- 15 Mount Royal
- 21 Gore Lake
- 22 Booth Lake
- 26 Grouse Lake
- 30 Notch Mountain

Strenuous
- 12 Buffalo Mountain
- 37 Hanging Lake

Map Legend

Transportation

═(70)═	Freeway/Interstate Highway
═(422)═	US Highway
═(82)═	State Highway
───────	Paved/Improved Road
═(90)═	County Road
═[FR851]═	Forest Road
= = = =	Unpaved Road
┼─┼─┼	Railroad
≠═≠═	Aqueduct/Tunnel
··········	Powerline
─ ─ ─	Ski Lift
─·─·─	County Boundary

Trails

─ ─ ─ ─	Selected Route
- - - - -	Trail
→	Direction of Route

Water Features

⬭	Body of Water
⩪	Swamp/Marsh
∿	River or Creek
⟋	Spring
⩘	Waterfall

Symbols

(20)	Trailhead
■	Building/Point of Interest
🅿	Parking
🚻	Restroom
✿	Scenic View/Overlook
❓	Visitor Center/Information
⛩	Picnic Area
▲	Campground
•─•	Gate
⏝	Bridge
○	Towns/Cities
🚌	Bus Stop
🎿	Ski Area
⏝	Pass
⊢──⊣	Tunnel
👥	Ranger Station

Land Management

⬚	National Forest/Wilderness Area

Breckenridge and Summit County

Second Eaglesmere Lake and Eagles Nest (hike 10)

Summit County is a high valley ringed with mountain ranges. Breckenridge lies at 9,600 feet near the southern end of the boomerang-shaped county. Native Americans hunted and fished in this area for over 7,000 years as evidenced by remains found at the top of Vail Pass. The Utes called the area Nah-oon-kara, meaning "where the river of the blue rises." Fur trappers rendezvoused in La Bonte's Hole, where Dillon Reservoir now stores water for thirsty Denver. Miners came in search of their fortunes, and many stayed to ranch in the high, harsh area.

The eighteen hikes in this section take you on a tour of Summit County. The area around Breckenridge and Keystone experienced a lot of mining from 1859 into the 1960s. High lakes nestled beneath the ridge of the Tenmile Range beckon hikers with their beauty. Waterfalls and wildflowers often reward your hike. Two hikes tour old mining areas with their wealth of history of intrepid and persistent humans.

Being on the eastern slope of the Gore Range, the forests, while still inundated with snow in the winter, are drier than on the western slope around Vail. The lodgepole pine forest, ravaged by pine beetles in the early 2000s, contains a lot of dead, gray tree trunks. Be careful when the wind blows, because the trees can be easily uprooted. Underneath what appears to be devastation, little trees and many plants, bushes, and grasses are growing and replacing the dead vegetation.

The northern end of the county escaped the mining frenzy because gold and silver didn't surface and attract the miners. Instead people built ranches to feed the hungry prospectors. The Eagles Nest Wilderness lies in this part of the county. The rugged peaks and high alpine lakes of the Gore Range provide a treat for any hiker.

White Falls along the McCullough Gulch Trail (hike 1)

McCullough Gulch Trail

This hike offers a little bit of almost everything to a high-altitude hiker. Mining remains, colorful wildflowers, a crystal clear creek, the cascades of White Falls, patterned rock slabs, and a high alpine lake tucked beneath the crags of 14,265-foot Quandary Peak make this short, but sometimes steep, hike a worthwhile adventure. Snow patches can linger into August up here. Enjoy your lunch along the lakeshore, but be sure to bring some warm clothes with you!

Start: At the orange gate near the McCullough Gulch sign
Distance: 3.0 miles out and back
Hiking time: 1.5 to 2.5 hours
Difficulty: Difficult due to an 840-foot elevation gain in 1.4 miles
Trail surface: Dirt and rocky trail
Best season: July through Sept
Other trail users: Equestrians
Canine compatibility: Dogs must be under voice control
Land status: National forest
Fees and permits: None required
Maps: USGS Breckenridge; Nat Geo Trails Illustrated 109 Breckenridge/Tennessee Pass; Latitude 40° Summit County Trails; Breckenridge & Summit County Hiking and Biking Trail Map; USFS White River National Forest map

Trail contact: USDA Forest Service, Dillon Ranger District, 680 Blue River Pkwy., Silverthorne; (970) 468-5400; www.fs.usda.gov/whiteriver; www.dillonranger district.com
Other: This popular trail means a lot of cars parked along the road. Please park responsibly and don't block the road or the gate.
Special considerations: Make sure to start hiking early to avoid afternoon thunderstorms and lightning above treeline at the lake. The trail is neither marked nor maintained for winter use; however, the McCullough Gulch Road is nice for snowshoeing and cross-country skiing.

Finding the trailhead: From I-70 exit 203 (Frisco/Breckenridge), head south on CO 9 for 18.6 miles through Breckenridge to Blue Lakes Road. (From Breckenridge at the corner of Main and South Park, Blue Lakes Road is 7.7 miles south on CO 9.) Turn right onto Blue Lakes Road, then turn right in 0.1 mile onto McCullough Gulch Road. In 1.6 miles the road forks; turn left. In another 0.6 mile you arrive at a dead end that is trailhead parking. Please park carefully on the south side of the road (left as you drive up) so you don't block the road or the gate—remember to leave space to turn around. No facilities are available at the trailhead. GPS: N39 24.06′ / W106 04.75′.

In the September 10, 1898, *Summit County Journal,* George W. Crow was reported as "taking out ore on his Alsatian lode at the head of the McCullough gulch which runs 150 ounces silver and nearly an ounce gold." Four years later the *Breckenridge Bulletin* had an article about prospecting: "McCullough gulch will repay careful prospecting. The glacial erosion has been so great in parts of the gulch that the veins may be seen in the bedrock." Two Swedes, S. and J. A. Anderson, worked the Charley Ross lode at the head of the gulch and sent their "good-grade" lead and gold ore by mule train to the gulch's mouth or over the ridge to Kokomo (now under the settling ponds of the Climax Molybdenum Mine). Mines such as the Diamond Jack, Thunderbolt, and Bondy-Greco contained gold, copper, lead, and/or silver. Prospectors were still finding what they hoped would be profitable mines in 1917. But with a few exceptions, the mining era near Breckenridge ended by the early 1930s.

About 0.3 mile up the trail, you'll pass a cabin with No Trespassing signs and another sign indicating that the use of national forest land is authorized by USDA Forest Service permit. The cabin is part of the Last Dollar Mine, an unpatented mining claim, meaning someone has claimed the right of possession of a piece of federal land, which contains a valuable mineral deposit. The person doesn't own the land, but instead is leasing it from the federal government. He has to apply for and be approved for a permit for the right to extract minerals.

Quandary Peak spires and White Falls

The Tenmile Range is part of the Colorado Mineral Belt, a northeast/southwest trending band that's 10 to 60 miles wide, starting in the La Plata Mountains west of Durango and ending in the Front Range foothills just north of Boulder. About 70 million years ago, the present-day Rockies started to rise during the Laramide Orogeny. While the rocks broke and buckled, mineral-rich solutions from magma below moved into the fractures and joints. When the solutions cooled, gold, silver, lead, and zinc were embedded in the rock.

Today's gold is water and snow, and near the trailhead is a water diversion structure owned by Colorado Springs Utilities. They own water rights in the Spruce, Crystal, and McCullough Gulch drainages and divert approximately 9,300 acre-feet of water through the Hoosier Tunnel under the Continental Divide (Hoosier Pass) to Montgomery Reservoir. The water then enters the Middle Fork of the South Platte River and flows to the Denver metro area.

The hike starts steeply on an old mining road. Willows line the trail along with little red elephants, a purplish flower that resembles an elephant's head, trunk, and ears. A sturdy bridge provides passage over the rushing creek that tumbles and cascades down McCullough Gulch. At 0.5 mile you'll turn left onto a singletrack trail that continues along the creek. Soon you'll come to a boulder field with a huge cairn to show the way. The trail wanders through thick spruce-fir forest, crossing some little creeks. Rocks in the trail provide nice stepping-stones, which keep you above what can be a muddy trail.

After 1 mile a loop trail proceeds left to the base of White Falls, a series of white frothy cascades dropping down granitic rock slabs with interesting patterns. A little farther, the trail splits. You can climb up the rock slab in front of you or head right for an easier way. To the left are more white cascades and a field of marsh marigolds and globeflowers. The trail passes through fabulous rock gardens, climbing to a pretty lake nestled in a bowl below the crags on Quandary Peak's north side. Glaciers carved the crags and left moraines and little lakes in this upper valley. Ribbons of water cascade down cliffs, while Fletcher Peak raises its head beyond. You're in the ecotone between subalpine and alpine, where krummholz with flag trees and miniature willows fight to live. Take time for lunch and to explore a little. Enjoy this beautiful piece of Summit County.

One story goes that miners found an unknown mineral on the flanks of the peak to the south of McCullough Gulch. Since they were in a dilemma about and having difficulty figuring out their find (meanings for "quandary"), they named the mountain Quandary Peak.

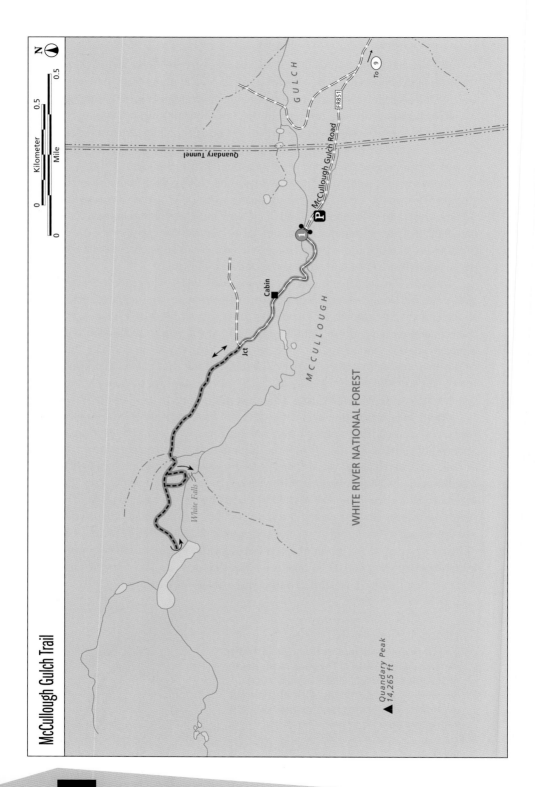

McCullough Gulch Trail

Quandary Peak
14,265 ft

WHITE RIVER NATIONAL FOREST

McCULLOUGH

Cabin

Jct

White Falls

GULCH

Quandary Tunnel

McCullough Gulch Road

FR851

To 9

N

Kilometer
0   0.5

Mile
0   0.5

0.0 Start at the gate near the McCullough Gulch sign. Elevation: 11,080 feet. Hike up the trail to the left.

0.3 Pass a cabin that is part of the Last Dollar Mine. No trespassing please!

0.5 Arrive at the junction of the road and singletrack trail. Turn left onto the singletrack. GPS: N39 24.22' / W106 05.13'. In about 250 feet you'll pass the remains of an old mine.

1.0 Come to the junction of the loop trail to White Falls. Turn left and hike about 250 feet to a rock slab near the base of the falls. Elevation: 11,600 feet. The trail loops back to the main trail from here. Turn left to continue the hike. (*Option:* You can turn around here for a moderate 2-mile out-and-back hike.)

1.3 The trail forks. You can either go right on the dirt trail or scramble up the rock slab in front of you—follow the cairns (rock piles).

1.4 Come to a trail junction. Turn right and head up a little rock band. The left branch goes to the lake's outlet.

1.5 Arrive at the lake. GPS: N39 24.39' / W106 05.84'. Elevation: 11,920 feet. Return the way you came.

3.0 Arrive back at the trailhead.

The lake at the end of the McCullough Gulch Trail

Local Information

Breckenridge Welcome Center, 203 S. Main St., Breckenridge; (877) 864-0868; www.gobreck.com

Breckenridge Resort Chamber, 111 Ski Hill Rd., Breckenridge; (888) 251-2417; www.gobreck.com

Local Events/Attractions

Country Boy Mine, 0542 French Gulch Rd., Breckenridge; (970) 453-4405; www.countryboymine.com

Breckenridge Heritage Alliance (various tours of mines and Breckenridge), 203 S. Main St., Breckenridge; (970) 453-9767 ; www.breckheritage.com

Backstage Theatre, 121 S. Ridge St., Breckenridge; (970) 453-0199; www.backstagetheatre.org

Breckenridge Music Festival, Riverwalk Center, CO 9 and W. Adams, Breckenridge; (970) 453-9142; www.breckenridgemusicfestival.com

National Repertory Orchestra, 111 S. Main St., Breckenridge; (970) 453-5825; www.nromusic.com

Organizations

Friends of the Dillon Ranger District, PO Box 1648, Silverthorne 80498; (970) 262-3449; www.fdrd.org

Sulphur flowers along Ridge Trail

Mohawk Lakes

Crystal clear Lower Mohawk Lake sits on a bench with a backdrop of craggy peaks, waterfalls, and mining relics. To reach this gem, hike along the Spruce Creek Trail as it gently climbs through thick forest for 1.5 miles. After the trail's junction with the Wheeler National Recreation Trail, various open areas provide glimpses of the silver ribbon of Continental Falls. After passing the remains of two old cabins, the trail switchbacks up a steep hill south of the falls through rock gardens of beautiful flowers with views to distant peaks. An optional hike takes you to treeline and Mohawk Lake.

Start: At the Spruce Creek Trail trailhead
Distance: 6.0 miles out and back to Lower Mohawk Lake
Hiking time: 2.5 to 5 hours
Difficulty: Difficult due to steep sections and a 1,430-foot elevation gain to Lower Mohawk Lake
Trail surface: Dirt trail and boulders
Best season: Late June to early Oct
Other trail users: Mountain bikers
Canine compatibility: Dogs must be under voice control
Land status: National forest
Fees and permits: None required
Maps: USGS Breckenridge; Nat Geo Trails Illustrated 109 Breckenridge/Tennessee Pass; Latitude 40° Summit County Trails; Breckenridge & Summit County Hiking and Biking Trail Map; USFS White River National Forest map
Trail contact: USDA Forest Service, Dillon Ranger District, 680 Blue River Pkwy., Silverthorne; (970) 468-5400; www.fs.usda.gov/whiteriver; www.dillonrangerdistrict.com
Special considerations: The lower part of the trail is nice for cross-country skiing in winter. Be aware of avalanche danger higher up. Hunters may use this area during hunting season.

Finding the trailhead: From I-70 exit 203 (Frisco/Breckenridge), drive south through Frisco and Breckenridge on CO 9 for 13.3 miles to Spruce Creek Road (The Crown subdivision). Turn right (west) onto Spruce Creek Road. At the first junction, stay to the right. At the second junction, turn left (southwest). The road is well marked with Spruce Creek Road signs at different intersections. Drive on Spruce Creek Road for about 1.3 miles to the trailhead parking area. The trail starts on the south side of the parking lot. No facilities are available at the trailhead. GPS: N39 26.22' / W106 03.03'.

Colorful wildflowers, ribbons of waterfalls, and spectacular peaks coupled with a close-up look at remains of the mining era make this trail a very popular hike. The first 1.5 miles of the trail are quite gentle and enjoyed by both hikers and mountain bikers. When you reach the Wheeler National Recreation Trail, take a quick walk to the right then left to a little viewpoint. Some logs provide seats to enjoy the view of Continental Falls and the peaks above Mohawk Lakes.

The trail intersects and joins an old road at 2 miles. Follow the road to find the trail again on the right below the diversion dam. The trail climbs steeply from here then levels out with more views of Continental Falls. If you have time, take the side trip to little Mayflower Lake and the remains of the old town. Back on the trail to the lakes, pass several more cabin ruins. After another climb you arrive at two cabins, one in ruins. To the right and a little downhill are the remains of an old mill. The Mohawk Company built the mill in 1888.

The trail passes between the two cabins and does not climb up along Continental Falls. However, a trail behind the cabin ruins takes you to a nice view of the lower part of the falls. After passing the cabins, the trail switchbacks up through some glorious fields of wildflowers. The rock gardens contain blue chiming bells, rosy and scarlet paintbrush, yellow sunflowers, and white bistort. Blue Colorado columbines bloom nearby. This hike is known as a "century" or "100 wildflower" trail because more than one hundred species of flowers can be found in the area.

Lower Mohawk Lake

Little side trips take you to overlooks of the falls. Across the forest below are views east to Baldy and Red Peak and north to Mount Helen. The trail occasionally crosses slabs of granite. After one slab you'll arrive at the remains of an old tram. The flywheel looks like those on today's ski lifts. This tram probably carried ore from the mines above down to the mill. A little farther up is Lower Mohawk Lake, where a little trail to the right leads to a rock shelf to enjoy the fantastic view.

Across the lake are the remains of an old building and behind it along the cliff are mine tailings. Look to the north to see another old mine tunnel. The Mount Gilead and Glen-Mohawk Mining Companies dug tunnels above treeline at the base of Pacific Peak at the turn of the century (1900). The 13,950-foot peak culminates the ridge to the south of Mohawk Lake (the upper lake). The tunnels bored into the mountain as much as 900 feet into veins of gold and silver ore.

Trout swim in the clear lake, fed from snowmelt and the waterfalls to the west. Watch for white-crowned sparrows flying overhead. These large sparrows can be identified by their black-and-white heads. They mate and nest in areas like Lower Mohawk Lake, at the boundary (ecotone) of the spruce-fir forest and the alpine tundra.

Along the edge of the lake, riparian-area flowers like the pink queen's crown or ruby king's crown flourish. Other flowers along the trail include white globe-flowers, yellow paintbrush, clover, daisies, pink Parry's primrose, lavender Jacob's ladder, and bright yellow alpine avens. Pink alpine lousewort hides under the plentiful willows.

If you have time, hike up to Mohawk Lake on the willow-lined trail with views of the lower lake, Breckenridge area, and Grays and Torreys Peaks.

MILES AND DIRECTIONS

0.0 Start at the Spruce Creek Trail trailhead bulletin board. Elevation: 10,370 feet. The trail splits not far from the trailhead; go straight and uphill.

1.5 Arrive at the junction with the Wheeler National Recreation Trail. Continue straight ahead on Spruce Creek Trail. GPS: N39 25.42' / W106 04.06'.

2.0 Arrive at a dirt road. Walk left on the road to a huge boulder and stay on the road around the boulder. Near the diversion dam, turn right (north) onto the trail by the trail sign. GPS: N39 25.29' / W106 04.51'.

2.3 The trail splits. Turn left (west) to Mohawk Lakes. (*Option:* The trail on the right goes to the remains of Mayflower town and to Mayflower Lake—a 0.25-mile out and back.) After crossing a creek, you'll pass cabin ruins then an area that is being restored. Please stay on the trail.

Mohawk Lakes

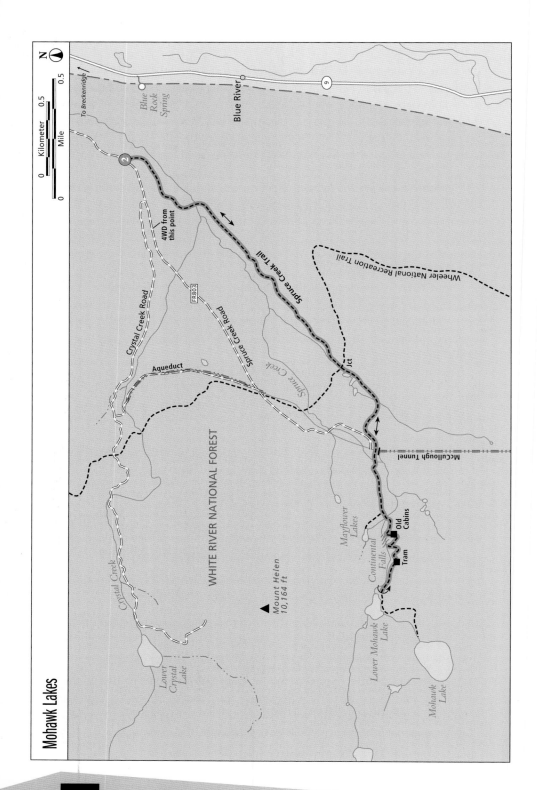

White River National Forest

Mount Helen
10,164 ft

Lower Crystal Lake

Crystal Creek

Crystal Creek Road

Spruce Creek Road

FR803

4WD from this point

Aqueduct

Spruce Creek

Spruce Creek Trail

Jct

Wheeler National Recreation Trail

McCullough Tunnel

Mayflower Lakes

Continental Falls

Old Cabins

Tram

Lower Mohawk Lake

Mohawk Lake

Blue Rock Spring

To Breckenridge

Blue River

9

N

Kilometer
0   0.5

Mile
0   0.5

2.5 The trail passes between two cabins (one in ruins) by a directional sign. GPS: N39 25.24' / W106 04.87'. Elevation: 11,385 feet. The trail leads away from the creek and switchbacks up a steep headwall with some rock slabs in the trail.

2.7 Pass a side trail to the right that offers an optional view of Continental Falls (about 265 feet out and back).

2.8 Arrive at the remains of an old tram. Past the tram, the trail curves left (west). Hike up the trail to the left up a boulder.

3.0 Trail splits. GPS: N39 25.27' / W106 05.17'. The right branch goes to a big rock slab with views of Lower Mohawk Lake, old mining remnants, and a cascade—a nice place for lunch if the wind isn't blowing. Elevation: 11,800 feet. The left branch continues around the lower lake and heads to Mohawk Lake (see option). Return the way you came.

6.0 Arrive back at the trailhead and parking lot.

Option
Mohawk Lake, at 12,105 feet, is 0.4 mile from Lower Mohawk Lake. Continue along the lower lake on the trail. At 3.1 miles (from the trailhead), a trail comes in from the right. The trail to Mohawk Lake clambers up the boulder before you and climbs up through some scratchy willows. At 3.4 miles you'll arrive at Mohawk

The view of Lower Mohawk Lake from the trail to Mohawk Lake

Lake. GPS: N39 25.14' / W106 05.37'. Enjoy the lake and great scenery. Return the way you came for a 6.8-mile out-and-back hike. Total elevation gain from the trailhead is 1,735 feet. Mohawk Lake is above treeline, so be aware of thunderstorms and lightning. Snow lingers here into July.

HIKE INFORMATION

Local Information
Breckenridge Welcome Center, 203 S. Main St., Breckenridge; (877) 864-0868; www.gobreck.com

Local Events/Attractions
Backstage Theatre, 121 S. Ridge St., Breckenridge; (970) 453-0199; www.backstagetheatre.org

Barney Ford Victorian House, 111 Washington Ave., Breckenridge; (970) 453-9767; www.breckheritage.com

Breckenridge Music Festival, Riverwalk Center, CO 9 and W. Adams, Breckenridge; (970) 453-9142; www.breckenridgemusicfestival.com

Country Boy Mine, 0542 French Gulch Rd., Breckenridge; (970) 453-4405; www.countryboymine.com

Edwin Carter Discovery Center, 111 N. Ridge St., Breckenridge; (970) 453-9767; www.breckheritage.com

Green Tip:
Never let your dog chase wildlife. It is illegal in Colorado for dogs to chase or harass wildlife, including chipmunks and squirrels.

Minnie Mine Loop

The sides of French Gulch sport golden wounds of mine tailings while the bottom is filled with boulder piles dredged from the creek bedrock in the endless quest for gold. Take a walk past historic mines on Prospect and Mineral Hills and the remains of an old gold dredge. An exhibit of a concentration mill jig explains how miners sorted the rocks and settled out the valuable minerals. Learn about the gold and silver mining history of Breckenridge through interpretive signs at several of the sites. While no active gold mines remain, the golden aspen make this hike a real treat in autumn!

Start: At the sign for the Reiling Dredge Trail across the road from the parking lot

Distance: 3.5-mile loop with spurs

Hiking time: 1.5 to 2.5 hours

Difficulty: Moderate due to distance and a 540-foot elevation gain and 120-foot loss

Trail surface: Dirt trail and old wagon roads

Best season: Mid-June through Oct

Other trail users: Mountain bikers and equestrians

Canine compatibility: Dogs must be on leash

Land status: Breckenridge and Summit County Open Space and Trails

Fees and permits: None required

Maps: USGS Breckenridge; Nat Geo Trails Illustrated 109 Breckenridge/Tennessee Pass; Latitude 40° Summit County Trails; Breckenridge & Summit County Hiking and Biking Trail Map

Trail contact: Town of Breckenridge Open Space and Trails, 150 Ski Hill Rd., Breckenridge; (970) 453-3160; www.breckenridge trails.org

Other: You can snowshoe or cross-country ski this loop in the winter (the trailhead parking lot is plowed). The Breckenridge Heritage Alliance offers tours of this area.

Special considerations: Bring water with you, as none is available along the trail.

Finding the trailhead: From I-70 exit 203 (Frisco/Breckenridge), head south on CO 9 for 9.5 miles. Turn left onto CR 450 at the 7-Eleven store. In 0.3 mile, turn right onto Reiling Road. In another 0.7 mile, turn left onto French Gulch Road. Drive 1.9 miles to the Reiling Dredge Trailhead. Turn left into the parking lot. No facilities are available at the trailhead. GPS: N39 29.11'/ W105 59.79'.

By 1858 men discouraged with the California gold fields swarmed to Colorado in search of their fortunes. Heading west from Denver in 1859, prospectors found gold in their pans along the Blue River near present-day Breckenridge. Hundreds of miners arrived and spread into the Blue's tributaries.

After the easy gold ran out, prospectors searched the nearby hills for the source of the metal that had washed into the streams. Miners dug holes and tunnels all over. Profitable hard-rock mines in French Gulch included the Extenuate (X10U8), Minnie, Lucky, Wellington, and Country Boy. The mines also produced silver, lead, and zinc over time. Along this hike you'll visit the Lucky, Minnie, Truax, and Rose of Breckenridge mine remains.

At mile 0.9 you cross the top of the tailings from the Minnie Mine, which operated from 1880 to 1958. The mine's production peaked in the 1920s and 1930s. An interpretive sign explains more about the mine and the precariously leaning Traylor Shaft. You can get an idea of the dredging operations along French Creek from the incredible rock piles below. From here you have a good view of the Breckenridge Ski Area, where today's white gold brings snowriders and their money to Breckenridge.

In addition to hard-rock mines, people wanted to dig deeper in the streambeds to extract more gold. Some type of gold panning machinery would fit the bill. The resulting barge floated in a pond and used small buckets in front moved

Remains of the Reiling Dredge

by a chain to dig into the bottom of the pond. As the buckets moved around the chain sprockets, the gravel and rocks dumped into a trommel (revolving screen) where water washed the finer material into a trough or sluice. The sands flowed through pans and tables with mercury traps, which settled out the gold for collection. Meanwhile the bigger rocks rode on a type of elevator that dumped them behind the barge. The pond filled in from behind, while the barge kept moving forward as it bit into the bedrock below. Thus the gold dredge came into existence.

Englishman Ben Stanley Revett brought the dredge boat to Breckenridge. The first dredge was installed in the Swan River north of French Gulch in 1898. His first attempts failed, being no match for the large boulders and depth of the deposits. He finally succeeded, and the remains of the Reiling Dredge are a stop along this hike. Originally steam powered the dredges, using wood then coal. Eventually electricity became available—resulting in electrocuted workers. By 1915 each dredge bucket could haul 16 cubic feet. A dredge could dig and wash an average of 300,000 cubic yards per month at a cost of less than three cents per cubic yard. The four dredges operating around Breckenridge reportedly produced over $500,000 each year. At one time the Reiling Dredge dug 40 feet to the bedrock in a 400-foot-wide band. By 1920 the dredges had retrieved the most valuable ore, and on November 19, 1922, the Reiling Dredge sank, never to dig again. Dredging ended in French Gulch that same year. Metal and machinery were salvaged from the Reiling Dredge during World War II.

The Boston & Breckenridge (B&B) Mines Company acquired mines and claims in French Gulch and land to the north. In 2005 the Town of Breckenridge and Summit County purchased 1,842 acres from B&B Mines—1,780 of these acres are protected as open space. The next year a partnership between the Town of Breckenridge, Summit County government, and Volunteers for Outdoor Colorado constructed the bridge and trail to the Reiling Dredge. The protected open space is part of the Golden Horseshoe, an 8,600-acre parcel managed by Summit County, the USDA Forest Service, and Breckenridge. Summit County and Breckenridge Open Space and Trails have created a wonderful system of trails on the B&B Mines lands, including installing interpretive signs in various places.

MILES AND DIRECTIONS

0.0 Start at the sign for the Reiling Dredge Trail across the road from the parking lot. Elevation: 10,080 feet. Walk down the trail and across the bridge.

0.1 Arrive at the junction to the Reiling Dredge interpretive sign. Turn left to the observation deck. Return back to the trail and turn left.

0.2 Arrive at the junction to another viewpoint for the Reiling Dredge. Turn left to the observation deck. Return back to the trail, turn right, and return back to the parking lot.

Minnie Loop

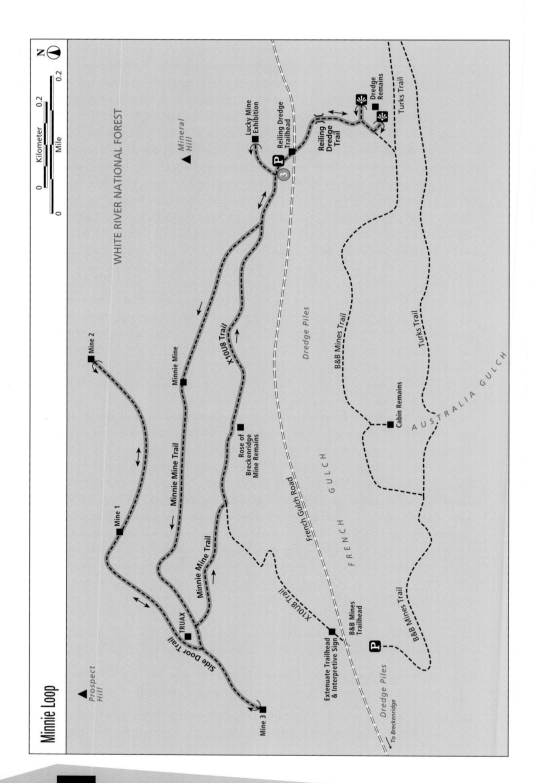

0.4 Come to French Gulch Road, cross it, and walk through the parking lot to the Minnie Mine Trail post. In about 100 feet, turn right and hike up the Interpretive Trail. Partway up on the left is a sign about the Lucky Mine. At the top is an exhibit of equipment from the Lucky Mine concentration mill jig. Elevation: 10,200 feet. Return the way you came and turn right onto the Minnie Mine Trail.

0.6 Arrive at the junction of the X10U8 and Minnie Mine Trails. Hike straight ahead on the Minnie Mine Trail.

0.9 Walk across the Minnie Mine area to the interpretive sign about the mine and the Traylor Shaft. Continue straight ahead on the trail. GPS: N39 29.24' / W106 00.15'.

1.3 Come to a sign that reads "Interpretive" and turn right to the sign about the remains of the Truax Mine. Return back to the main trail and turn right.

1.4 Arrive at the junction with the Side Door Trail and "To Minnie Mine Trail" sign. Turn right and hike up Side Door Trail. You pass the other side of the Truax Mine.

1.7 Walk through an old mining area complete with partial cabin, ore cart tracks, and the remains of an old stove or boiler.

2.0 Come to another mine with cables and ore cart tracks. GPS: N39 29.35' / W106 00.12'. Elevation: 10,500 feet. Turn around here and return the way you came.

2.5 Arrive at the same junction as at 1.4 miles and turn right.

2.6 Arrive at the top of a tailings pile. You can see the Extenuate Mine buildings and tailings below. GPS: N39 29.15' / W106 00.69'. Return the way you came to the junction at 1.4 miles.

2.7 Arrive back at the same junction as at 1.4 miles and go right and downhill.

2.8 Come to the junction with the Minnie Mine Trail. Turn right and head downhill.

3.0 Arrive at the junction with the Minnie Mine and X10U8 Trails. Turn left onto X10U8. GPS: N39 29.19' / W106 00.34'.

3.1 Come to the interpretive sign for the Rose of Breckenridge Mine.

3.4 Arrive at the junction of the Minnie Mine and X10U8 Trails. Continue straight ahead to the parking lot.

3.5 Arrive back at the Reiling Dredge parking lot.

Local Information

Breckenridge Welcome Center, 203 S. Main St., Breckenridge; (877) 864-0868; www.gobreck.com

Local Events/Attractions

Backstage Theatre, 121 S. Ridge St., Breckenridge; (970) 453-0199; www.back stagetheatre.org

Barney Ford Victorian House, 111 Washington Ave., Breckenridge; (970) 453-9767; www.breckheritage.com

Breckenridge Music Festival, Riverwalk Center, CO 9 and W. Adams, Brecken-ridge; (970) 453-9142; www.breckenridgemusicfestival.com

Country Boy Mine, 0542 French Gulch Rd., Breckenridge; (970) 453-4405; www.countryboymine.com

Edwin Carter Discovery Center, 111 N. Ridge St., Breckenridge; (970) 453-9767; www.breckheritage.com

Guided Historical Tours

Breckenridge Heritage Alliance, 203 S. Main St., Breckenridge; (970) 453-9767; www.breckheritage.com

Lucky Mine concentration mill jig exhibit

Iowa Hill

The Iowa Hill Hydraulic Placer Mine is explored along this historical interpretive trail. The hike takes you back over 125 years in history to the days when miners panned for gold then developed techniques using water cannons, called hydraulic giants or monitors, to wash the dirt on the sides of gulches into sluice boxes to capture gold particles. Mining History News *rates this trail as having "one of the best hydraulic mining exhibits in the world." The restored two-story log Miners' Boarding House on the trail can be toured with a guide.*

Start: At the Iowa Hill Trailhead sign
Distance: 1.2-mile lollipop including 4 side spurs
Hiking time: 1 to 2 hours
Difficulty: Moderate due to a 290-foot elevation gain in a short distance
Trail surface: Dirt trail
Best season: Late May to late Oct (snowshoe in winter)
Other trail users: Hikers only
Canine compatibility: Dogs must be on leash
Land status: Breckenridge Open Space and Trails
Fees and permits: None required
Maps: USGS Frisco; Nat Geo Trails Illustrated 108 Vail/Frisco/Dillon; Latitude 40° Summit County Trails; Breckenridge & Summit County Hiking and Biking Trail Map

Trail contact: Town of Breckenridge Open Space and Trails, 150 Ski Hill Rd., Breckenridge; (970) 453-3160; www.breckenridgetrails.org
Other: If the trail is muddy, please walk through the mud puddles and not on the vegetation around the trail. Trampled vegetation results in bigger mud puddles! Please stay on the trail to avoid trespassing on nearby private properties. The Breckenridge Heritage Alliance offers tours of the boardinghouse and Iowa Hill year-round.
Special considerations: No water is available along the trail. The trail is neither marked nor maintained for winter use, and the trailhead parking lot is not plowed.

Finding the trailhead: From I-70 exit 203 (Frisco/Breckenridge), drive south on CO 9 for 9 miles to Valley Brook Road. Turn right and travel 0.2 mile to Airport Road. Turn right onto Airport Road, then left in 0.3 mile, then immediately right onto the dirt road by the Iowa Hill Trail sign. Drive 0.1 mile to the parking lot. (A Breckenridge Free Ride bus stop is located near the trailhead.) No facilities are available at the trailhead. GPS: N39 30.14' / W106 03.14'.

The Iowa Hill interpretive displays were created by researching old pictures and documentation of how the miners first panned for gold in streams and then evolved hydraulic techniques to remove gold from the hills.

The interpretive signs begin with explanations of gold panning and use of a rocker box and Long Tom for greater efficiency. A sluice box exhibit comes complete with a resident pine squirrel chattering at hikers. Other exhibits contain a blacksmith shop, a guard station, an old derrick, a hydraulic monitor, an ore car used in bank blasting, and examples of flumes. At the top of the hike is the pressure box and headgate, which provided the force required to run the hydraulic guns (also called monitors). A flume was reconstructed in summer 2005, and the remains of the original wood from the flume can still be seen in the area.

Pan, rocker box, and Long Tom exhibit

Miners' Boarding House

A real gem on this hike is the restored and furnished Miners' Boarding House. Breckenridge Heritage Alliance offers guided tours of the building. Once inside, you're transported back over 125 years. The tour explains how the miners lived their lives after returning from a hard day of work. If you ever wondered what hobnailed boots looked like, a pair survives in the house. Historians think eight men lived in the boardinghouse. Bunks in the cabin were re-created from pictures. Sample boxes of herbs used to cure ills line a shelf near the old wood cookstove. The boardinghouse dates back to at least 1876. One picture on the wall shows snow up to the eaves of a cabin.

Hiking up the trail through dry forest (recently thinned due to pine beetle–killed lodgepole pine trees) begs the question of, where did the miners get the water for the hydraulic monitors? At the turn of the twentieth century, the Banner Placer Company owned the mine and built a reservoir to provide water. According to the October 15, 1904, *Breckenridge Bulletin,* the Banner Placer Mining Company, managed by Colonel Lemuel Kingsbury, was preparing to operate the well-known Iowa placer on Iowa Hill in 1905. "A storage reservoir is being built on a portion of the Boom placer (ten acres of which were purchased for that purpose) to hold water for supplying a couple of 'giants' under a head of pressure of over 200 feet." Another report stated the reservoir was located between the head of the north fork of Cucumber Creek and South Barton Creek. Kingsbury picked a series of sites for little reservoirs so when one filled, the overflow would fill the others. Headgates were placed in two of the lakes. The company built a road to the storage reservoirs and dug miles of ditches to make the hydraulic placer operation a success. The water dropped over 200 feet in elevation through a 3,200-foot-long, 22-inch steel pipe. The headgate now on display was once used in another mining operation in Illinois Gulch south of town. Pressure generated was estimated at 260 pounds per square inch. Lateral pipes ran three 6-inch nozzles, which played on the 18- to 40-foot-high gravel banks. The gravel passed through a 4-foot-wide sluice with riffles that caught the gold. Two Acme concentrating tables separated gold, which in the past had been hard to reclaim from the heavy black sand. A dynamo run by water generated power for the tables and lights for night work. In addition to gold the black sand also contained some platinum. Kingsbury filed the articles of incorporation for the Summit Banner Placer Mining and Milling Company in Summit County in December 1904 with a capital stock of $500,000. On August 31, 1905, Colonel Kingsbury invited the whole town of Breckenridge to come celebrate the completion of the Banner placer "plant"—all the equipment and reservoirs needed to work the rich gravel of Iowa Hill. The *Summit County Journal* reported that he purchased a ton of Rocky Ford watermelons for the party.

The newspapers also reported that Kingsbury exhibited several beautiful gold nuggets from Iowa Hill, one of which resembled a bear's foot. Gold nuggets from Iowa Hill were also exhibited at the 1893 Chicago World's Fair.

Hike back into time and learn about some of Breckenridge's mining history.

MILES AND DIRECTIONS

0.0 Start at the Iowa Hill Trail trailhead sign. Elevation: 9,450 feet. In 325 feet, the trail splits. Turn left (south) and follow the trail, which leads you to many interpretive signs. Take time to explore the side trails to several signs and displays.

0.4 The trail splits. Turn left (west) to the hydraulic giant display and sign then return to the junction and the Derrick Interpretive sign. Head uphill from here.

0.6 The trail splits. Turn left and head uphill (southwest) for more interpretive signs. GPS: N39 30.12' / W106 03.30'.

0.75 Arrive at the pressure box and headgate. GPS: N39 30.06' / W106 03.42'. Elevation: 9,740 feet. Return back to the last junction.

> *The December 30, 1905, issue of the* **Summit County Journal** *reported that Banner gold had a value of $19 per ounce.*

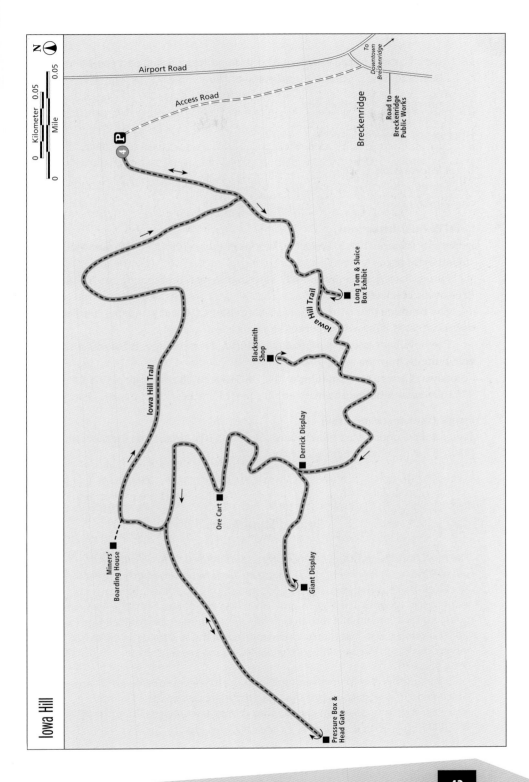

Iowa Hill

Airport Road

Access Road

P

4

Iowa Hill Trail

Iowa Hill Trail

Miners' Boarding House

Ore Cart

Derrick Display

Giant Display

Blacksmith Shop

Long Tom & Sluice Box Exhibit

Pressure Box & Head Gate

Breckenridge

To Downtown Breckenridge

Road to Breckenridge Public Works

N

Kilometer 0   0.05

Mile 0   0.05

0.9 Back at the 0.6-mile junction, turn left and head down past the Miners' Boarding House. Continue on the downhill trail.

1.2 Arrive back at the trailhead.

HIKE INFORMATION

Local Information
Breckenridge Welcome Center, 203 S. Main St., Breckenridge; (877) 864-0868; www.gobreck.com

Local Events/Attractions
Backstage Theatre, 121 S. Ridge St., Breckenridge; (970) 453-0199; www.back stagetheatre.org

Barney Ford Victorian House, 111 Washington Ave., Breckenridge; (970) 453-9767; www.breckheritage.com

Breckenridge Music Festival, Riverwalk Center, CO 9 and W. Adams, Breckenridge; (970) 453-9142; www.breckenridgemusicfestival.com

Country Boy Mine, 0542 French Gulch Rd., Breckenridge; (970) 453-4405; www.countryboymine.com

Edwin Carter Discovery Center, 111 N. Ridge St., Breckenridge; (970) 453-9767; www.breckheritage.com

Public Transportation (free)
Town of Breckenridge Free Ride Transit System, 1105 Airport Rd., Breckenridge; (970) 547-3140; www.breckfreeride.com

Guided Mine Tours

The Breckenridge Heritage Alliance offers guided tours to Iowa Hill and two other mines near Breckenridge. The Lomax Placer Mine was another hydraulic placer mining operation. In addition to learning about the mine, you can learn to pan for gold. The Washington Mine was one of Breckenridge's largest gold and silver operations with over 10,000 feet of underground workings. Gold panning is also offered. To learn more about the tours and times, check the Breckenridge Heritage Alliance website at www.breckheritage.com or call (970) 453-9767.

The Country Boy Mine offers tours into the former gold mine on French Gulch Road. You walk over 1,000 feet into the mine during the 45-minute tour. Check on tour details at www.countryboymine.com or call them at (970) 453-4405.

Lenawee Trail

The Lenawee Trail provides some fantastic views of Summit County and into Eagle County as you wind your way along the alpine tundra. The trail climbs 1,650 feet in the first 2 miles through thick forest. Once above treeline the trail mellows a little and the views are expansive the higher you climb. The long ridge of Lenawee Mountain lies before you. Eventually you traverse its south flank to a narrow ridge with a rocky outcrop. Continue along the trail, dropping to the top of Arapahoe Basin's Zuma Lift for more fantastic views and colorful wildflowers. Keep an eye open for mountain goats!

Start: At the Lenawee Trail sign
Distance: 6.8 miles out and back
Hiking time: 3.5 to 4.5 hours
Difficulty: Difficult due to a 2,170-foot elevation gain
Trail surface: Dirt and rocky trail
Best season: July through Sept
Other trail users: Equestrians and mountain bikers
Canine compatibility: Dogs must be under voice control
Land status: National forest
Fees and permits: None required
Maps: USGS Montezuma; Nat Geo Trails Illustrated 104 Idaho Springs/Loveland Pass; Latitude 40° Summit County Trails; USFS White River National Forest map

Trail contact: USDA Forest Service, Dillon Ranger District, 680 Blue River Pkwy., Silverthorne; (970) 468-5400; www.fs.usda.gov/whiteriver; www.dillonrangerdistrict.com
Other: This trail is popular with mountain bikers, who ride up Arapahoe Basin Ski Area's service roads and zoom downhill on the Lenawee Trail to Peru Creek Road.
Special considerations: Bring water, as there is no reliable water source along the trail. Start hiking early to avoid afternoon thunderstorms and lightning above treeline. Trail is neither marked nor maintained for winter use; but Peru Creek Road is nice for snowshoeing and cross-country skiing.

Finding the trailhead: From I-70 exit 205 (Silverthorne/Dillon), head south on US 6 for 7.9 miles through Keystone to Montezuma Road. Turn right onto Montezuma Road and, in another 4.6 miles at the big right curve with the guardrail, turn left onto Peru Creek Road (wide for winter parking). Peru Creek Road (FR 260) is dirt and sometimes bumpy. After crossing the bridge, the road narrows to about 1.5 cars wide. Drive a total of 1.7 miles up Peru Creek Road, watching carefully for the Lenawee Trail sign on the left among the trees. Find a wide spot to park, being sure not to block the road. There are several wide spots within about 0.1 mile of the trailhead. No facilities at the trailhead. GPS: N39 36.09' / W105 50.83'.

THE HIKE

Gold was first discovered in Summit County near Breckenridge in 1859. The area would never again be the peaceful, high-altitude basin where deer, elk, and bison provided summer hunting opportunities for the Utes. Miners swarmed all over the mountains, hoping to strike it rich. In 1863 John Coley found silver in the Snake River district near Sts. John. A rough trail opened over Loveland Pass, bringing miners from Georgetown and points east. The town of Montezuma, a little farther up Montezuma Road from the Peru Creek turnoff, saw its first hotel in 1868. Miners developed various silver mines along Peru Creek in the 1870s, and by 1880 the little town of Chihuahua was incorporated just past the Lenawee Trail trailhead. The mountains along the Snake River and Peru Creek became a top silver-producing area in the late 1800s.

According to an article in the *Colorado Miner,* September 4, 1880, W. D. Bradford discovered the Eliza Jane lode on Lenawee Mountain on July 15, 1880. The discovery was disputed by Hunt and Shavallia (no first names recorded), who filed an injunction against Bradford, claiming they had previously discovered the lode. Instead of fighting a prolonged legal battle, all parties decided to consolidate and each own a share, allowing them to proceed with mining the mountain instead of each other in court. Their find was patented as the American Eagle Mine, but locals called it the Eliza Jane. They built a little house over its entrance so they could work during the winter. In summer 1884 two carloads of ore from the previous winter were shipped and averaged $400 per ton.

Cascade in Thurman Gulch below Lenawee Mountain

Isaac Filger along with S. C. and William Hoskinson discovered the Winning Card mine on July 14, 1882, high on Lenawee Mountain near the Eliza Jane. The mine produced good silver ore, and by 1885 people talked about starting a town called Filger City on Lenawee Mountain. The town at one time had a mayor, but didn't succeed. Both the Eliza Jane and the Winning Card were reported as "the pride of Lenawee Mountain," due to the fine quality of the ore being mined. In July 1885 the *Montezuma Millrun* reported that an ore shipment from the Winning Card was "probably the richest load of ore ever shipped from Snake River valley." The ore contained both silver and copper. Filger died in 1903 after a long illness. In his obituary the *Summit County Journal* reported, "Forty thousand dollars was taken from the mine in two months." The Winning Card was still shipping ore in 1906.

The trail starts climbing through lodgepole pine and subalpine fir forest then enters an aspen grove with bushy common juniper, blue harebells, and silver-green buffaloberry growing beneath. Make sure to turn off at the viewpoint at 1.3 miles to check out the nice view of Buffalo Mountain and Uneva Peak, Frisco, some ski runs at Keystone, and a glimpse of the Tenmile Range. Lenawee Mountain, a long ridge, comes into view the higher you climb. A long, thin cascade drops from a bowl below the American Eagle Mine remains at the top of pretty Thurman Gulch. Around 11,850 feet the trees stop growing and are replaced by short willows and wondrous wildflowers. Yellow paintbrush, large yellow-orange old-man-of-the-mountain (sunflower), pink moss campion, white pussytoes, yellow alpine avens, and pale green sage outline the trail. It continues to wind along the tundra until it traverses Lenawee's southern flank. Note that the trail is higher on Lenawee Mountain than the elevation shown on the USGS topographical map. Keep an eye open for mountain goats! You'll pass below the old American Eagle Mine. Take a moment to think about Isaac Filger and other miners working high on Lenawee Mountain in the thin cold air, especially in the winter! The trail is narrow along here until it switchbacks up to the ridge near a rock outcropping. You can turn around here, but the views to the northwest of the rugged Gore Range are fantastic if you walk a little farther along the trail. The top of Arapahoe Basin's Zuma Lift is 0.1 mile from the ridge. A nice view of the Continental Divide, Loveland Pass, and beyond treats you from near the lift. Take a walk back into history and enjoy the fantastic scenery and flowers along the way!

The big golden sunflowers that tower over the smaller plants are old-man-of-the-mountains, or **Rydbergia grandiflora.** *These giants can grow for twelve to fifteen years to gather and store enough energy to bloom. Once the flower fades away, the plant dies.*

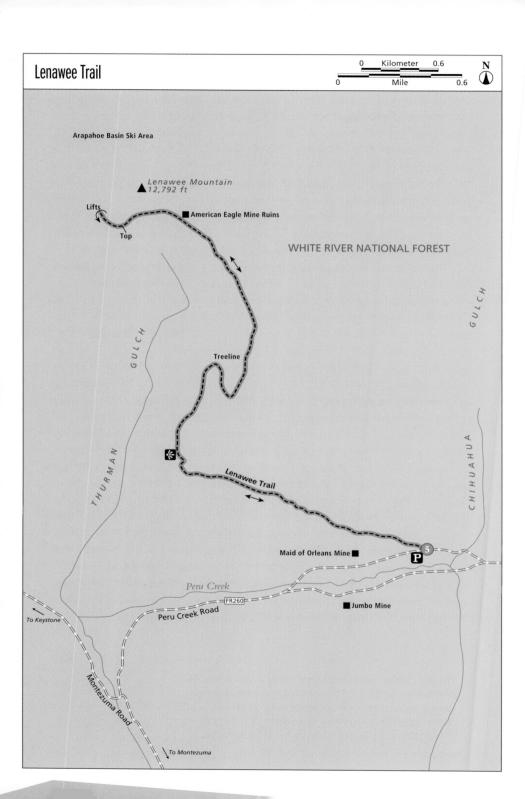

Lenawee Trail

0 Kilometer 0.6
0 Mile 0.6

N

Arapahoe Basin Ski Area

Lenawee Mountain
▲ 12,792 ft

Lifts

American Eagle Mine Ruins

Top

WHITE RIVER NATIONAL FOREST

GULCH

GULCH

Treeline

THURMAN

CHIHUAHUA

Lenawee Trail

Maid of Orleans Mine ■

P 5

Peru Creek

FR260

Jumbo Mine ■

Peru Creek Road

To Keystone

Montezuma Road

To Montezuma

MILES AND DIRECTIONS

0.0 Start at the Lenawee Trail sign. Elevation: 10,350 feet.

1.3 Come to a right switchback with a view area to the left. Enjoy the scenery and a rest break. GPS: N39 36.45' / W105 52.02'. Elevation: 11,500 feet.

1.8 You are now in the ecotone (boundary) between the subalpine and the alpine zones.

2.0 Come to a big left switchback. Check out the layered rocks to your right. You're definitely in the land above the trees.

3.0 The trail appears to split. Stay on the trail to the left; the right branch climbs steeply to the American Eagle Mine remains.

3.3 Arrive at the ridge. GPS: N39 37.32' / W105 52.26'. Elevation: 12,520 feet. This place, or if it's windy walk a little way down the trail you came up, is a nice lunch spot. (You can turn around here for a 6.6-mile out-and-back hike.) Continue another 0.1 mile to the top of Arapahoe Basin Ski Area for views of the Continental Divide, Gore Range, and more.

3.4 Come to the top of the Zuma Lift. Return the way you came.

6.8 Arrive back at the trailhead.

HIKE INFORMATION

Local Information
Keystone Neighbourhood Company, Keystone; (800) 919-0038; www.keystone neighbourhood.com

Local Events/Attractions
Bluegrass and Beer Festival, Keystone; (800) 919-0038; www.keystonefestivals.com
Keystone Wine and Jazz Festival, Keystone River Run Village; (800) 919-0038; www.keystonefestivals.com
Blue Ribbon Bacon Tour, Keystone; (800) 919-0038; www.keystonefestivals.com

Organizations
Friends of the Dillon Ranger District, PO Box 1648, Silverthorne 80498; (970) 262-3449; www.fdrd.org

In late December 1884 John Preston reported to the **Montezuma Millrun** *that on the way down from the American Eagle Mine, he ran into 5-foot-deep drifts in the timber, with the snow over his head in a few places.*

What Is Wilderness?

Twenty of the hikes in this book are in congressionally designated wilderness areas. What is wilderness? What makes wilderness different from any other part of national forest or Bureau of Land Management (BLM) land?

Wilderness areas are very special places. The American people, through acts of Congress, designate certain pristine and primitive sections of undeveloped federal land as wilderness. The Wilderness Act of 1964, which created a National Wilderness Preservation System (NWPS), gives Congress the authority to designate lands as wilderness.

First a little history. Back in the 1870s, people became alarmed at the rapid rate of development in America and the overuse of natural resources on public lands. Efforts were made to conserve and preserve certain areas. Yellowstone became our first national park in 1872. The first primitive area, a forerunner of wilderness, was designated in 1930. Concerns about development and abuse of public lands didn't stop then. Some believed that certain areas should be saved in their pristine condition. In 1955 the first draft legislation outlining the NWPS was written. After nine years of negotiations and rewrites, the Wilderness Act became law.

The purpose of the NWPS is to assure that Americans now and in the future have the benefits of a wilderness resource. Those benefits include "outstanding opportunities for solitude or a primitive and unconfined type of recreation" and "the public purposes of recreational, scenic, scientific, educational, conservation, and historical use." The Wilderness Act specifically states "A wilderness, in contrast with those areas where man and his works dominate the landscape, is hereby recognized as an area where the earth and its community of life are untrammeled by man, where man himself is a visitor who does not remain . . . an area of undeveloped Federal land retaining its primeval character and influence, without permanent improvements or human habitation, which is protected and managed so as to preserve its natural conditions and which . . . generally appears to have been affected primarily by the forces of nature . . ."

The Wilderness Act prohibits certain uses in wilderness, such as motorized equipment, landing of aircraft, nonmotorized mechanical transport (like mountain bikes), roads, and structures except in emergencies or administrative necessity. However, Congress allowed other uses to continue, such as grazing, hunting, and fishing. Since the end of 1983, new mining claims are prohibited, but patented claims existing prior to 1984 may be worked under certain restrictions. Water in wilderness is a very touchy issue, especially in Colorado, where most of its major rivers originate within the state and flow outward. The state has historically held authority over water rights. Occasionally a wilderness area surrounds private or state lands. The Act assures these landowners "reasonable access" that is consistent with wilderness preservation. As a result you might see a building in the middle of a wilderness area!

Wilderness can be designated in national forests, BLM lands, national parks and monuments, and national wildlife refuges. The agency responsible for the land administers the wilderness. Designation of new wilderness areas on national public lands is still ongoing. By mid-2013, Colorado contained forty-three wilderness areas: thirty-nine areas managed by the USDA Forest Service and/or the BLM and four managed by the National Park Service. The US Fish & Wildlife Service helps manage Mount Massive Wilderness.

Public lands managers face an interesting challenge in trying to provide solitude and a primitive and unconfined type of recreation while preserving the wilderness character of the lands "unimpaired for future use," lands that are primarily affected by natural forces. Human visitation is bound to leave scars on the land and impact other visitors unless each of us is very careful. Wilderness managers therefore strive to manage human behavior, mainly through education, access limitations, and regulations. Several wilderness areas require that dogs be on leash to minimize harassment of wildlife and other visitors. A self-issue free permit system for overnight camping has been implemented in the Holy Cross Wilderness to obtain accurate wilderness visitor data and to educate visitors. Land agencies alone can't preserve and protect wilderness areas. Each of us plays an important role.

As you hike or backpack in a wilderness area, remember you are in a very special place. Keeping groups small, understanding the ecosystems enough to make good decisions about where to hike and camp, keeping water clean, minimizing traces of your presence (for example, preventing fire rings and scars), and respecting wildlife and other visitors are all extremely important. One hiker may not make a huge impact, but we are now hundreds of thousands of hikers each year. By understanding what designated wilderness is and taking the responsibility to act appropriately, we can preserve these special areas for ourselves and future generations.

For further information, check out:

Leave It Wild, The Pew Charitable Trusts, 901 E St. NW, Washington, DC 20004; (202) 552-2000; www.leaveitwild.org

White River National Forest, Supervisor's Office, 900 Grand Ave., Glenwood Springs, CO 81601; (970) 945-2521; www.fs.usda.gov/whiteriver

Wilderness Land Trust, PO Box 1420, Carbondale, CO 81623; (970) 963-1725; www.wildernesslandtrust.org

The Wilderness Society, 1615 M St. NW, Washington, DC 20036; (800) 843-9453; www.wilderness.org

www.wilderness.net, an Internet-based tool about wilderness

Dillon Nature Preserve

The Dillon Reservoir Recreation Area offers easy-to-moderate hiking opportunities in the Dillon Nature Preserve Open Space. The mostly flat, gated service road to the West Portal of the Roberts Tunnel is hikable year-round, while the forested Meadow Loop and Ridge Trails can sometimes be obscured by snow. Because the trail is lower than many in central Summit County, the snow melts faster and the flowers bloom earlier here. Keep your eyes open for fox, pine squirrels, deer, red-tailed hawks, and ospreys. Enjoy the beautiful views of the Gore Range and the Tenmile Range across the blue waters of Dillon Reservoir.

Start: At the gate at the end of the parking lot off US 6 across from Cemetery Road

Distance: 4.8-mile lollipop with a spur

Hiking time: 2 to 2.5 hours

Difficulty: Easy due to mostly gentle trails and a 235-foot elevation gain

Trail surface: Paved recreational path, service road, and dirt trail

Best season: Late May to late Oct (service road is year-round)

Other trail users: Bikers on paved recreation trail

Canine compatibility: Dogs must be on leash

Land status: Town of Dillon Open Space

Fees and permits: None required

Maps: USGS Frisco; Nat Geo Trails Illustrated 109 Breckenridge/ Tennessee Pass; Latitude 40° Summit County Trails

Trail contact: Town of Dillon, 275 Lake Dillon Dr., Dillon; (970) 468-2403; www.townofdillon.com

Other: New seedlings have been planted to replace the removed trees that were killed by pine beetles, so if you walk off-trail, please watch where you step to avoid trampling the new vegetation. Part of this hike is the service road for Denver Water, so you may occasionally see a vehicle on it.

Special considerations: Other than Dillon Reservoir, no water exists along these trails so bring some with you. Please stay on the established Ridge Trail and its spurs. Avoid getting too close to any steep or rocky slopes (cliffs).

Finding the trailhead: From I-70 exit 205 (Silverthorne/Dillon), drive approximately 3.5 miles east on US 6 to Cemetery Road (on the left), just east of mile marker 212. Turn right (southwest) across from Cemetery Road and drive 0.1 mile to the recreation path parking lot. No facilities are available at the trailhead. GPS: N39 36.65' / W106 01.34'.

THE HIKE

The Dillon Nature Preserve contains two hiking trails but is first and foremost a nature preserve. This peninsula, which juts out into Dillon Reservoir along the Snake River inlet, has seen many changes over time. Bison (buffalo), deer, elk, and antelope used to feed in the lush valley now covered by water. Indians, mainly Utes, followed the game here in summer. Mountain men once rendezvoused in La Bonte's Hole where the Snake and Blue Rivers and Tenmile Creek converged. (Today the confluence lies underwater southeast of Dillon Dam.) La Bonte the man remains a mystery—perhaps a French Canadian trapper lent his name to the area.

The rush for gold in the 1860s brought miners to the south and east of La Bonte's Hole. With the Homestead Act of 1862, homesteaders claimed their 160 acres of public land by building a house and working the land. Ranchers around Dillon and down the Lower Blue Valley grew crops and raised cattle, which fed the miners and other Summit County residents.

By the early 1870s, entrepreneurs built a stage stop and trading post near the confluence of the rivers in La Bonte's Hole. The growing settlement gained a post office in 1879. The Denver & Rio Grande Railroad reached Dillon in 1882, and the rival Denver, South Park, and Pacific arrived in 1883. The town of Dillon incorporated on January 26, 1883, on the northeast side of the Snake River. Dillon soon moved just south of the confluence of the three rivers to be closer to both railroads. Later, citizens again moved their town, west of Tenmile Creek but still close to transportation. Dillon became a hub for the ranches and farms of the area.

View from the first overlook on Meadow Loop

Herds of cattle bound for Denver were driven along roads to the Dillon depot. Ore and lumber hauled by wagon to Dillon were loaded onto trains for transport.

Dillon moved a fourth time when the Denver Water Board (DWB) started to build a reservoir to provide water for its customers. As early as 1910, plans were drawn to divert water from the Blue River drainage to the east slope for growing Denver. DWB started buying water rights on the west slope. In 1927 alternate plans were filed showing a dam across the Blue River just below the three-river confluence. A 23.3-mile tunnel would transport the water to the South Platte River and on to Denver. When times were tough during the Depression, DWB purchased many properties in and around Dillon at tax sales. In 1955 DWB met with citizens of Dillon to discuss their plans and hear concerns. Despite opposition, plans for the dam and tunnel progressed. Dillon would be moved to a hill to the north. Some people moved and others stayed in place. The DWB informed the remaining residents that they had to evacuate Dillon by August 1, 1961. Clearing for the dam started in April 1960. The earthen dam required 12 million tons of fill dirt. Some buildings from Old Dillon moved to New Dillon and some to the Silverthorne area. Over 300 graves had to be moved from the Dillon Cemetery, established in 1885, to the new cemetery along US 6.

Workers completed the dam in July 1963, and water storage began in September of that year. Dillon Reservoir has a 24.5-mile shoreline and can store about 85.5 billion gallons of water.

MILES AND DIRECTIONS

0.0 Start at the gate at the northwest end of the parking lot. Elevation: 9,110 feet. Turn right (northwest) and walk on the paved recreation path heading northwest.

0.3 Arrive at the Dillon Nature Preserve Open Space sign and junction with the Dillon Peninsula Road. Turn left (northwest) and walk past the gate onto the service road.

0.8 Come to the junction of the service road and the Ridge Trail and Meadow Loop. Turn left (south) here and follow the trail up the meadow. GPS: N39 37.05' / W106 02.05'.

1.3 Arrive at the junction of Ridge and Meadow Loop Trails. Continue straight ahead on Meadow Loop Trail.

1.4 Come to a faint unmarked trail to the left. Continue straight ahead and uphill.

1.5 Curve to the right then arrive at the junction of Meadow Loop Trail and a spur trail to an overlook to the left. A bench is approximately 210 feet out and back.

Dillon Nature Preserve

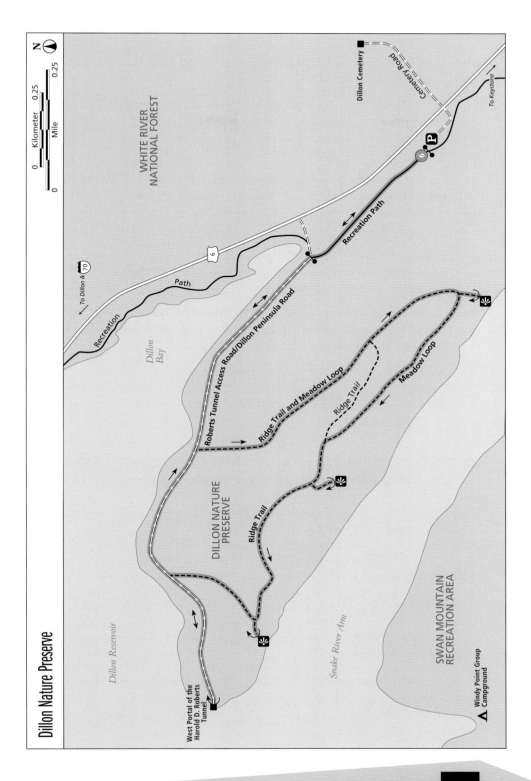

N

| 0 | Kilometer | 0.25 |
| 0 | Mile | 0.25 |

WHITE RIVER
NATIONAL FOREST

Dillon Cemetery

Cemetery Road

To Keystone

P

6

Recreation Path

To Dillon & 70

6

Recreation Path

Dillon
Bay

Roberts Tunnel Access Road/Dillon Peninsula Road

Ridge Trail and Meadow Loop

Ridge Trail

Meadow Loop

DILLON NATURE PRESERVE

Ridge Trail

Dillon Reservoir

Snake River Arm

West Portal of the
Harold D. Roberts Tunnel

SWAN MOUNTAIN
RECREATION AREA

Windy Point Group
Campground

2.0   Come to the junction of Ridge and Meadow Loop Trails. Turn left (north-west) here to hike Ridge Trail.

2.1   Come to a junction with a trail to an overlook with two benches. Turn left for the overlook, which is approximately 425 feet out and back. Return back to this point to continue on Ridge Trail. Climb up to the high point at approximately 9,275 feet.

2.5   Come to a low rock ledge next to the trail with a good view of Frisco, Mount Royal, and Peaks 1 and 2.

2.7   Arrive at a junction with a trail to an overlook. GPS: N39 36.95' / W106 02.46'. Turn left (west) to the overlook. The trail goes up a rocky stretch and ends at a Denver Water Board boundary (approximately 0.1 mile out and back). Return the way you came to the junction. Turn left if you went to the overlook or right if you didn't.

3.0   Arrive at the junction of Ridge Trail and Dillon Peninsula Road. GPS: N39 37.13' / W106 02.36'. Turn left (southwest) and walk on the service road to the West Portal of the Roberts Tunnel.

3.4   Arrive at the end of the service road near the West Portal of the Roberts Tunnel. Enjoy the nice views over Dillon Reservoir. GPS: N39 37.03' / W106 02.69'. Elevation: 9,040 feet. Turn around to start your return on the service road back to the parking lot.

Dillon Peninsula Becomes Open Space

Over the years, the Denver Water Board (DWB) had purchased many acres of land for their water projects. By the 1990s, DWB decided it best not to keep land it wasn't using. DWB and the Town of Dillon entered into discussions about excess DWB land near Dillon Reservoir. DWB gave Dillon 173 acres for parks and open space but kept 49 acres adjacent to US 6, which the town zoned for fourteen single-family residences while allowing that density to be transferred to other DWB land on the east side of US 6. DWB also kept 18 acres at the peninsula's tip, where the Roberts Tunnel West Portal is located.

The Town of Dillon, DWB, and Summit County reached an agreement on July 16, 1996, to protect the 173 acres of open space as a conservation ease-ment. In 1998 Dillon's town manager asked Volunteers for Outdoor Colorado (VOC) if they would be interested in building a formal trail system the fol-lowing summer. VOC enthusiastically agreed to the project. These partner-ships deserve the credit for creating the wonderful hiking area along Dillon Reservoir.

4.0 The junction of the road and the Ridge and Meadow Loop Trails is to your right. Continue on the service road.

4.5 Come back to the Dillon Nature Preserve Open Space sign and junction with the gated Dillon Peninsula Road. Turn right (southeast) here onto the paved recreation path.

4.8 Arrive back at the parking lot.

Options

1. Dillon Peninsula Road. Follow the directions above to start, but stay on the service road for an easy, year-round 2.9-mile out-and-back hike.
2. Meadow Loop Trail. Follow the directions above but at mile 2.0, turn right at the junction with the Ridge Trail, head downhill to a junction, and turn left and continue downhill. Turn right onto the service road to return to the parking lot. This option is an easy, 3.6-mile lollipop hike.
3. Ridge Trail. Follow the directions above but at mile 1.3 turn right onto Ridge Trail and hike until it meets the service road. Turn right to return to the parking lot on the service road. This option is an easy, 3.4-mile lollipop hike.

HIKE INFORMATION

Local Information

Colorado Welcome Center at Silverthorne, Outlets at Silverthorne, 246 Rainbow Dr., Silverthorne; (970) 468-0353; www.colorado.com/official-colorado-welcome-centers

Town of Dillon, 275 Lake Dillon Dr., Dillon; (970) 468-2403; www.townof dillon.com

Local Events/Attractions

Friday Farmers Market, Buffalo and Main Streets; Town of Dillon, 275 Lake Dillon Dr., Dillon; (970) 468-2403; www.townofdillon.com

Sunset at the Summit Concert Series, Dillon Amphitheatre; Town of Dillon, 275 Lake Dillon Dr., Dillon; (970) 468-2403; www.townofdillon.com

Krystal 93 BBQ at the Summit, Dillon; www.summitrotaryevents.com/ BBQ-at-the-Summit.php

Dillon Schoolhouse Museum, 403 La Bonte St., Dillon; (970) 468-2207; www .summithistorical.org

Lake Dillon Theatre, 176 Lake Dillon Dr., Dillon; (970) 513-1151; www.lake dillontheatre.org

The Ptarmigan Trail climbs steadily through various ecosystems including sagebrush meadow, lodgepole pine, aspen, spruce-fir, and alpine tundra—the land above the trees. While thick forest envelops the trail between 1.7 and 4.2 miles, a few open spaces provide great views of the Gore Range or the lower Blue River valley. As you hike above treeline, keep your eyes open on the north ridge for the resident elk herd. The long hike is rewarded by beautiful vistas from the top, including four 14,000-foot peaks, much of the craggy Gore Range, the Tenmile Range, and Dillon Reservoir. A shorter, difficult 5.2-mile option is noted.

Start: At the Angler Mountain Trail trailhead bulletin board
Distance: 12.4 miles out and back
Hiking time: 6 to 10 hours
Difficulty: Most difficult due to a 3,818-foot elevation gain and altitude
Trail surface: Dirt road and dirt trail
Best season: July to early Oct
Other trail users: Equestrians on Angler Mountain Trail and in Ptarmigan Peak Wilderness. Mountain bikers can ride the Ptarmigan Trail to the wilderness boundary.
Canine compatibility: Dogs must be on leash in the wilderness; under voice control elsewhere.
Land status: National forest and wilderness
Fees and permits: None required. Limit of 15 people per group in the wilderness.
Maps: USGS Dillon; Nat Geo Trails Illustrated 108 Vail/Frisco/Dillon; Latitude 40° Summit County Trails; USFS White River National Forest map

Trail contact: USDA Forest Service, Dillon Ranger District, 680 Blue River Pkwy., Silverthorne; (970) 468-5400; www.fs.usda.gov/white river; www.dillonrangerdistrict .com
Other: The first part of the trail is on an easement through the Angler Mountain subdivision. Please stay on the designated trail. Starting at mile 4.5 the trail enters the Ptarmigan Peak Wilderness. Please comply with wilderness regulations.
Special considerations: Water is very sparse on the Ptarmigan Trail. Make sure to bring plenty. Because the trail travels about 1.7 miles one way above treeline, start early to avoid thunderstorms and lightning. Bring clothing layers because the wind can be very chilly on top. Hunters use this area during hunting season. The lower part of the trail is used by snowshoers, winter walkers, and cross-country skiers. The trail is neither marked nor maintained for winter use.

Finding the trailhead: From I-70 exit 205 (Silverthorne/Dillon), head north on CO 9 about 2.2 miles and turn right onto Bald Eagle Road at The Ponds sign. Drive 0.6 mile to where the road curves left, then turn right into the trailhead parking lot. No facilities are available. GPS: N39 39.18′ / W106 04.37′.

THE HIKE

The Angler Mountain Trail climbs steeply up a sagebrush hillside then mellows as it winds up through aspen forest, which is gorgeous when decked in gold in late September. Blue columbines, the Colorado state flower, bloom under the aspen canopy. After the national forest boundary, the trail continues through sagebrush meadow where yellow arrowleaf balsamroot and blue lupine bloom profusely in June. Take a moment to enjoy the view of Dillon Reservoir and the Daley Ranch. You reach the Ptarmigan Trail after steadily gaining 1,120 feet in 2.1 miles. Notice how the vegetation differs dramatically between the lush aspen groves and the drier lodgepole ecosystem. Flowers blooming along the trail include white yarrow, white pussytoes, purple fringe (phacelia), and yellow sulphur flowers.

After you turn left onto the Ptarmigan Trail, keep an eye open to the left near mile 2.6 for a scenic view and nice log to sit on. This spot is a good turnaround for a shorter hike or a winter walk. From here the trail climbs and switchbacks

Ptarmigan Peak Wilderness boundary

through lodgepole pine and spruce-fir forest. Just before the wilderness boundary, the trail heads south through more open forest with fields of red paintbrush, blue lupine, and yellow cinquefoil and dandelions.

After the wilderness portal sign, the trail climbs steadily through the ecotone where subalpine forest and alpine tundra meet. The trees grow sparser and smaller where the winds blow harder, creating lower temperatures. Summer temperatures here average less than 50°F. Speaking of wind, a chilly breeze (or wind that makes you walk like a drunk) usually blows over these open spaces, and rare is the day when you can sit on the summit without wearing a jacket. Finally you are in the land above the trees, with its miniature plants and flowers that somehow survive where summer may only last for six weeks. One wet area with miniature willows provides a small dribble of water.

The flowers bloom brilliantly after the Fourth of July. Patches of blue forget-me-nots grow along the trail, accompanied by grayish-green stalks of sage, the bright yellow of alpine avens and cinquefoil, pink moss campion, white alpine phlox, yellow paintbrush, and bistort. Plants such as the moss campion grow in cushions for protection against wind and ice particles. Their taproots may reach

Ptarmigan Peak Wilderness

The Ptarmigan Peak Wilderness is just a sliver of protected area along the ridge and west side of the Williams Fork Mountains. The parcel was originally part of the Williams Fork Further Planning Area; environmentalists requested designation of a 74,770-acre wilderness area that started farther down on the west side and continued east into the two drainages of the South Fork and Middle Fork of the Williams Fork and to Bobtail Creek, Pettingell Peak, and Jones Pass. The area ranked as one of the highest in Colorado in the USDA Forest Service's Wilderness Attribute Rating System in the 1980s. But the Denver Water Board owned easements in the area and wanted to be able to divert water from the South and Middle Forks to their growing consumer base in the Denver area. The Federal Timber Purchasers Association also opposed wilderness designation for the larger area. By the time everyone took a bite, the Colorado Wilderness Act of 1993 proposed the Farr Wilderness Area with 13,175 acres. When the Act was approved in August 1993, it created the 13,175-acre Ptarmigan Peak Wilderness and renamed the Granby Pumping Plant the Farr Pumping Plant.

The Farr Pumping Plant is part of the Colorado–Big Thompson Project, which diverts water from the upper Colorado River from Grand Lake to Mary's Lake near Estes Park. The pumping plant lifts water from Lake Granby to Shadow Mountain Reservoir, which then goes into Grand Lake. The Farr family, in particular W. D. Farr, was honored for its contributions to water development, agricultural innovations, and conservation in Colorado.

4 to 5 feet underground to find moisture and anchor against the winds. The moss campion grows slowly—about one-quarter inch a year. The big golden sunflowers that tower over the smaller plants are old-man-of-the-mountains, or *Rydbergia grandiflora*. These giants can grow for twelve to fifteen years to gather and store enough energy to bloom. Once the flower fades away, the plant dies.

For all their seeming toughness, alpine plants are quite fragile. Frequent trampling by boots can destroy them. A piece of paper covering a small cushion plant may deny it the energy needed to make it through the winter. If no trail exists and it's necessary to walk across alpine tundra, walk on rocks as much as possible, and spread out so no two footsteps land on the same plant.

Gentle Ptarmigan Peak has a false summit, so keep hiking. When you reach a sign that says "Ute Peak Trail" left and "Ptarmigan Trail" right, turn right and carefully walk up to the summit cairn, where it's easy to think that the other spot over there is a tad higher! If the wind is blowing mercilessly, hike down the east side of the ridge from the cairn. Dropping below the ridge just a few feet makes a huge difference in the wind, and you can enjoy the view of Ptarmigan Pass, the South Fork of the Williams Fork drainage, peaks on the Continental Divide, and 14,200-foot Grays and Torreys Peaks to the southeast. A large elk herd spends the summers grazing nearby. They can often be seen along the ridge to the north or down by the little lake to the southeast. Enjoy the views, especially of the Gore and Tenmile Ranges, on your way back down.

MILES AND DIRECTIONS

0.0 Start at the Angler Mountain Trail trailhead bulletin board. Elevation: 8,680 feet.

1.1 Come to the national forest boundary. Just beyond are good views to the south.

2.1 Arrive at the junction with the Ptarmigan Peak Trail. Turn left and head uphill. GPS: N39 39.47' / W106 03.23'.

2.6 To the left of the trail is a log that provides a nice place to sit with a great view of Silverthorne, the Gore Range, and over to the Tenmile Range. GPS: N39 39.76' / W106 03.29'. Elevation: 10,050 feet. (**Option:** Turn around and return the way you came for a 5.2-mile out-and-back hike with a 1,370-foot elevation gain.)

4.1 An opening in the trees provides a nice view to the north of the lower Blue River valley.

4.5 The trail reaches the Ptarmigan Peak Wilderness boundary. GPS: N39 40.30' / W106 02.43'.

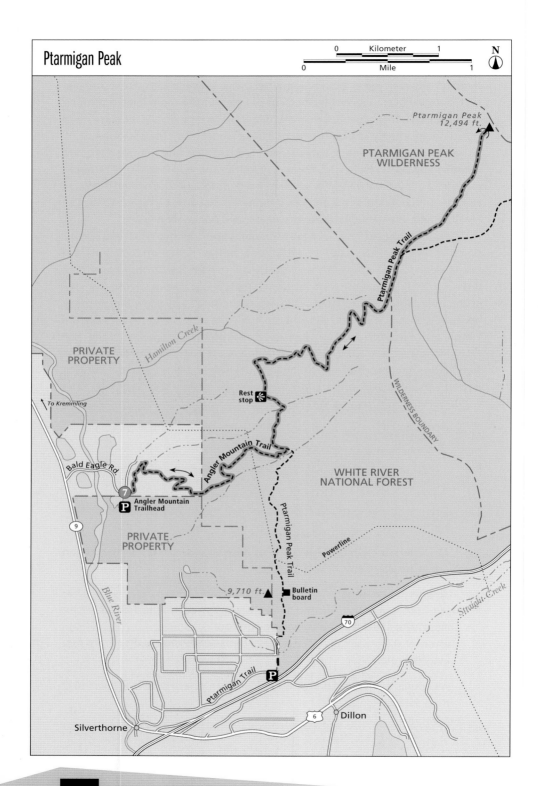

Ptarmigan Peak

Ptarmigan Peak
12,494 ft.

PTARMIGAN PEAK
WILDERNESS

Ptarmigan Peak Trail

PRIVATE
PROPERTY

Hamilton Creek

WILDERNESS BOUNDARY

To Kremmling

Rest
stop

Angler Mountain Trail

Bald Eagle Rd.

WHITE RIVER
NATIONAL FOREST

7

Angler Mountain
Trailhead

PRIVATE
PROPERTY

9

Powerline

Ptarmigan Peak Trail

Blue River

9,710 ft.

Bulletin
board

70

Straight Creek

Ptarmigan Trail

P

6

Dillon

Silverthorne

Kilometer

Mile

N

Ptarmigan Peak
summit cairn

5.0 You're now in the land above the trees by a trail sign. The faint trail to the right leads to Ptarmigan Pass. Go straight ahead to reach the peak. Sometimes the trail disappears, but just continue along the left (north) side of the ridge and you'll find the trail again.

6.1 A trail sign marks the place to turn right to reach the summit cairn.

6.2 You've made it to the Ptarmigan Peak summit cairn. GPS: N39 41.45'/W106 01.58'. Elevation: 12,498 feet. Enjoy the 360-degree view to the Mount of the Holy Cross, the Gore Range, over to Longs Peak, Grays and Torreys Peaks, and the valleys below. Return the way you came.

12.4 Arrive back at the trailhead.

HIKE INFORMATION

Local Information
Colorado Welcome Center at Silverthorne, Outlets at Silverthorne, 246 Rainbow Dr., Silverthorne; (970) 468-0353; www.colorado.com/official-colorado -welcome-centers

Local Events/Attractions
Friday Farmers Market, Buffalo and Main Streets; Town of Dillon, 275 Lake Dillon Dr., Dillon; (970) 468-2403; www.townofdillon.com
    Sunset at the Summit Concert Series, Dillon Amphitheatre; Town of Dillon, 275 Lake Dillon Dr., Dillon; (970) 468-2403; www.townofdillon.com
    Krystal 93 BBQ at the Summit, Dillon; www.summitrotaryevents.com/BBQ -at-the-Summit.php

Organizations
Friends of the Eagles Nest Wilderness, www.fenw.org, or call the Dillon Ranger District, (970) 468-5400, for the current contact.

8

South Willow Creek Falls

Most of this hike follows the route originally proposed for I-70, but today it takes you to a set of waterfalls beneath craggy spires on the north side of Buffalo Mountain. The trail wanders through lodgepole pine forest interspersed with a few aspen. Mountain pine beetles killed many of the pines in the first decade of the 2000s. While this hike is longer than some, the elevation gain is spread out, with the steepest section coming after 3.6 miles. Part of the trail is downright flat! South Willow Creek Falls is worth the effort, especially in early summer during runoff.

Start: At the Mesa Cortina Trailhead

Distance: 9.0 miles out and back

Hiking time: 3.7 to 6 hours

Difficulty: Moderate due to distance and an 820-foot elevation gain

Trail surface: Dirt trail

Best season: Late June to early Oct

Other trail users: Equestrians

Canine compatibility: Dogs must be on leash

Land status: National forest and wilderness

Fees and permits: None required. Limit of 15 people per group.

Maps: USGS Dillon, Willow Lakes, and Vail East; Nat Geo Trails Illustrated 108 Vail/Frisco/Dillon; Latitude 40° Summit County Trails; USFS White River National Forest map

Trail contact: USDA Forest Service, Dillon Ranger District, 680 Blue River Pkwy., Silverthorne; (970) 468-5400; www.fs.usda.gov/whiteriver; www.dillonranger district.com

Other: The trail is mainly within the Eagles Nest Wilderness area. Please comply with wilderness regulations.

Special considerations: Hunters use this area during hunting season. The trail is neither marked nor maintained for winter use, but many locals use the trails during winter for walking, snowshoeing, and cross-country skiing at least to the meadow at mile 3.6. After the meadow, be careful of avalanches the rest of the way to the falls and beyond.

Finding the trailhead: From I-70 exit 205 (Silverthorne/Dillon), head north on CO 9 for 0.2 mile to Wildernest Road by the 7-Eleven store. Turn left (south) and follow Wildernest Road for 0.3 mile to the second traffic light. Go straight ahead onto Buffalo Mountain Drive. (Lowe's will be on your left.) Drive up a steep hill for 0.7 mile to Lake View Drive. Make a sharp right turn (north) and drive up Lake View Drive for 0.5 mile then curve to the left (south) onto Aspen Drive. Turn right in 0.1 mile into the parking lot for the Mesa Cortina Trailhead. GPS: N39 37.44' / W106 04.92'.

If the Colorado Department of Transportation's (CDOT) wish had been granted back in the mid-1960s, you would be driving along South Willow Creek instead of hiking. CDOT proposed a route for I-70 that would turn at Silverthorne and head up South Willow Creek. At an elevation of about 10,700 feet, a two-lane tunnel would burrow under Red-Buffalo Pass for about 6,500 feet. On the west side of the pass, I-70 would travel down Gore Creek and then curve west past Vail.

CDOT chose the route because it would cut 11 miles off the alternate route of US 6 through Tenmile Canyon and over Vail Pass. Calculations estimated that the shorter route would save travelers $4 million annually over the next twenty years. Cost projections for the shorter route including the tunnel came in at $42 million plus an extra $21 million for a second tunnel. The Vail Pass route estimate was $22 million.

Not everyone agreed with CDOT about the appropriateness and cost savings of the Red-Buffalo route. CDOT held public meetings in 1966 and 1967. Some concerns mentioned included known avalanche paths along the corridor and poor sun exposure during winter because of Buffalo Mountain and other peaks along Gore Creek.

Residents of Summit County and Leadville voiced their apprehension that the Red-Buffalo route would bypass easy access to those communities. They wondered if CDOT had considered the additional cost of maintaining US 6 as well as the new I-70.

Buffalo Mountain and a meadow along the trail

The proposed route cut through the Gore Range-Eagles Nest Primitive Area, which was scheduled for congressional hearings in 1968 for designation as a wilderness area. Because the route would cross national forest lands, the then-secretary of agriculture, Orville Freeman, had the final say on CDOT's request. In May 1968, according to a USDA Forest Service press release, Freeman denied the request, noting "the public benefits of preserving this priceless wilderness area far outweigh any other considerations."

After many other battles involving timber and water, Congress designated the Eagles Nest Wilderness in 1976.

The trail traverses the hillside above the town of Silverthorne, crossing meadows interspersed with forest. You can see the Williams Fork Mountains and Ptarmigan Peak to the east. Before reaching the Gore Range Trail (GRT), the path widens where a road once carried people to their house. After turning onto the GRT and going up a little hill, the trail is basically flat until you reach the meadow at 3.6 miles. Look to the left for old bedsprings and other remains of the house that once sat at the meadow's edge. The house burned down around 1983. Enjoy the wonderful wildflowers on this section of trail. In early spring (June in this area), pasqueflowers, with their nodding purplish heads, line the trail. This meadow is a good turnaround place for a cross-country ski tour or snowshoe trip, as avalanche paths cross the trail farther up. From here the trail narrows and becomes rocky. At 4.2 miles you'll pass a huge house-size boulder along the trail. The trail climbs up past a small avalanche chute and is usually lined with

South Willow Creek Falls from above

5

5

beautiful blue columbines, Colorado's state flower. Just before the junction to the falls, a large rock outcrop next to the trail provides a nice view down valley.

South Willow Creek Falls is a great place for a picnic. A big flat rock provides a close-up view of and occasional spray from the upper falls, and you are at the top of the lower falls. Although not included in this hike's mileage, you can walk up to the top of the falls by going back to the GRT, turning left, and switchbacking up the trail about 0.1 mile. The trail passes a rock slab—to the left you can walk over to see the top of the falls. The rock slab is another good lunch spot. If you continue up the GRT, you can hike all the way to Frisco over Eccles Pass (one-way total of about 10.8 miles) or to East Vail over Red-Buffalo Pass (one-way total of 14.9 miles).

MILES AND DIRECTIONS

0.0 Start at the Mesa Cortina Trailhead. Elevation: 9,215 feet.

0.8 Come to the Eagles Nest Wilderness boundary.

1.6 The Leopold Trail from Wildernest comes in from the left. Continue to the right on the Mesa Cortina Trail.

2.3 Arrive at a trail junction to private property. Stay to the left on the Mesa Cortina Trail.

2.4 The South Willowbrook Trail comes in from the right. Hike straight ahead on the Mesa Cortina Trail.

2.8 Reach the junction of Mesa Cortina Trail and the Gore Range Trail. GPS: N39 38.23' / W106 06.73'. Turn left (west) onto the Gore Range Trail (GRT).

3.6 The trail crosses a meadow with a good view of Buffalo Mountain. Look to the left for old bedsprings from a house that burned down here.

3.8 The South Willow/Buffalo Cabin Connect Trail comes in from the left. GPS: N39 37.95' / W106 07.66'. Continue straight ahead (west) on the GRT.

4.4 Come to a signed junction with the trail to South Willow Creek Falls. Turn left (southwest).

An interesting rule of thumb: For every 1,000 feet of elevation gained, the temperature drops between 5.4°F when sunny or about 3.3°F when cloudy. So when it's 80°F in Denver at 5,280 feet, it may be 60°F in Frisco at 9,100 feet.

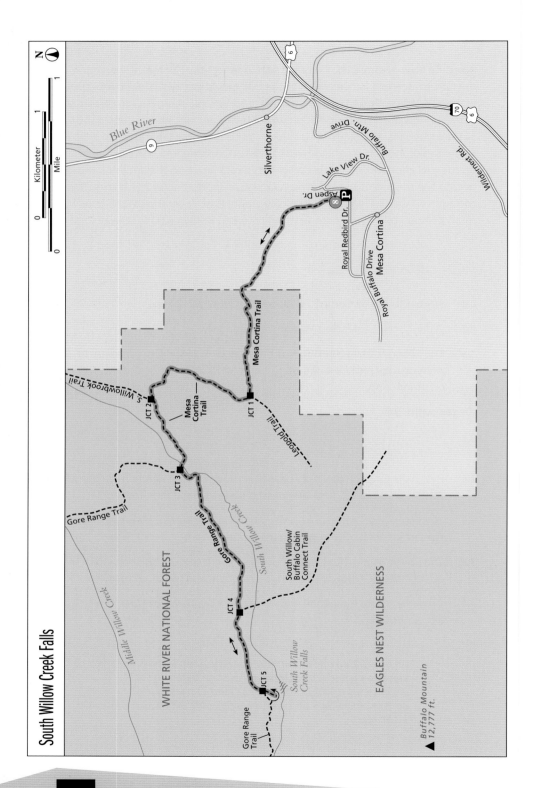

South Willow Creek Falls

N

White River National Forest

Middle Willow Creek

Gore Range Trail

S. Willowbrook Trail

JCT 2

Mesa Cortina Trail

JCT 3

Gore Range Trail

Gore Range Trail

JCT 4

JCT 5

South Willow Creek Falls

South Willow Creek

South Willow/ Buffalo Cabin Connect Trail

JCT 1

Mesa Cortina Trail

Leopold Trail

Mesa Cortina Trail

Lake View Dr.

Aspen Dr.

Royal Redbird Dr.

Buffalo Mtn. Drive

Royal Buffalo Drive

Mesa Cortina

Silverthorne

Blue River

9

6

6

70

Wildernest Rd.

EAGLES NEST WILDERNESS

Buffalo Mountain
12,777 ft.

Kilometer

Mile

4.5 To reach the falls, stay on the trail to the right of the cabin remains. Head downhill toward the creek to reach upper South Willow Creek Falls. GPS: N39 37.76' / W106 08.22'. Elevation: 10,040 feet. Trails go every which way in this area. Enjoy your visit to the falls. Return the way you came.

9.0 Arrive back at the trailhead.

HIKE INFORMATION

Local Information
Colorado Welcome Center at Silverthorne, Outlets at Silverthorne, 246 Rainbow Dr., Silverthorne; (970) 468-0353; www.colorado.com/official-colorado-welcome-centers

Local Events/Attractions
Friday Farmers Market, Buffalo and Main Streets; Town of Dillon, 275 Lake Dillon Dr., Dillon; (970) 468-2403; www.townofdillon.com

Sunset at the Summit Concert Series, Dillon Amphitheatre; Town of Dillon, 275 Lake Dillon Dr., Dillon; (970) 468-2403; www.townofdillon.com

Krystal 93 BBQ at the Summit, Dillon; www.summitrotaryevents.com/BBQ-at-the-Summit.php

Organizations
Friends of the Eagles Nest Wilderness, www.fenw.org, or call the Dillon Ranger District, (970) 468–5400, for the current contact.

Despite what some maps show, the Continental Divide National Scenic Trail does NOT follow the Gore Range Trail! Neither does the CDNST traverse the Eagles Nest Wilderness. It crosses through Summit County passing Gold Hill north of Breckenridge and over the Tenmile Range to Copper Mountain.

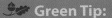 **Green Tip:**
Carry a reusable water container that you fill at the tap or from a water filter while you are out hiking. Bottled water is expensive; lots of petroleum is used to make the plastic bottles; and they're a disposal nightmare. It's best to pre-cycle by not buying plastic items to begin with, even if you can recycle them.

Kettle Ponds

This gentle, uncrowded hike follows an old mining road then travels on the Gore Range Trail (GRT), climbing a lateral moraine left by two epochs of glaciers. The GRT wanders around the top of the forested glacial debris, past many small ponds, some covered with lily pads. Conifers grow thickly on the moraine—mainly lodgepole pine interspersed with a few aspen, spruce, and fir. You'll notice many dead lodgepole pines, killed by the mountain pine beetle. Dropping down to cross South Rock Creek, the trail crosses a few boggy areas then climbs to an unnamed lake. The peaceful destination provides views of Red Peak, with its craggy ridge, and the Thorn.

Start: At the North Rock Creek Trail trailhead bulletin board

Distance: 6.4 miles out and back

Hiking time: 2.5 to 4.5 hours

Difficulty: Moderate due to distance and a 600-foot elevation gain

Trail surface: Dirt trail

Best season: Mid-June to mid-Oct

Other trail users: Equestrians

Canine compatibility: Dogs must be on leash

Land status: National forest wilderness

Fees and permits: None required. Limit of 15 people per group.

Maps: USGS Willow Lakes; Nat Geo Trails Illustrated 108 Vail/Frisco/Dillon; Latitude 40° Summit County Trails; USFS White River National Forest map

Trail contact: USDA Forest Service, Dillon Ranger District, 680 Blue River Pkwy., Silverthorne; (970) 468-5400; www.fs.usda.gov/whiteriver; www.dillonranger district.com

Other: The trail is mainly within the Eagles Nest Wilderness. Please comply with wilderness regulations.

Special considerations: This area is very popular during hunting season. The winter parking lot (small) is at the junction of Rock Creek Road and FR 1350, 1.6 miles from the summer trailhead. Rock Creek Road is popular for cross-country skiing and snowshoeing in winter. The trail is neither marked nor maintained for winter use.

Finding the trailhead: From I-70 exit 205 (Silverthorne/Dillon), drive about 7.8 miles north on CO 9 to Rock Creek Road, just past mile marker 109 and across from Blue River Campground, and turn left. Follow the dirt road about 1.3 miles to the Rock Creek trailhead sign. Turn left onto FR 1350. The road narrows and becomes bumpy. It dead-ends at the North Rock Creek Trail trailhead in 1.6 miles. No facilities are available at the trailhead. GPS: N39 42.63' / W106 10.03'.

THE HIKE

Between 150,000 and 12,000 years ago, two periods of glaciation (Bull Lake and Pinedale) deposited thick sheets of ice in this area. As the glaciers crept forward, they eroded the land underneath and pushed the resulting sediments out of the way, creating ridges known as lateral moraines. Hunks of ice sometimes became embedded in the moraines then melted, creating small ponds. Geologists call these depressions kettle ponds or kettle holes.

This hike starts on the old Boss Mine Road (Rock Creek Trail) then turns south onto the Gore Range Trail (GRT). The GRT descends to a nice bridge. A local group, Friends of the Eagles Nest Wilderness, provided the labor to help the USDA Forest Service build this bridge and a good horse crossing. From here the GRT travels through lodgepole pine forest to switchback steadily up the side of a moraine. Once on top, the trail undulates along the moraine. Various kettle ponds appear along the trail—some are filled with green goop, some contain lily pads or grasses, while others have dried out. Some ponds hide in the forest not far off the trail.

The lodgepole forest has sparse understory including buffaloberry bushes, heartleaf arnica, yellow paintbrush, whortleberry, and harebells. Occasionally a large boulder, probably left by a glacier, sits near the trail, watching history march on. Pine squirrels scold hikers passing too close to their favorite trees.

The GRT eventually drops down and crosses sparkling South Rock Creek on a fancy bridge complete with handrails. A quick climb out of the drainage brings

North Rock Creek view of Gore Range

you to a ditch that takes water from South Rock Creek to Maryland Creek. In a few more steps the trail comes to a small lake, the destination of this hike. Take some time to enjoy the scenery of the Gore Range and its reflections. The peak to the left is on the ridge of Red Peak. Spindly spires form the ridge to Red Peak's high point to the west. On the other side of the rounded ridge lie Salmon and Willow Lakes. The craggy peak above is known locally as East Thorn or the Thorn. The peak to the right of East Thorn is unnamed, as are many in the Eagles Nest Wilderness.

The Gore Range was uplifted with the present Rocky Mountains starting about 70 million years ago in an episode called the Laramide Orogeny. These mountains lifted along the Blue River Frontal Fault, and the lower Blue River valley dropped as a block.

A regional uplift occurred between 5 and 2 million years ago, raising the Rockies and the Colorado Plateau as much as 5,000 feet. The climate changed and snow remained year-round, growing deeper with each season. Eventually only the tops of the highest peaks poked above the glaciers. The Gore Range is unusual in that both sides of the range were glaciated. In other mountain ranges only the east slopes, which filled with snow blown by west winds, developed glaciers. The sharp arêtes of the Gore Range were created as the ice stripped away rock and dirt, leaving behind sharp ridges and points.

While a few mines were discovered and worked in the Gore Range, like the Boss Mine, the mountains and creeks did not contain the wealth of minerals

South Rock Creek bridge

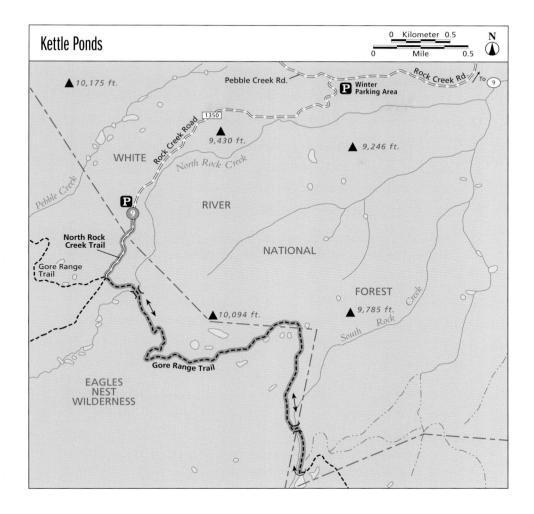

Kettle Ponds

found in other parts of Summit County. The Eagles Nest Wilderness is therefore less disturbed by human activity than areas that were mined.

This section of the GRT is lightly traveled except during hunting season and provides a pleasant escape from the more crowded trails in Summit County.

MILES AND DIRECTIONS

0.0 Start at the North Rock Creek Trail trailhead bulletin board. Elevation: 9,470 feet.

0.1 Arrive at the Eagles Nest Wilderness boundary.

0.4 The trail intersects with the Gore Range Trail (GRT). Turn left and hike south on the GRT. GPS: N39 42.33' / W106 10.20'.

0.6 The trail crosses North Rock Creek on a nice bridge.

0.8 The trail crosses a boggy area with a little footbridge. (*Note:* Look back as you cross this area because the trail is not as obvious on the return trip.)

1.6 The trail reaches the top of the moraine. High point: 10,070 feet.

2.0 The trail passes several kettle ponds with grass and one with lily pads.

2.9 The trail crosses South Rock Creek on a bridge with handrails. On both sides of the creek, the trail traverses boggy areas.

3.1 The trail splits at a ditch. Cross the ditch and head uphill to the left.

3.2 Arrive at an unnamed lake with beautiful views of the craggy Gore Range. GPS: N39 41.38' / W106 09.05'. Elevation: 10,060 feet. Return the way you came.

6.4 Arrive back at the trailhead.

HIKE INFORMATION

Local Information
Colorado Welcome Center at Silverthorne, Outlets at Silverthorne, 246 Rainbow Drive, Silverthorne; (970) 468-0353; www.colorado.com/official-colorado-welcome-centers

Local Events/Attractions
Friday Farmers Market, Buffalo and Main Streets, Town of Dillon, 275 Lake Dillon Dr., Dillon; (970) 468-2403; www.townofdillon.com

Friday Night Concerts at the Amphitheatre, Dillon Amphitheatre, Town of Dillon, 275 Lake Dillon Dr., Dillon; (970) 468-2403; www.townofdillon.com

Krystal 93 BBQ at the Summit, Dillon; www.summitrotary.com/BBQ-at-the-Summit.php

Buffaloberry

One of the shrubs found in lodgepole pine forests is the buffaloberry. Its thick oval leaves look gray green with fuzzy silver undersides. The red berries are rich in both vitamin C and iron and can be eaten fresh, although they taste bitter. Favorite uses include jelly, syrup, or whipped with water into a foamy dessert called "Indian ice cream." The berries can also be used as soap after being crushed or boiled. If eaten in large quantities—much like soap—the fruit can cause diarrhea. Bears and little forest critters like chipmunks and ground squirrels enjoy the berries.

Eaglesmere Lakes

Surrounded by spruce-fir forest, Eaglesmere Lakes, remnants from the last ice age, are slowly filling in with grass. A great view of craggy Eagles Nest, the peak after which the Eagles Nest Wilderness was named, treats your eye from the trail and at the farthest lake. At 13,310 feet, Eagles Nest is the second-highest peak in the Gore Range, while nearby Mount Powell at 13,566 feet is the highest. The lakes are a nice backpacking destination, but are also a great day hike, especially during autumn when the aspen leaves turn gold.

Start: At the Eaglesmere Trail trailhead
Distance: 7.6 miles out and back
Hiking time: 3 to 5 hours
Difficulty: Difficult due to a 1,670-foot elevation gain
Trail surface: Dirt trail
Best season: Mid-June to early Oct
Other trail users: Equestrians
Canine compatibility: Dogs must be on leash in the Eagles Nest Wilderness
Land status: National forest and wilderness
Fees and permits: None required. Limit of 15 people per group.
Maps: USGS Mount Powell; Nat Geo Trails Illustrated 107 Green Mountain Reservoir/Ute Pass; Latitude 40° Summit County Trails; USFS White River National Forest map

Trail contact: USDA Forest Service, Dillon Ranger District, 680 Blue River Pkwy., Silverthorne; (970) 468-5400; www.fs.usda.gov/whiteriver; www.dillonrangerdistrict.com
Other: The trail is mainly within the Eagles Nest Wilderness. Please comply with wilderness regulations.
Special considerations: Campfires are prohibited at Eaglesmere Lakes. Bring your own water or be prepared to treat water. Hunters use this area during hunting season. The road is closed in winter about 1.3 miles from the trailhead. The trail is neither marked nor maintained for winter use. Cataract Creek Road is nice for cross-country skiing, walking, or snowshoeing past the winter closure.

Finding the trailhead: From I-70 exit 205 (Silverthorne/Dillon), drive north through Silverthorne on CO 9 for 16.9 miles to Heeney Road (Summit CR 30). Turn left and drive on Heeney Road for 5.6 miles to the Cataract Creek Road sign. Make a sharp left (southwest) and follow Cataract Creek Road for 2.2 miles to FR 1726. Turn right and drive 0.4 mile to the trailhead. Please park only in the few designated spaces. More parking is available at the Surprise Lake and Lower Cataract Lake trailheads. An outhouse is available near the trailhead. GPS at trailhead bulletin board: N39 50.37' / W106 18.83'.

If you reached the trailhead by driving on CR 30 from the south, you passed the Knorr Ranch. Judge William Guyselman came to Breckenridge in 1880 and obtained land along the lower Blue River. Some pioneers homesteaded their land while others purchased land from the original homesteaders. William Knorr immigrated from Germany and, with his brother, mined around Breckenridge and Montezuma. In 1902 Knorr married Judge Guyselman's daughter, Corinne, and they settled on a ranch along the Blue River. Ranches typically consisted of a house, barn(s), corral, icehouse, chicken coop, and pigpen. Fields for crops, especially timothy, alfalfa, clover, and wild grasses for winter feed for the animals, and a winter grazing area lay nearby. Hungry miners, happy for local produce that didn't cost as much as food that had to be shipped into Summit County, purchased vegetables, meat, and dairy products from the ranchers. Hardy vegetables that grew well during the short summers included radishes, carrots, lettuce, turnips, potatoes, spinach, peas, cabbage, and onions. One ranch at Slate Creek produced 17 tons of potatoes in 1914. Cattle and sheep were driven along the road that is now CO 9 to Dillon or Kremmling to the railroad for shipment to Denver. People raised chickens for eggs and meat. In summer and fall, ranching families used trails into the area above Lower Cataract Lake to fish, hunt, and trap.

Between 1940 and 1942, Green Mountain Reservoir was built as part of the Colorado–Big Thompson Project, which transports water from the west slope to thirsty Denver residents and agriculture on the east slope. The Knorrs' original

First of two Eaglesmere Lakes

ranch soon lay under water. They moved uphill to their present site, at one time owning about 10,000 acres. They raised more than 700 cows, 35 draft horses, and some saddle horses. Hay for winter feed is still a common crop, and occasionally you can see an old hay stacker along the road.

The Eaglesmere Trail starts in a beautiful aspen forest. The five-petaled pink flowers are Woods' rose, a common plant that grows beneath aspen. Other flowers include blue columbines, white yarrow, purple asters, and white geraniums along with currant bushes. At 0.8 mile, the trail traverses a sagebrush meadow, which affords a wonderful view of Lower Cataract Lake and Eagles Nest. After crossing a small drainage, the trail winds through spruce-fir forest before coming to the Eagles Nest Wilderness boundary. After turning onto the Gore Range Trail, you pass several damp or marshy areas, precursors to the lakes.

The USDA Forest Service built sections of the Gore Range Trail during the 1930s and early 1940s to allow access to fight fires in remote areas. Trail workers included men from local ranches and towns. The trail is approximately 54 miles long, starting at Copper Mountain in the south, first crossing the Gore Range, then traversing its east side to Mahan Lake in the north.

When you arrive near the first Eaglesmere Lake, a side trail takes you to some boulders to the right where you can enjoy the peace and quiet. Continue a little farther to a flat area between the two lakes. A rock ridge provides views of both lakes. Walk a little farther to the left of the ridge on the north side of the lake for a view of craggy Eagles Nest to the south. Enjoy your time at quiet Eaglesmere Lakes.

MILES AND DIRECTIONS

0.0   Start at the Eaglesmere Trail trailhead bulletin board. Elevation: 8,727 feet.

0.8   Arrive at a view of Lower Cataract Lake, Eagles Nest, and Dora Mountain. The trail splits here. Head right and uphill. GPS: N39 50.31' / W106 19.48'.

2.25   Enter the Eagles Nest Wilderness.

3.1   Arrive at the junction with the Gore Range Trail. Turn right.

> **🌿 Green Tip:**
> *If you plan to camp, please find a spot at least 100 feet away from the trail, from the flat spot between the lakes, and from the water. A trail on the east side of the lake takes you to some potential campsites. Remember to treat lake water for drinking.*

Eaglesmere Lakes

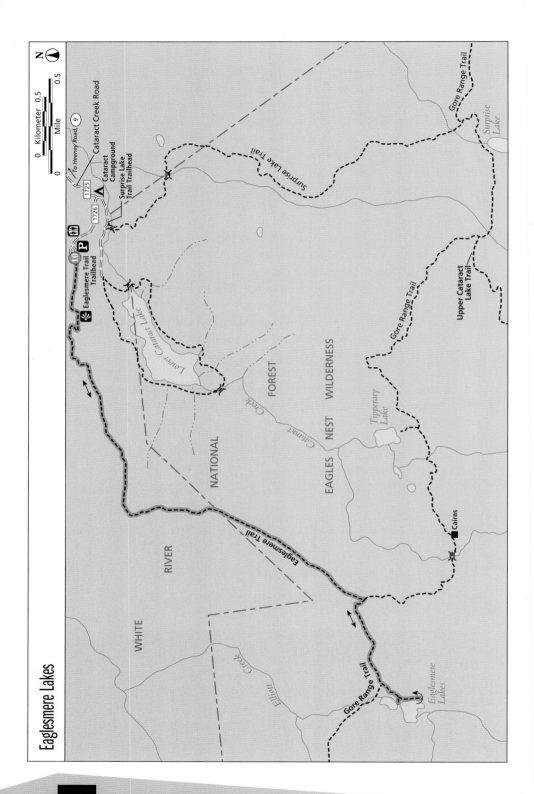

N

0 Kilometer 0.5

0 Mile 0.5

To Heeney Road, 9

Cataract Creek Road

1725

Cataract
Campground

Surprise Lake
Trail Trailhead

Surprise Lake Trail

Surprise
Lake

Gore Range Trail

1726

Eaglesmere Trail
Trailhead

P

Lower Cataract Lake

Upper Cataract
Lake Trail

Gore Range Trail

Cataract Creek

WHITE

RIVER

NATIONAL

FOREST

EAGLES

NEST

WILDERNESS

Tipperary
Lake

Eaglesmere Trail

Elliott Creek

Cairns

Gore Range Trail

Eaglesmere
Lakes

3.7 Come to the junction with the Eaglesmere Lake Spur. Go straight ahead (Gore Range Trail heads to the right). GPS: N39 49.01' / W106 21.37'.

3.8 Arrive at a flat area between the two Eaglesmere Lakes. GPS: N39 48.92' / W106 21.48'. Elevation: 10,400 feet. Enjoy the two lakes, eat lunch, and explore a little. Return the way you came.

7.6 Arrive back at the trailhead.

Option

A 12.3-mile four-lake loop hike/backpack to Surprise, Tipperary, and Eaglesmere Lakes.

0.0 Park your car at the Eaglesmere Trail trailhead and walk back down the road to FR 1725, turn right, and walk 0.2 mile to the Surprise Lake Trail trailhead. GPS: N39 50.22' / W106 18.65'.

0.6 Head up the Surprise Lake Trail.

3.3 Arrive at the junction with the Gore Range Trail. Turn right.

3.5 Surprise Lake is to the south of the trail. GPS: N39 48.54' / W106 18.16'.

4.0 Arrive at the junction with the Upper Cataract Lake Trail. Stay on the Gore Range Trail, which goes straight ahead.

Lower Cataract Lake from Eaglesmere Trail

5.4 Come to the trail junction for Tipperary Lake. GPS: N39 48.83' / W106 19.87'. It's 0.2 mile out and back to the lake, which is at elevation 9,765 feet. Return the way you came to the Gore Range Trail and turn right (west) to continue the loop.

6.9 The trail Ys. Turn right as marked by the cairn.

7.8 Arrive at the trail junction with the Eaglesmere Trail. Turn left and head uphill.

8.4 Come to the junction with the Eaglesmere Lake Spur. Go straight ahead (Gore Range Trail heads to the right).

8.5 Come to the flat area between the two Eaglesmere Lakes. Return the way you came to the junction of the Eaglesmere Lake Spur and Gore Range Trails. Turn right.

9.2 Arrive at the trail junction with the Eaglesmere Trail (same as mile 7.8). Turn left and head downhill.

12.3 Arrive at the Eaglesmere Trail trailhead.

HIKE INFORMATION

Local Information
Colorado Welcome Center at Silverthorne, Outlets at Silverthorne, 246 Rainbow Dr., Silverthorne; (970) 468-0353; www.colorado.com/official-colorado-welcome-centers

Local Events/Attractions
Friday Farmers Market, Buffalo and Main Streets; Town of Dillon, 275 Lake Dillon Dr., Dillon; (970) 468-2403; www.townofdillon.com

Sunset at the Summit Concert Series, Dillon Amphitheatre; Town of Dillon, 275 Lake Dillon Dr., Dillon; (970) 468-2403; www.townofdillon.com

Krystal 93 BBQ at the Summit, Dillon; www.summitrotaryevents.com/BBQ-at-the-Summit.php

Organizations
Friends of the Eagles Nest Wilderness, www.fenw.org, or call the Dillon Ranger District, (970) 468-5400, for the current contact.

> **Mere *means sea, lake, pool, or pond. Eaglesmere Lakes probably were named for the view of Eagles Nest from the south lake.***

Lower Cataract Lake

This easy and family-friendly loop trail travels through fields of colorful wildflowers, thick spruce-fir forest, and past the beautiful cascades of Cataract Creek. After hiking, spend some time picnicking along the shores of the lake enjoying views of Cataract Falls and Eagles Nest. The pointy peak is the second highest in the Gore Range and is the namesake for the Eagles Nest Wilderness area.

Start: At the Cataract Loop Trail trailhead
Distance: 2.4-mile loop
Hiking time: 1 to 2.5 hours
Difficulty: Easy due to distance and only a 100-foot elevation gain
Trail surface: Dirt trail and a short section of dirt road
Best season: Mid-May to mid-Oct
Other trail users: Hikers only
Canine compatibility: Dogs must be on leash
Land status: National forest and wilderness
Fees and permits: None required. Limit of 15 people per group.
Maps: USGS Mount Powell; Nat Geo Trails Illustrated 107 Green Mountain Reservoir/Ute Pass; Latitude 40° Summit County Trails; USFS White River National Forest map
Trail contact: USDA Forest Service, Dillon Ranger District, 680 Blue River Pkwy., Silverthorne; (970) 468-5400; www.fs.usda.gov/whiteriver; www.dillonranger district.com
Other: The trail is mainly within the Eagles Nest Wilderness. Please comply with wilderness regulations.
Special considerations: Bring your own water or be prepared to treat water. The USDA Forest Services discourages hiking to the waterfalls because the area is hazardous due to the slippery and steep terrain. The road is closed by snow in the winter 1.3 miles from the trailhead. The trail around the lake is neither marked nor maintained for winter use. Cataract Creek Road is nice for cross-country skiing, walking, or snowshoeing from the winter closure to Cataract Lake.

Finding the trailhead: From I-70 exit 205 (Silverthorne/Dillon), drive north through Silverthorne on CO 9 for 16.9 miles to Heeney Road. (Summit CR 30). Turn left and drive on Heeney Road for 5.6 miles to the Cataract Creek Road sign. Turn left and follow Cataract Creek Road 2.7 miles to its end. (*Note:* At 2.2 miles the road splits. Stay on the road to the left.) A vault toilet is available at the trailhead. GPS at trailhead bulletin board: N39 50.24' / W106 18.97'.

THE HIKE

Back in the late 1800s locals enjoyed Cataract Lake, which Howard Hill owned. He also ran a fish hatchery and stocked trout in the pretty lake. The *Summit County Journal* in July 1899 noted that "Mountain trout, from Cataract Lake, the proprietor holding a state license to market fish, [is] on sale at George E. Moon's every Friday." An article in the *Breckenridge Bulletin,* September 23, 1905, stated that Hill "has already placed 1,500,000 fish in the lake since he became its owner."

Cataract Falls and hikers on the trail

Hill sold Cataract Lake and 400 surrounding acres in late 1916 to O. K. Gaymon. At $15,000 the price was considered modest in those days. Hill reportedly headed back to Maine to care for his aging mother. The article reporting the sale mentioned the attractions of the area, which included fishing and hunting, a clubhouse, summer cottages, and high-class resort facilities. Gaymon had plans to improve the roads and trails, construct cabins, and add a motorboat to the existing primitive boats that plied that lake.

In the 1950s and 1960s, John Rockwell from Phoenix owned the lake. A nice lodge existed along with the various cabins. In the late 1960s the USDA Forest Service purchased the area. Photos taken in 1975 show cabins and a boat dock.

Cataract Lake had been just outside the boundary of the Gore Range-Eagles Nest Primitive Area. This special area consisting of 32,400 acres in the Arapaho National Forest was established on June 19, 1932. Another 47,250 acres in the Holy Cross National Forest was added to the primitive area in 1933. In December 1941 the primitive area was reduced by 18,425 acres for the construction of US 6 over Vail Pass.

Originally Cataract Lake was not included in the plans for the proposed Eagles Nest Wilderness area. In 1971 the USDA Forest Service proposed an 87,755-acre wilderness. The boundary had been drawn west of the Gore Range Trail. Old timber cuts existed along today's Surprise Lake Trail. Other possible timber sales and cuts could be made in the area. The Denver Water Board (DWB) developed plans to build the 40-mile East Gore Collection System, which would bring about 70,000 acre-feet of water from numerous branches of the Blue River back to Dillon Reservoir. Some of the tributaries included Cataract Creek and Slate Creek. The boundary for the Eagles Nest Wilderness excluded the area where the East Gore Range Canal would be built. However, the DWB only had claims to water in the area, and a water referee denied them in a ruling in 1975.

After several years of negotiations, Colorado congressional representative Jim Johnson penned a bill for the Eagles Nest Wilderness that added acreage near Frisco and Maryland Creek to protect the Gore Range Trail. Main trails leading into other wilderness areas in Colorado, such as Mount Zirkel, had not been included in the designated area, and problems arose with motorized incursions into wilderness. The Gore Range Trail provides access to about 70 percent of the Eagles Nest Wilderness and was included in the final boundaries.

Starting about 70 million years ago, the Gore and Williams Fork Ranges were uplifted, and what is now the Blue River valley dropped as a block (a graben in geological terms). Water flowing over the edge of the uplift into the graben became Cataract Falls.

11

The Eagles Nest Wilderness, in its own bill, was officially designated on July 12, 1976, in Public Law 94-352. In November 1997 another 160 acres in the Slate Creek area were added to the Eagles Nest Wilderness in Public Law 105-75, contingent upon acquisition of the parcel by the United States, which has been completed.

The hike around Lower Cataract Lake is a treat starting in about mid-June when wildflowers blanket the hills along the southern shore. Since the slopes face north, they retain more snow and moisture from winter. You'll find giant green gentians, which can grow to 6 feet. Their beautiful flowers consist of overlapped parts in fours, radiating from a center "button." After flowering, the plant dies (after living for twenty to eighty years!). Each flower can produce as many as sixty seeds, while 600 flowers might bloom on a single stalk. Even though the plant blooms only once, it makes sure the species will continue.

Other spring flowers include blue lupines, which often bloom in stretches along the access road. Blue columbines (Colorado's state flower) grow in and near aspen, making for stunning photos. White to orange sulphur flowers provide a contrast to the surrounding blue flowers.

Make sure to hike the trail again toward the end of September when the golden glow of the aspen stand out against a crisp blue autumn sky. The north side of the lake typically turns color sooner, probably due to less moisture. From the south side of the lake, the reflections of the north-side aspen make for great photos.

Lower Cataract Lake and Cataract Falls

Lower Cataract Lake

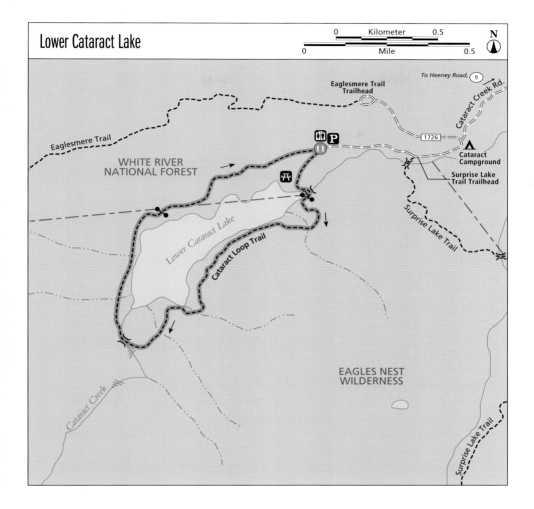

Eaglesmere Trail Trailhead

To Heeney Road, 9

Cataract Creek Rd.

1726

Eaglesmere Trail

WHITE RIVER NATIONAL FOREST

Cataract Campground

Surprise Lake Trail Trailhead

Lower Cataract Lake

Cataract Loop Trail

Surprise Lake Trail

EAGLES NEST WILDERNESS

Cataract Creek

Surprise Lake Trail

MILES AND DIRECTIONS

0.0   Start at the Cataract Loop Trail trailhead at the fence at the end of the parking lot. Elevation: 8,650 feet. Be sure to read the trailhead bulletin board, which contains area information and regulations. Walk down the trail that heads to the lake (not the trails to the left or right). (**Option:** You can walk this loop in either direction.)

0.1   Arrive at a trail junction. Turn left (south). The trail straight ahead goes to a picnic table and the lake.

0.2   Come to another trail junction. Turn right (east) and walk across the bridge over Cataract Creek. In about 200 feet, pass through the wooden Z gate at the Eagles Nest Wilderness boundary. Follow the trail signs in the next trail section.

0.8 Come to a nice view of Cataract Falls.

1.25 Arrive at the bridge over the lower cascades of Cataract Creek. GPS: N39 49.70' / W106 19.58'. Elevation: 8,630 feet.

1.4 Enter a meadow with views of the lake and the Williams Fork Range to the northeast.

1.8 There's a nice view of the lake, falls, and Eagles Nest (peak). In about 400 feet, pass through a wooden Z gate and exit the Eagles Nest Wilderness.

2.2 Come to a junction with a service road. GPS: N39 50.19' / W106 19.16'. Turn left (east) and walk down the dirt road to the trailhead.

2.4 Arrive back at the trailhead.

HIKE INFORMATION

Local Information
Colorado Welcome Center at Silverthorne, Outlets at Silverthorne, 246 Rainbow Dr., Silverthorne; (970) 468-0353; www.colorado.com/official-colorado-welcome-centers

Local Events/Attractions
Friday Farmers Market, Buffalo and Main Streets; Town of Dillon, 275 Lake Dillon Dr., Dillon; (970) 468-2403; www.townofdillon.com

Sunset at the Summit Concert Series, Dillon Amphitheatre; Town of Dillon, 275 Lake Dillon Dr., Dillon; (970) 468-2403; www.townofdillon.com

Krystal 93 BBQ at the Summit, Dillon; www.summitrotaryevents.com/BBQ-at-the-Summit.php

Organizations
Friends of the Eagles Nest Wilderness, www.fenw.org, or call the Dillon Ranger District, (970) 468-5400, for the current contact.

Buffalo Mountain

The huge granite dome called Buffalo Mountain towers above Dillon Reservoir and the towns of Silverthorne and Frisco. Such an imposing mountain attracts climbers, and over the years people scrambled up, creating "climbers' trails" to the summit. Buffalo Mountain now boasts a summit trail that, while still difficult, is much more hiker and environmentally friendly. "Still difficult" means a 23 percent grade for 0.6 mile through a boulder field. The climb is well worth the effort for the views, beautiful tundra flowers, and a chance to see the mountain goat family that grazes on the high slopes.

Start: At the Buffalo Cabin Trail trailhead
Distance: 6.0 miles out and back
Hiking time: 3 to 7 hours
Difficulty: Strenuous due to a 3,017-foot elevation gain and altitude
Trail surface: Dirt trail and boulders
Best season: July to late Sept
Other trail users: Hikers; equestrians on lower part of trail
Canine compatibility: Dogs must be on leash
Land status: National forest and wilderness
Fees and permits: None required. Limit of 15 people per group.
Maps: USGS Vail Pass and Frisco; Nat Geo Trails Illustrated 108 Vail/Frisco/Dillon; Latitude 40° Summit County Trails; USFS White River National Forest map
Trail contact: USDA Forest Service, Dillon Ranger District, 680 Blue River Pkwy., Silverthorne; (970) 468-5400; www.fs.usda.gov/whiteriver; www.dillonranger district.com
Other: The trail is mainly within the Eagles Nest Wilderness. Please comply with wilderness regulations.
Special considerations: Very little water can be found along this trail and none above Buffalo Cabin. Make sure to bring plenty. Bring clothing layers because the wind can be very chilly on top. Lightning from thunderstorms can be deadly on the upper 1.1 miles of the trail. Make sure to start early and be down below treeline before thunderstorms develop. Hunters may use this area during hunting season. Avalanches have left two big scars on the east face of Buffalo. Weather can change quickly and unexpectedly, including snow in the middle of July. The trail to Buffalo Cabin is a nice ski or snowshoe tour in winter. The trail is neither marked nor maintained for winter use.

Finding the trailhead: From I-70 exit 205 (Silverthorne/Dillon), head north on CO 9 about 0.2 mile to Wildernest Road by the 7-Eleven store and across from Wendy's. Turn left and follow Wildernest Road (which becomes Ryan Gulch Road) for 3.5 miles. The parking lot for the Buffalo Cabin Trail trailhead is on the left (east) as the road curves. (You can also ride the Summit Stage for free from the Silverthorne Transfer Center to the bus stop around the curve just south of the Buffalo Cabin Trail trailhead.) Make sure to start at the Buffalo Cabin Trail trailhead and not the Lily Pad Lake Trailhead! No facilities are available at the trailhead. GPS: N39 37.21' / W106 06.59'.

THE HIKE

Buffalo Mountain has long been a landmark in Summit County. Called Buffalo by early settlers who thought it looked like a buffalo's back, the peak towered over La Bonte's Hole below, at the intersection of the Blue River, the Snake River, and Tenmile Creek. Bison (buffalo) grazed in the lush valley during the summer, retreating over Hoosier Pass to South Park for the long winters. Ute Indians summered in the valleys, hunting the plentiful game.

The east face of Buffalo sports two cirques created by glaciers, not a crater formed by volcanic action. The mountain's dome shape is the result of its granite eroding off like layers of an onion, not from glaciation. The two avalanche paths show the destructive force of Mother Nature. Trees are growing again in the smaller path. An avalanche in 1986 created the larger path, knocking down hundreds of trees as the white death roared off the tundra after a major snowstorm. Trees still standing at the bottom had other trees skewered in their tops like spears. After another period of heavy snow in 2003, a second avalanche widened and lengthened the path.

The Buffalo Cabin Trail starts innocently enough, passing wetlands and traveling through lodgepole pine forest. Before the wilderness boundary, many of the lodgepole pines, which had been killed by mountain pine beetles, have been removed. When you reach the four-way trail junction and head left (west), make sure to look back to remember what the junction looks like, including the trail sign. People have a tendency to miss the turnoff on their return and find themselves miles from their car.

Miners probably used the cabins—locals call the highest cabin ruins Buffalo Cabin. From here a trail built by the USDA Forest Service trail crew and the Rocky Mountain Youth Corps (RMYC) in summer 2004 switchbacks and climbs steadily through the forest behind the cabin then up through the boulder field. Friends of the Eagles Nest Wilderness (FENW) received a grant from State Parks/Trails to hire RMYC for four weeks of strenuous work. Various community businesses and The

Hikers on top of Buffalo Mountain

Summit Foundation donated matching funds for the grant. The Forest Service crew worked mainly in the boulder field and above for four weeks. In the rough terrain a pair of work gloves typically lasted only eight days. After the crews completed the trail, FENW volunteers spent two days building cairns to mark the trail through the boulder field. Volunteers for Outdoor Colorado spent two days revegetating the old braided trail system that hikers had created over time.

The trail through the boulder field is steep, but a great improvement over the old trail, which was even steeper and consisted of slippery ball-bearing soil. Wildflowers grow between boulders in places and trees struggle to gain a toehold in soil between the rocks. A sub-peak blocks the view of any incoming weather, and any sound of thunder should advise a quick retreat.

12

Once above the boulder field, keep an eye open for the family of mountain goats that calls the summit home. They may cooperate and stand still for pictures, while keeping a watchful eye and comfortable distance. Please make sure dogs are on leashes and respect the goats so others may enjoy seeing them.

Buffalo Mountain provides great views of much of Summit County and the Vail area. The scenery, wildlife, and wildflowers reward a successful climb!

MILES AND DIRECTIONS

0.0   Start at the Buffalo Cabin Trail trailhead. Elevation: 9,760 feet.

0.4   Reach the Eagles Nest Wilderness boundary. The trail is fairly flat for the next 0.2 mile.

0.6   Reach a four-way junction. Turn left (southwest) and head uphill.

Friends of the Eagles Nest Wilderness

When local journalist M. John Fayhee tagged along on a three-day backpack in the Eagles Nest Wilderness one summer with two USDA Forest Service wilderness rangers, he was appalled by their lack of resources. The wilderness boundaries were not well marked—only three wilderness portal signs existed in the two wildernesses in those days. He wrote a column about their financial plight in the *Summit Daily News* that spurred the formation of Friends of the Eagles Nest Wilderness (FENW) in May 1994. The group began to help the Dillon Ranger District of the White River National Forest maintain and preserve the Summit County portions of the Eagles Nest and Ptarmigan Peak Wildernesses, which make up about 25 percent of Summit County. Since its inception the group has received grants and raised funds with which the group has installed portal signs and bulletin boards with interpretive posters; purchased tools, which are shared with other volunteer groups, for trail maintenance projects throughout Summit County; developed a volunteer wilderness ranger program; and treated noxious weeds in the wilderness. Each year FENW sponsors at least three trail maintenance projects in the Eagles Nest Wilderness. In 2006, FENW expanded its programs and volunteer opportunities to help the Holy Cross Ranger District to maintain and preserve the Eagle County portions of the Eagles Nest and Holy Cross Wildernesses. The group also advocates for wilderness issues. To help FENW with their efforts or for more information about how a grassroots group can make a difference, log onto www.fenw.org or contact the Dillon Ranger District, (970) 468-5400, for the current contact. Citizen support may be what protects and maintains the Eagles Nest, Holy Cross, and Ptarmigan Peak Wilderness areas throughout time.

Buffalo Mountain

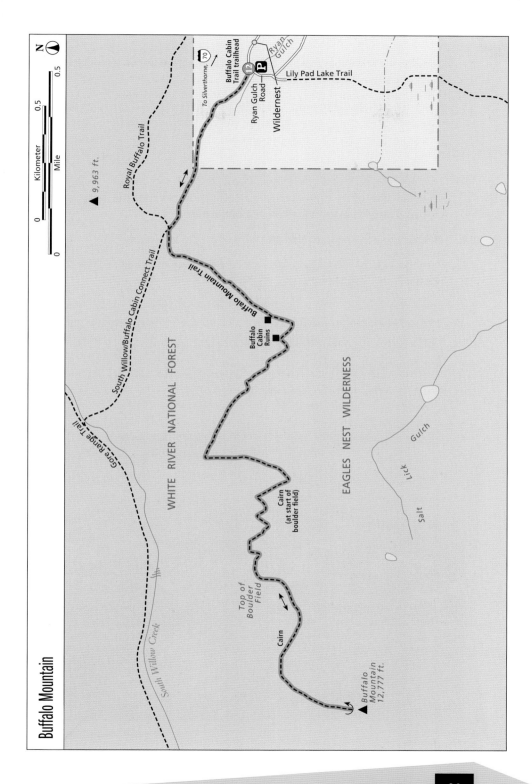

Top of Boulder Field

Cairn

Cairn (at start of boulder field)

Buffalo Mountain 12,777 ft.

Buffalo Cabin Ruins

Gore Range Trail

South Willow/Buffalo Cabin Connect Trail

WHITE RIVER NATIONAL FOREST

South Willow Creek

Royal Buffalo Trail

Buffalo Mountain Trail

▲ 9,963 ft.

EAGLES NEST WILDERNESS

Salt

Lick

Gulch

Buffalo Cabin Trail trailhead

To Silverthorne, 70

Ryan Gulch Road

Ryan Gulch

Wildernest

Lily Pad Lake Trail

N

Kilometer

Mile

0   0.5

0   0.5

0.9 Come to the first cabin ruins by a little creek, which is the last water along the trail—if the creek is running.

1.1 Reach the Buffalo Cabin ruins. GPS: N39 37.14' / W106 07.42'. The ruins provide a good rest place—the trail climbs steeply from here. (*Option:* You can turn around here for a 2.1-mile out-and-back hike with a 600-foot elevation gain.)

1.9 The trail enters a boulder field by a large cairn (rock pile). Walk to the right (downhill side) of the cairn. Look for smaller cairns that mark the rocky trail. Do not walk up the dirt trail to the left of the big cairn.

2.45 The trail exits the boulder field and crosses the alpine tundra.

2.8 Come to a cairn with a post that marks the final summit climb. Follow the ridgeline.

3.0 Reach the summit. GPS: N39 37.00' / W106 08.57'. Elevation: 12,777 feet. Two rock windbreaks about 200 feet apart provide some shelter and great views. Return the way you came.

6.0 Arrive back at the trailhead.

View west from the summit of Buffalo Mountain

12

Local Information

Colorado Welcome Center at Silverthorne, Outlets at Silverthorne, 246 Rainbow Dr., Silverthorne; (970) 468-0353; www.colorado.com/official-colorado-welcome-centers

Local Events/Attractions

Friday Farmers Market, Buffalo and Main Streets; Town of Dillon, 275 Lake Dillon Dr., Dillon; (970) 468-2403; www.townofdillon.com

Sunset at the Summit Concert Series, Dillon Amphitheatre; Town of Dillon, 275 Lake Dillon Dr., Dillon; (970) 468-2403; www.townofdillon.com

Krystal 93 BBQ at the Summit, Dillon; www.summitrotaryevents.com/BBQ-at-the-Summit.php

Organizations

Friends of the Eagles Nest Wilderness, www.fenw.org, or call the Dillon Ranger District, (970) 468-5400, for the current contact.

Public Transportation (free)

Summit Stage, PO Box 2179, Frisco 80443; (970) 668-0999; www.summitstage.com

People have argued for years whether mountain goats are indigenous to Colorado. The Colorado Division of Wildlife once reported that mountain goats were introduced into Colorado in 1947 to provide trophy-hunting opportunities. However, after two years of historical research, which found documentation that mountain goats roamed Colorado in the 1880s, the Colorado Wildlife Commission declared them a native species.

13

Lily Pad Lake

Lily Pad Lake is a very popular destination reachable from two different trailheads. This hike description starts on the Meadow Creek Trail near Frisco, which provides the most diverse scenery and wildflowers. Lily Pad Lake itself contains only a few lily pads (yellow pond lilies), but a nearby smaller lake contains many, especially along the shore. Buffalo Mountain towers above the lake. Good views of the Frisco area can be seen along the trail.

Start: At the Meadow Creek Trailhead near Frisco
Distance: 3.4 miles out and back
Hiking time: 1.5 to 2.5 hours
Difficulty: Moderate due to distance and a 750-foot elevation gain
Trail surface: Dirt trail
Best season: June to mid-Oct
Other trail users: Equestrians
Canine compatibility: Dogs must be on leash
Land status: National forest and wilderness
Fees and permits: None required. Limit of 15 people per group.
Maps: USGS Frisco; Nat Geo Trails Illustrated 108 Vail/Frisco/Dillon; Latitude 40° Summit County Trails; USFS White River National Forest map

Trail contact: USDA Forest Service, Dillon Ranger District, 680 Blue River Pkwy., Silverthorne; (970) 468-5400; www.fs.usda.gov/whiteriver; www.dillonranger district.com
Other: The trail is mainly within the Eagles Nest Wilderness. Please comply with wilderness regulations.
Special considerations: Bring your own water because it is sparse along most of the trail. Hunters may use this area during hunting season. The trail is neither marked nor maintained for winter use, but many locals use the trails during winter for walking, snowshoeing, and cross-country skiing.

Finding the trailhead: From I-70 exit 203 (Frisco/Breckenridge), drive around the "elk" roundabout on the north side of I-70 and turn right (southwest) onto the dirt frontage road (not the one with the Private Drive sign). The dirt road dead-ends at the trailhead in 0.6 mile. (Or take the free bus: The Frisco Transfer Center for the Summit Stage is located behind Safeway on the south side of I-70, about a 1-mile walk from the trailhead.) No facilities are available at the trailhead. GPS: N39 35.34' / W106 06.36'.

THE HIKE

When you arrive at Lily Pad Lake, the bigger of the two lakes, you might wonder why it has so few water lilies on it. The lake used to be smaller, but beavers built a dam and enlarged it. (Look for the old beaver lodge near the southwest shore.) The yellow pond lilies did not like the enlarged lake, perhaps because of the change in depth or water flow. They prefer shallow (no more than 6 feet deep) and quiet water. The pond lilies' leaves (pads) are connected to a stem that is attached to a rootstock (a rhizome with roots) that grows sideways. Rootstocks

Buffalo Mountain reflected in Lily Pad Lake

are buried in sediment under the lake. Many stems, pads, and flowers can grow from the same rhizome, similar to aspen trees. Pond lilies can sprout from either seeds or rhizomes. Beavers enjoy the pads and roots of the showy plant. Native Americans used the seeds from the pond lily to produce a food similar to popcorn. They ground dried popped kernels into flour. Roasted or boiled and peeled rootstocks were used in stews or dried and ground into flour. Medicinal uses for the rootstocks included treating sore throats, venereal disease, and heart problems. The smaller lake is probably a kettle pond left over from glacial times, and it sports a large quantity of yellow pond lilies. Watch closely for duck families that enjoy swimming among the lilies. The little ducklings appear to be walking on water as they waddle across the green pads.

As you hike up Meadow Creek Trail to the south end of the Lily Pad Lake Trail, you'll pass an ore chute for the Foremost Mine on the left (southwest). The mine is farther up the flank of Chief Mountain to the south and produced lead ore into the early 1900s. The Surprise Mine lies farther yet up the mountain and also produced lead ores.

Along the Lily Pad Lake Trail, a few viewpoints offer you vistas of Frisco and Dillon Reservoir. Much of the land under the reservoir and the area along I-70 used to be ranch land. To the south and east of Lily Pad Lake, the Giberson family owned 720 acres where they raised beef cattle, ten to twelve milk cows, and ten to twelve horses. The ranch started small at 160 acres in 1909. In 1916, through provisions of the Homestead Act of 1862, the Gibersons added 160 acres to their spread. They used all the land behind the ranch for grazing, including the lake the family called Pond Lily (today's Lily Pad Lake). Even back in those days, the US government charged a fee of about fifty cents a head to graze cattle on national forest lands. The family didn't own a tractor at first, and planting and harvesting hay was done manually with the help of a team of horses. The annual cattle sale brought cash to the family. The Gibersons also sold dairy products to people in the area and shipped cream via train to creameries in Denver. The family leased then purchased an additional 400 acres.

Time marched on, and the ranch was slowly purchased for water storage and highways. Since the 1920s the Denver Water Board (DWB) had been planning to build a dam across the Blue River near its confluence with Tenmile Creek and the Snake River. During the Depression, DWB purchased many properties around Dillon at tax sales. By 1959 only a few properties remained to be procured for the reservoir behind the dam. The DWB purchased 380 acres of the Gibersons' ranch. The Colorado Division of Transportation (CDOT) bought land to reroute US 6, which would soon be under water. Later, CDOT obtained another 51 acres of the Gibersons' remaining land for I-70, and developers purchased additional acreage. Safeway, Holiday Inn, Best Western, a shopping center, and several subdivisions now stand where cattle once grazed.

Today only 189 acres remain of the Giberson Ranch. Of those, 179 acres are a conservation easement called the Giberson Preserve, held by the Continental Divide Land Trust. The preserve is private (no public access), protecting elk habitat, meadows, wetlands, forest, and the view corridor from Frisco.

As you hike to Lily Pad Lake, reflect on the changes this area has seen in the last one hundred years or so. What will it look like one hundred years from now?

MILES AND DIRECTIONS

0.0 Start at the Meadow Creek Trailhead. Elevation: 9,157 feet.

0.5 Look for old mine relics to your left.

0.6 Arrive at the junction of Meadow Creek and Lily Pad Lake Trails. Turn right (northeast) onto Lily Pad Lake Trail. GPS: N39 35.45' / W106 06.80'.

0.8 Cross Meadow Creek on a nice bridge and in a few feet find the Eagles Nest Wilderness portal sign.

1.3 Stop to enjoy the view of Mount Guyot, Baldy, Frisco, and Dillon Reservoir.

1.6 Arrive at a nice view of Lily Pad Lake and Buffalo Mountain. Sit on the rocks and enjoy! A little farther up the trail on the right is a little lake with lily pads in it. GPS: N39 35.97' / W106 06.93'.

1.7 Come to the junction with the Lily Pad Lake Trail to Ryan Gulch Road on the right (northeast) here. Walk a few feet to the right for a better view of the little lake. To the left you can walk down the hill to Lily Pad Lake. Elevation: 9,905 feet. Return the way you came.

3.4 Arrive back at the trailhead.

Option

You can do a 3.3-mile point-to-point hike starting at the Meadow Creek Trailhead and ending at the Lily Pad Lake Trail trailhead along Ryan Gulch Road. This hike requires a car shuttle, riding the Summit Stage (free bus), or hiking 6.6 miles round-trip. To leave a vehicle at the Lily Pad Lake Trail trailhead near Silverthorne: From I-70 exit 205 (Silverthorne/Dillon), head north on CO 9 about 0.2 mile to the traffic light by Wendy's and the 7-Eleven. Turn left onto Wildernest Road (which becomes Ryan Gulch Road) and

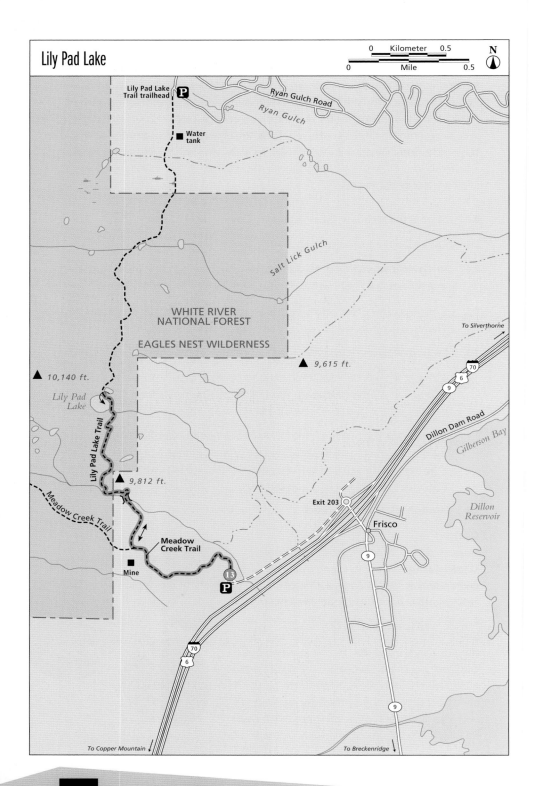

Lily Pad Lake

0 Kilometer 0.5
0 Mile 0.5

N

Lily Pad Lake
Trail trailhead ☐ P

Ryan Gulch Road

Ryan Gulch

■ Water
tank

Salt Lick Gulch

WHITE RIVER
NATIONAL FOREST

EAGLES NEST WILDERNESS

▲ 9,615 ft.

To Silverthorne

▲ 10,140 ft.

70
6
9

Lily Pad
Lake

Dillon Dam Road

Gilberson Bay

Lily Pad Lake Trail

▲ 9,812 ft.

Dillon
Reservoir

Exit 203

Meadow Creek Trail

Frisco

Meadow
Creek Trail

■
Mine

13

P

9

70
6

9

To Copper Mountain

To Breckenridge

drive 3.5 miles. The parking lot for the Lily Pad Lake Trail trailhead is on the left (east) side of the road as it curves left. (The Summit Stage has a bus stop near the parking area.) To reach the trailhead, walk south on the road to where another road comes in from the right. You'll see the trailhead sign. (*Note:* This parking area also serves the Buffalo Cabin Trail, so be sure to find the correct trailhead.) No facilities are available at the trailhead. GPS: N39 37.14' / W106 06.63'.

From mile 1.7 above, turn right onto the Lily Pad Lake Trail and pass the little lake full of pond lilies.

At 2.2 miles, reach the junction with the Salt Lick Trail. Continue straight ahead.

At mile 3.0, leave the Eagles Nest Wilderness. Soon you'll pass a water tank on your right and head downhill on a dirt service road. The Lily Pad Lake Trail trailhead bulletin board is near the junction with Ryan Gulch Road. The parking lot and bus stop are to the left. (Take the Wildernest Route bus to the Silverthorne Transfer Center then take the bus to the Frisco Transfer Center. It's about 1 mile back to the Meadow Creek Trailhead.)

HIKE INFORMATION

Local Information
Frisco Information Center, 300 Main St., Frisco; (970) 668-5547, (800) 424-1554; www.friscococ.com

Local Events/Attractions
Colorado BBQ Challenge, 1 Main St., Frisco; (800) 424-1554; www.townoffrisco .com/events/bbq-challenge

Concert in the Park Series, 120 Main St. (Gazebo), Frisco; (800) 424-1554; www.townoffrisco.com/events/concert-in-the-park/

Fall Fest, Main Street event, Frisco; (800) 424-1554; www.townoffrisco.com/ events/fallfest/

Organizations
Friends of the Eagles Nest Wilderness, www.fenw.org, or call the Dillon Ranger District, (970) 468-5400, for the current contact.

Public Transportation (free)
Summit Stage, PO Box 2179, Frisco 80443; (970) 668-0999; www.summitstage .com

14

Meadow Creek Trail

The high meadows full of wonderful, colorful wildflowers make this hike a must-do. The trail starts in a mixed forest of aspen and lodgepole pine, which then transitions to lodgepole as it climbs steadily. The grade finally mellows where the sparkling creek tumbles near the trail. You'll pass stumps left behind by loggers then wander through the glorious meadows, which also offer great views of the Tenmile Range, Buffalo Mountain, Bald Mountain, Mount Guyot, and Eccles Pass. From the top of Eccles Pass, the view of Red Peak, Red-Buffalo Pass, and the South Willow Creek drainage is a piece of heaven.

Start: At the Meadow Creek Trailhead near Frisco
Distance: 10.2 miles out and back
Hiking time: 5 to 7 hours
Difficulty: Difficult due to distance and a 2,740-foot elevation gain
Trail surface: Dirt trail
Best season: July to early Oct
Other trail users: Equestrians
Canine compatibility: Dogs must be on leash in the wilderness; under voice control elsewhere
Land status: National forest and wilderness
Fees and permits: None required. Limit of 15 people per group.
Maps: USGS Frisco and Vail Pass; Nat Geo Trails Illustrated 108 Vail/Frisco/Dillon; Latitude 40° Summit County Trails; USFS White River National Forest map

Trail contact: USDA Forest Service, Dillon Ranger District, 680 Blue River Pkwy., Silverthorne; (970) 468-5400; www.fs.usda.gov/whiteriver; www.dillonranger district.com
Other: The trail is mainly within the Eagles Nest Wilderness. Please comply with wilderness regulations.
Special considerations: Start early and head down from the pass before thunderstorms start. Hunters may use this area during hunting season. Bring your own water because it is sparse along much of the trail. The trail is neither marked nor maintained for winter use, but many locals use the trail during winter for walking, snowshoeing, and cross-country skiing.

Finding the trailhead: From I-70 exit 203 (Frisco/Breckenridge), drive around the "elk" roundabout on the north side of I-70 and turn right (southwest) onto the dirt frontage road (not the one with the Private Drive sign). The dirt road dead-ends at the trailhead in 0.6 mile. (Or take the free bus: The Frisco Transfer Center for the Summit Stage bus is located behind Safeway on the south side of I-70, about a 1-mile walk from the trailhead.) No facilities are available at the trailhead. GPS: N39 35.34' / W106 06.36'.

THE HIKE

As you hike up the Meadow Creek Trail, you pass old mining remains and evidence that the logging industry once existed. In 1899 plans were made to build a good wagon road to the head of Meadow Creek "to open up the Red Peaks country . . . the richest undeveloped territory in Colorado." The wide first part of the trail is probably the remains of that road or a subsequent one. By 1921, L. A. Wildhack of Frisco owned silver claims on the north side of Eccles Pass at the head of South Willow Creek. Wildhack became the Frisco postmaster in 1914—the post office and his general store were located together in a building that today houses Foote's Rest Sweet Shoppe and Eatery at 510 Main St.

At 0.5 mile, look to your left for the old ore chute for the Foremost Mine. The mine itself is farther up the side of Chief Mountain to the southwest and produced lead ore into the 1910s. James H. Myers wrote about Chief Mountain's geology in the *Breckenridge Bulletin* in June 1906. He described the mountain as being about 3 miles long and 2 miles wide at its base, composed of "metamorphosed mica chist, granetic rock." Mineral-bearing quartz veins, from 7 to 30 feet wide, reportedly contained mainly lead and iron with a little copper. The mined ore consisted of 8 to 25 ounces of silver and 0.5 to 3 ounces of gold per ton.

At 0.8 mile there's an open spot where you can see parts of Frisco, Dillon Reservoir, Keystone Mountain, Keystone's ski runs, Grays and Torreys Peaks, and southeast to Mount Guyot near Breckenridge. Purple lupine, yellow cinquefoil,

Gore Range Trail and Eccles Pass

white yarrow, purple daisies, blue harebells, and pink fireweed line the trail and meadows. The trail climbs steeply, but occasionally almost levels out so you can catch your breath before the next climb. By 2.2 miles you're out of the thickest part of the lodgepole pine forest. Look for little yellow stonecrop, red and yellow paintbrush, pussytoes, and yellow sulphur flowers along this section. As you continue up the trail, the forest changes to mixed conifers with spruce and fir joining the lodgepole pine. Notice the tall stumps, some charred, near the trail. The mines needed lumber for support beams, and railroads used wood for ties. Without electricity, people who lived in Frisco and on nearby ranches needed a lot of wood for both buildings and fires for their woodstoves to cook and stay warm. Logging was easier in winter, when horses could drag the cut timber along the snow, thus the tall stumps. Sometimes trees were burned before cutting to dry them out.

Cross pretty little Meadow Creek and its small cascades lined with a plethora of colorful wildflowers at 4.2 miles. The trail winds through flower-filled meadows both before and after the junction with the Gore Range Trail at mile 4.4. Broadleaf arnica, purple daisies (or asters), white bistort, and rosy (subalpine) paintbrush towering over green leaves create a lush carpet at the base of the Gore Range ridge. Eccles Pass is the low point on the ridge to the right. The trail switchbacks up past huge rock slabs and shorter trees to the top. To the southeast is the Tenmile Range. The rounded hulk of mountain to the northeast is Buffalo Mountain, which sports very different faces on each side. Red Peak towers to the north, and the beautiful pond-studded upper meadows of South Willow Creek lie below. Find a good place to sit, enjoy lunch, and savor the beautiful scenery in this little piece of Summit County heaven.

MILES AND DIRECTIONS

0.0   Start at the Meadow Creek Trailhead bulletin board. Elevation: 9,157 feet.

0.6   Arrive at the junction with the Lily Pad Lake Trail to the right. GPS: N39 35.45' / W106 06.80'. Continue straight ahead and uphill. In about 300 feet you'll enter the Eagles Nest Wilderness.

1.4   Cross Meadow Creek on a sturdy bridge.

2.2   The forest starts changing from lodgepole to less dense, mixed conifers.

3.1   Cross Meadow Creek and enjoy the creek tumbling nearby.

4.2   Cross Meadow Creek and enter the upper meadows.

4.4   Come to the junction of the Gore Range Trail to the left. Look behind you for a great view of the Tenmile Range. GPS: N39 36.07' / W106 10.15'. Elevation: 11,400 feet.

Meadow Creek Trail

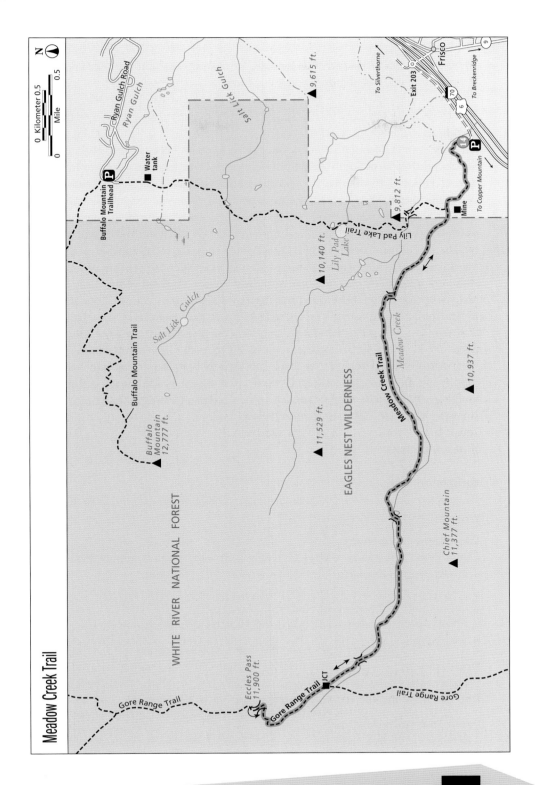

Buffalo Mountain Trailhead

Ryan Gulch Road

Ryan Gulch

Salt Lick Gulch

9,615 ft.

To Silverthorne

Exit 203

Frisco

To Breckenridge

Water tank

9,812 ft.

Mine

To Copper Mountain

Lily Pad Lake Trail

Lily Pad Lake

10,140 ft.

Salt Lick Gulch

Buffalo Mountain Trail

Buffalo Mountain 12,777 ft.

Meadow Creek

Meadow Creek Trail

EAGLES NEST WILDERNESS

11,529 ft.

10,937 ft.

Chief Mountain 11,377 ft.

WHITE RIVER NATIONAL FOREST

Eccles Pass 11,900 ft.

Gore Range Trail

Gore Range Trail

JCT

Gore Range Trail

N

0 Kilometer 0.5

0 Mile 0.5

5.1   You made it to the top of Eccles Pass! GPS: N39 36.43' / W106 10.32'. Elevation: 11,900 feet. Return the way you came.

10.2   Arrive back at the trailhead.

Option

For a car shuttle hike of 10.8 miles, you can head down Eccles Pass to the trail on the north side of South Willow Creek and down to the Mesa Cortina Trail trailhead above Silverthorne. The trail down South Willow Creek crosses several avalanche chutes, filled with wonderful wildflowers. After you pass the junction with the short side trail to South Willow Creek Falls, continue heading downhill, past the South Willow/Buffalo Cabin Connect Trail on the right. You'll come to the junction of the Gore Range and Mesa Cortina Trails. Go straight ahead on the Mesa Cortina Trail for 2.8 miles to the parking lot where you left another vehicle. Finding the Mesa Cortina Trail trailhead: From I-70 exit 205 (Silverthorne/Dillon), head north on CO 9 for 0.2 mile to Wildernest Road by the 7-Eleven store and across from Wendy's. Turn left (south) and follow Wildernest Road for 0.3 mile to the second traffic light just after the bridge over the Blue River. Go straight ahead onto Buffalo Mountain Drive. (Lowe's will be on your left.) Follow Buffalo Mountain Drive up a steep hill for 0.7 mile to Lake View Drive. Make a sharp right turn (north) and drive up Lake View Drive for 0.5 mile then curve to the left (south) onto Aspen Drive. Turn right in 0.1 mile into the parking lot for the Mesa Cortina Trailhead. GPS: N39 37.44' / W106 04.92'.

HIKE INFORMATION

Local Information

Frisco Information Center, 300 Main St., Frisco; (970) 668-5547, (800) 424-1554; www.friscococ.com

Local Events/Attractions

Colorado BBQ Challenge, 1 Main St., Frisco; (800) 424-1554; www.townoffrisco .com/events/bbq-challenge

Concert in the Park Series, 120 Main St. (Gazebo), Frisco; (800) 424-1554; www.townoffrisco.com/events/concert-in-the-park/

Fall Fest, Main Street event, Frisco; (800) 424-1554; www.townoffrisco.com/ events/fallfest/

Organizations

Friends of the Eagles Nest Wilderness, www.fenw.org, or call the Dillon Ranger District, (970) 468-5400, for the current contact.

Public Transportation (free)

Summit Stage, PO Box 2179, Frisco 80443; (970) 668-0999; www.summitstage.com

Winter Hiking

When winter covers Colorado's mountains under a blanket of snow, don't hibernate! Cross-country skis and snowshoes open a new world to summer hikers. Many trails are still used in the winter, and ski trails are often marked with blue diamonds (but not in wilderness areas). Orange diamonds denote snowmobile routes. Unmarked trails may be extremely hard to find, as a snow-blanketed forest looks very different. Also be aware of and avoid avalanche danger.

The type of equipment you buy depends on how you are going to use it. Lightweight, small snowshoes are great on packed trails, but sink in deep, off-trail snow where larger snowshoes work better. Snowshoeing is like walking with wide and long feet. Hiking or ski poles can help with balance.

For backcountry skiing, wider skis than those made for groomed Nordic center trails are typically used. For novices or spring skiing, waxless skis are the way to go. As you gain skill, Colorado's snow is great for waxed skis. Waxes grip the snow so you don't slide backwards while going uphill, but let you slide downhill. Waxless skis work the same but are usually less efficient. Skins placed on the bottom of your skis can help you climb interestingly steep or hard-packed hills (remember avalanche danger though). Backcountry skiers use free-heel bindings, which are great for both touring and for telemarking (a downhill turn).

Colorado has fantastic backcountry hut systems. Traveling to these huts requires good winter backcountry and route-finding skills and equipment. Trails may not be obvious, and many a skier has camped overnight outdoors without finding the hut.

Summer hiking trails may or may not be the best winter ski trails. Check with the local land management agency for recommended winter trails. Then have a great winter "hike" on your snowshoes or skis!

This trail is a pleasant family hike as far as Masontown. It starts on the paved recreation path that follows the route of the defunct Colorado & Southern Railroad and passes by the old Frisco Tunnel. Explore the interesting remains of the former mining town and mill, which nature is slowly reclaiming. The hike from Masontown to Mount Royal is strenuous but passes more mine and cabin ruins. The upward grunt is worth the climb for the views, especially the straight-down, bird's-eye view of I-70 in Tenmile Canyon. Limber pine, which grow in harsh conditions, live on the ridges.

Start: At the park-and-ride parking lot at the west end of Frisco's Main Street
Distance: 3.8 miles out and back
Hiking time: 2 to 4 hours
Difficulty: Most difficult because of an 840-foot elevation gain beyond Masontown (1,300-foot total gain)
Trail surface: Paved recreational path and dirt trail
Best season: June through Oct
Other trail users: Mountain bikers and equestrians
Canine compatibility: Dogs must be on leash on paved recreation path; under voice control elsewhere
Land status: National forest
Fees and permits: None required

Maps: USGS Frisco; Nat Geo Trails Illustrated 108 Vail/Frisco/ Dillon; Latitude 40° Summit County Trails; USFS White River National Forest map
Trail contact: USDA Forest Service, Dillon Ranger District, 680 Blue River Pkwy., Silverthorne; (970) 468-5400; www.fs.usda.gov/ whiteriver; www.dillonranger district.com
Other: Remember to leave artifacts where you find them.
Special considerations: Bring water because there is none along the trail. Hunters may use this area during hunting season. Be aware of avalanche danger near and above Masontown in winter. These trails are neither marked nor maintained for winter use.

Finding the trailhead: From I-70 exit 201 (Frisco Main Street), drive east approximately 0.1 mile toward town to a parking lot on your right (south). Turn right into the parking lot and park. (Summit Stage bus stops are located close to the trailhead.) Portable toilets are usually available at the trailhead in the summer. GPS: N39 34.49' / W106 06.66'.

THE HIKE

While walking along the paved recreation path toward the Mount Royal Trail, imagine the sounds of the old trains that steamed along here. Two railroads served Frisco. The first, the Denver & Rio Grande (D&RG), came from Leadville down Tenmile Canyon, arriving in town in summer 1882. The Denver, South Park & Pacific, later called the Colorado & Southern (C&S), chooed and chugged down today's recreation path from Breckenridge, arriving in Frisco in July 1883. The depot for the C&S once stood at mile 0.3 of this hike. Across the field you can see the tailings from the Frisco Tunnel, which operated into the 1930s. The D&RG ended service in 1911, while the C&S ran until 1937.

Mount Royal Trail

In 1866 General Buford discovered gold and copper leads above Rainbow Lake on the side of Royal Mountain. He built a road from the lake to the site—the old path still exists today. Buford built a mill, and a little town started to grow. In 1880 the Victoria mine produced about $10,000 in gold. Lack of affordable transportation created problems. The nearest railroad stopped in Georgetown, and ore had to be shipped via mule or wagons over Argentine or Loveland Passes.

From here the story varies depending on what one reads. Several history books indicate that the Masontown Mining and Milling (M&M) Company planned to build a reduction works in 1872, and that the company leased the Victoria mine. The *Summit County Journal* reported in its September 26, 1903, issue that Lars Matsson sold the 115-acre Victoria-Eureka property to Masontown M&M Company.

J. V. Hoover of Masontown, Pennsylvania, served as president of the well-capitalized company. The article also reported that about 2,000 feet of work had been done in the mine, exposing a large body of low-grade gold, and that the new owners were building a mill.

The *Summit County Journal*'s June 4, 1904, issue reported that the Masontown mill was fully operational with electric lighting and "runs with the accuracy of a watch." A tram brought ore from the mine to the mill. The ore then passed through a Blake crusher to automatic feeders that sent it to four battery boxes containing twenty stamps, a double discharge, and amalgamating plates. The pulp then passed to four concentrating tables that extracted the sulphides and heavy minerals. The remaining pulp flowed into cyanide tanks, where the solution percolated for some appropriate amount of time. That solution ran into a tank and then into zinc boxes. The precipitates were treated in a room with an acid tank, filter box, vacuum pump, centrifugal pump, and drying and melting furnaces. The process produced gold amalgam, cyanide precipitates, and auriferous sulphides. The first two became gold bars, and the concentrates were shipped to smelters. The paper further reported the ore's value at $5 to $20 per

Friends of Dillon Ranger District

In early 2004, Friends of the Dillon Ranger District (FDRD) formed to help "bridge the gap caused by increased visitation and costs and declining congressionally appropriated budgets." Their mission is "to promote stewardship of the White River National Forest in Summit County through partnerships, volunteer service, education, and support." FDRD volunteers help to maintain local trails, educate visitors, control invasive weeds, plus other projects. Over 75 percent of Summit County is part of the White River National Forest. To help FDRD with their efforts, log onto www.fdrd.org or contact them at (970) 262-3449.

ton in gold, while the costs of mining and milling ran about $3 per ton. The June 11, 1904, *Breckenridge Bulletin* stated the sulphide ore containing gold and silver was assaying at $12 to $80 per ton.

Disagreements among the company's owners closed the operation for about a year, according to articles in July 1905 in both the *Breckenridge Bulletin* and the *Summit County Journal.* By December 1905 the *Breckenridge Bulletin* reported Masontown M&M Company as "preparing for aggressive work."

Frisco mining played out about 1910. Some legends say that while Masontown's residents partied in Frisco on New Year's Eve in 1912, a snow slide roared down Mount Victoria, taking Masontown's buildings with it. Other accounts relate the snow slide that wiped out Masontown occurred in 1926, leaving only a few cabins on the north side (see the option at mile 1.2 below).

MILES AND DIRECTIONS

0.0   Start at the bulletin board before the bridge. Elevation: 9,110 feet. Cross Tenmile Creek on the wooden bridge. At the junction with the paved recreation path, turn left (east) onto the paved path.

0.25   Look to your right across an open area. The big mine tailings are the remains of the Frisco Tunnel.

0.4   Arrive at the start of the Mount Royal Trail on the right (west). GPS: N39 34.35' / W106 06.27'. Read the signs and bulletin board for more information about the area. The trail climbs fairly steeply from here. Ignore any trails coming in from the left as you hike.

0.8   Arrive at a junction. Continue uphill on the right (southwest) branch.

0.9   Arrive at a hunk of metal and some mining holes in the ground. The trail appears to go in three directions; take the middle path, which is lined with rocks in places.

1.0   Arrive in the remains of Masontown. Take some time to wander around and see old bricks, twisted metal, and other artifacts. When the trail appears to split in three directions, continue straight ahead. GPS: N39 33.91' / W106 06.19'. (*Option:* Turn around here for a 2-mile moderate hike.)

1.2   A faint trail takes off to the left as the main trail curves to the right. (An optional 0.1-mile out and back on the faint trail takes you to the remains of a cabin that escaped the avalanche that wiped out Masontown.) The trail continues to climb steeply.

1.7   Arrive at a trail junction. Turn right (northwest) and head uphill.

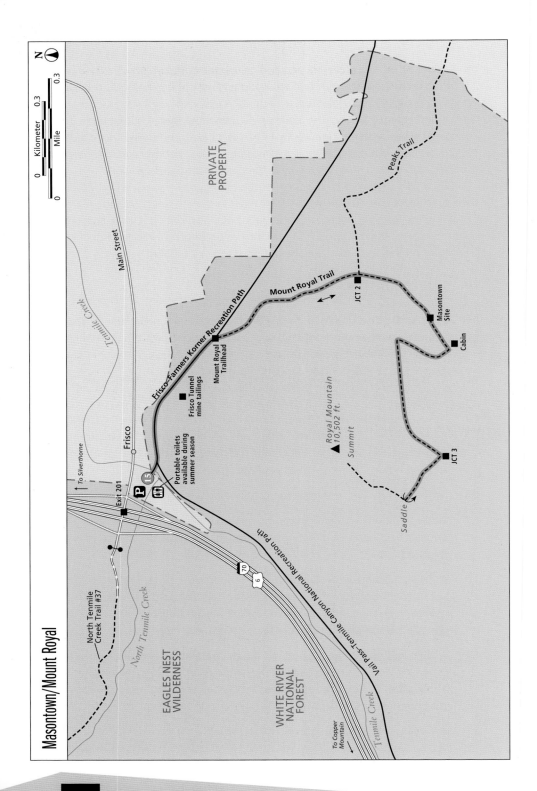

Masontown/Mount Royal

1.9 Arrive at the big cairn in a saddle that locals call Mount Royal. Elevation: 10,421 feet. Enjoy the views. GPS: N39 33.96' / W106 06.71'. Return the way you came. (*Option:* Hike from the Mount Royal saddle to the "top" of Mount Royal, a 0.4-mile, moderate out-and-back trek, by following the trail to the right [northeast]. A cairn marks the summit [or one of the summits]. GPS: N39 34.08' / W106 06.61'.)

3.8 Arrive back at the trailhead.

HIKE INFORMATION

Local Information
Frisco Information Center, 300 Main St., Frisco; (970) 668-5547, (800) 424-1554; www.friscococ.com

Local Events/Attractions
Colorado BBQ Challenge, 1 Main St., Frisco; (800) 424-1554; www.townoffrisco .com/events/bbq-challenge

Concert in the Park Series, 120 Main St. (Gazebo), Frisco; (800) 424-1554; www.townoffrisco.com/events/concert-in-the-park/

Fall Fest, Main Street event, Frisco; (800) 424-1554; www.townoffrisco.com/ events/fallfest/

Public Transportation (free)
Summit Stage, PO Box 2179, Frisco 80443; (970) 668-0999; www.summitstage.com

Cairn at the top of the Mount Royal Trail

Wheeler Lakes

Wind through lodgepole pine and aspen forest then climb through thick spruce-fir forest and flower-filled meadows to a pair of small but beautiful lakes that reflect the Colorado sky and surrounding woods. The trail sports a few steep spots and some mucky areas (after a good rain), but Wheeler Lakes are worth the effort. This hike starts on the southern part of the Gore Range Trail, which traverses to the east side of the range then contours north along the base of the rugged mountains. The hike description takes you to the first lake, but you can continue on to the nearby second lake if you have time. Enjoy exploring this pretty area.

Start: At the Gore Range Trailhead bulletin board
Distance: 6.6 miles out and back
Hiking time: 3.5 to 4.7 hours
Difficulty: Difficult due to distance and a 1,410-foot elevation gain
Trail surface: Dirt trail
Best season: July to early Oct
Other trail users: Equestrians
Canine compatibility: Dogs must be on leash
Land status: National forest and wilderness
Fees and permits: None required. Limit of 15 people per group.
Maps: USGS Vail Pass; Nat Geo Trails Illustrated 109 Breckenridge/ Tennessee Pass; Latitude 40° Summit County Trails; USFS White River National Forest map
Trail contact: USDA Forest Service, Dillon Ranger District, 680 Blue River Pkwy., Silverthorne; (970) 468-5400; www.fs.usda.gov/ whiteriver; www.dillonranger district.com
Other: The trail is mainly within the Eagles Nest Wilderness. Please comply with wilderness regulations.
Special considerations: Bring your own water; not much is available along the trail. Hunters may use this area during hunting season. The trail is neither marked nor maintained for winter use.

Finding the trailhead: From westbound I-70, travel 1.5 miles south of exit 198 (Officers Gulch) and turn into the scenic overlook parking. If you're heading eastbound on I-70, get off at exit 198, turn under the highway, and get back on heading westbound.

You can also park near the Conoco station to the east of the traffic light at Copper Mountain's entrance at exit 195. The Summit Stage bus goes to Copper Mountain with a stop near the entrance by CO 91. Walk back across the bridge over I-70 to a trail on the left that joins this hike at mile 0.8.

The trail starts on the right (west) side of the scenic overlook. GPS: N39 31.06' / W106 08.81'

Many summer moons ago, Ute Indians camped in this area and hunted bison, deer, elk, antelope, and mountain sheep in the surrounding high open areas. The discovery of gold near Denver in 1859 started a gold rush to the Rockies. Miners found gold by panning in the Blue River, and Breckenridge was born. The easy gold played out by 1863, and miners left for new gold fields. Silver was discovered in Tenmile Canyon in 1878 between Copper Mountain and the top of Fremont Pass. The mines and buildings needed lumber, and Judge John S. Wheeler built the first sawmill in Tenmile Canyon that same year. He and seven legislators purchased numerous mining claims in Tenmile Canyon, operating as the Federal Silver Mining Company of Colorado.

In 1879 Wheeler purchased 320 acres, now part of Copper Mountain Resort, and started a hay ranch. The next year silver miners arrived, finding silver on Copper Mountain's slopes. The ranch became a town known by various names: Wheeler's Ranch, Wheeler Station, Wheeler's, Wheeler, and Wheeler Junction. Wheeler prospered with a hotel, saloons, and a post office. By 1881 the town had 225 residents. Six sawmills provided lumber for the numerous mines along Tenmile Creek from Frisco to the top of Fremont Pass.

Despite its status as a mining town, Wheeler attracted tourists for the beautiful scenery and excellent fishing. In 1884 the Colorado & Southern Railroad finished laying tracks to Wheeler on the east side of Tenmile Creek. Their trains arrived over Boreas Pass to Breckenridge and on to Frisco. The railroad station at

First Wheeler Lake

Wheeler was named Solitude Station. On the other side of the creek, the Denver & Rio Grande Railroad built a line with a station called Wheeler's. The Denver & Rio Grande serviced this area from 1880 to 1911. The Colorado & Southern ended its rail service around 1937.

Wheeler also became a logging center. Silver-ore smelters in the area ran on charcoal fuel. Loggers often set fire to the forest because dry timber proved best for making charcoal. By 1899 loggers had basically stripped the mountains of trees, and the charcoal industry put itself out of business.

Today Copper Mountain has been developed into a popular ski area. Ski lifts across I-70 can be seen from various points along the trail. Skiing, other forms of outdoor recreation, and vacation homes have replaced mining in a new "gold rush" to the Rockies. The view of the Tenmile Range is also excellent from many places along the trail.

The lower part of the trail passes through sagebrush—yes, sagebrush grows on drier slopes in both Summit and Eagle Counties. Blue flax, yellow potentillas, and yellow-clustered sulphur flowers line the trail while scarlet gilia (sky rockets) trumpet your passing. Keep an eye out for an interesting large boulder along the right (north) side of the trail after mile 0.8. Colorful lichens cover the top while the lower part contains swirling ridges. As you climb into thicker forest, tiny Jacob's ladder grows in the shade. The snow lingers longer here so flowers bloom later than on the open sunny slopes below. After the steep climb through dark forest, you are greeted by a beautiful, open, flower-filled meadow. The ridge in the distance to the northwest is Shrine Ridge just west of Vail Pass. If directions seem weird, remember that Copper Mountain is to the south. The side trail into the lake passes through green grassy areas polka-dotted with flowers and clumps of trees. The trail can be a tad muddy after a rain. Some nice lunch spots can be found at the first lake. Take some time to explore and enjoy this quiet and peaceful area.

MILES AND DIRECTIONS

0.0 Start at the Gore Range Trailhead bulletin board. Elevation: 9,671 feet. After about 200 feet arrive at the Wheeler Trail bulletin board. Read the information then turn left and follow the old dirt road.

0.75 The trail goes along the I-70 off ramp for Copper Mountain. Curve right onto the singletrack. In about 200 feet a trail comes in from the left from CO 91. Continue curving right on the Gore Range Trail.

1.7 Enter the Eagles Nest Wilderness.

2.6 Arrive at a beautiful meadow. Continue following the trail.

3.1 Come to the junction with the Wheeler Lakes Spur. Turn right here.

Wheeler Lakes

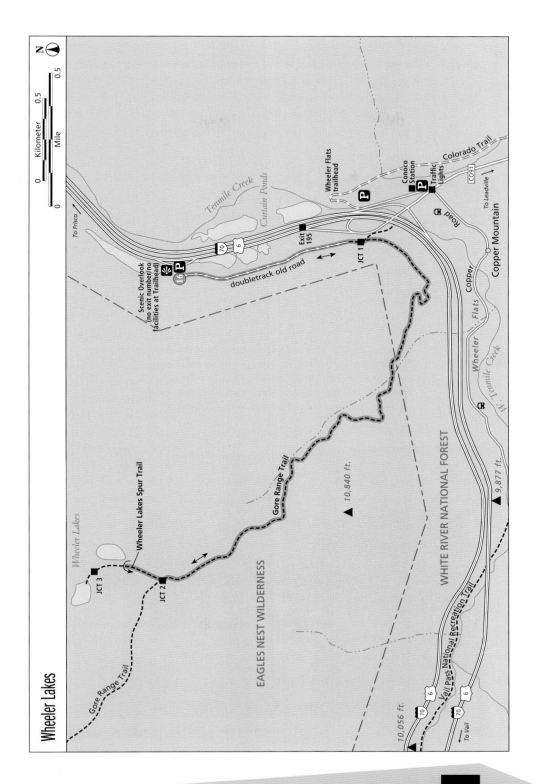

N

Kilometer
0   0.5   0.5

Mile
0   0.5   0.5

To Frisco

Tenmile Creek

Curtain Ponds

70 6

Exit 195

Scenic Overlook
(no exit number/no
facilities at Trailhead)

doubletrack old road

JCT 1

Wheeler Flats
trailhead

Conoco
Station

Traffic
Lights

Colorado Trail

CO91

To Leadville

Copper Road

Copper Mountain

Wheeler Flats

W. Tenmile Creek

10,840 ft.

Gore Range Trail

WHITE RIVER NATIONAL FOREST

9,877 ft.

Wheeler Lakes Spur Trail

Wheeler Lakes

JCT 3

JCT 2

Gore Range Trail

EAGLES NEST WILDERNESS

10,056 ft.

Vail Pass National Recreation Trail

70 6

70 6

To Vail

3.3 Arrive at the first lake. GPS: N39 31.27′ / W106 10.09′. Elevation: 11,079 feet. Return the way you came. (***Option:*** Proceed to the second lake. At mile 3.4 the trail splits. The left branch takes you along the west shore of the second lake. The right branch goes around the east edge of the lake to a ridge with a view down Tenmile Canyon and beyond. Return the way you came.)

6.6 Arrive back at the trailhead.

HIKE INFORMATION

Local Information
Copper Mountain Resort Chamber, 0189 Ten Mile Circle, Copper Mountain 80443; (970) 968-6477; www.copperchamber.com

Frisco Information Center, 300 Main St., Frisco; (970) 668-5547, (800) 424-1554; www.friscococ.com

> *Back in 1860 the Richard Sopris expedition named the Ten Mile Range because it was 10 miles from Breckenridge to the mouth of Tenmile Canyon near today's Frisco. The name of the range and creek is now spelled Tenmile according to the US Geological Survey.*

Second Wheeler Lake

Local Events/Attractions

Colorado BBQ Challenge, 1 Main St., Frisco; (800) 424-1554; www.townoffrisco.com/events/bbq-challenge

Concert in the Park Series, 120 Main St. (Gazebo), Frisco; (800) 424-1554; www.townoffrisco.com/events/concert-in-the-park/

Fall Fest, Main Street event, Frisco; (800) 424-1554; www.townoffrisco.com/events/fallfest/

Copper Mountain Resort hosts various events throughout the year, (866) 841-2481; www.coppercolorado.com

Organizations

Friends of the Eagles Nest Wilderness, www.fenw.org, or call the Dillon Ranger District, (970) 468-5400, for the current contact.

Public Transportation (free)

Summit Stage, PO Box 2179, Frisco 80443; (970) 668-0999; www.summitstage.com

Leave No Weeds

On January 16, 2004, USDA Forest Service chief Dale Bosworth talked about the four threats to our nation's forests and grasslands. One threat is the spread of invasive species. The chief said, "These are species that evolved in one place and wound up in another, where the ecological controls they evolved with are missing. They take advantage of their new surroundings to crowd out or kill off native species, destroying habitat for native wildlife."

Even if you do your best to Leave No Trace, did you Leave No Weeds? Weed seed can cling to anything. After a hike you might unknowingly transport these seeds to a new location and start a new infestation. Here are some ideas of how to prevent spreading weed seed from one area to another.

1. **Be aware and prepare.** Learn to identify noxious weeds. Rid camping gear and clothes of mud and weed seed before each trip and at each campsite. Brush animals before and after hiking trips to remove weed seed.

2. **Camp and travel in weed-free areas.** Wash your vehicle, boots, hiking poles, tents, and clothes before and after each outing. Stay on established roads and trails. Avoid camping in or hiking through weed-infested areas. Avoid soil-disturbing activities and practices.

3. **Report it.** Report weed infestations to your local Forest Service or Bureau of Land Management office.

For more information on noxious weeds, contact the Colorado Weed Management Association at (970) 361-8262 or www.cwma.org.

Guller Creek Trail

Wander across some of Copper Mountain's west-side ski trails filled with wildflowers on section eight of the 483-mile Colorado Trail, then wind down to the confluence of Jacque and Guller Creeks. Remnants of the old days of mining and logging mix with today's white gold (snow riding) along this trail. Hike along beautiful willow-lined Guller Creek through little meadows filled with colorful flowers to the remains of an old cabin. A shorter, 6.4-mile out-and-back hike is also listed.

Start: At the mini-golf course near the bottom of American Eagle Lift
Distance: 9.2 miles out and back
Hiking time: 4 to 6 hours
Difficulty: Moderate due to distance and a 1,060-foot elevation gain
Trail surface: Dirt trail and dirt road
Best season: Late June to early Oct (whenever Copper Mountain starts snowmaking)
Other trail users: Equestrians and mountain bikers
Canine compatibility: Dogs must be under voice control
Land status: National forest
Fees and permits: None required in summer. Daily fee required in winter.
Maps: USGS Copper Mountain; Nat Geo Trails Illustrated 109

Breckenridge/Tennessee Pass; Latitude 40° Summit County Trails; USFS White River National Forest map
Trail contact: USDA Forest Service, Dillon Ranger District, 680 Blue River Pkwy., Silverthorne; (970) 468-5400; www.fs.usda.gov/white river; www.dillonrangerdistrict.com
Other: This trail is popular with mountain bikers. Copper Stables uses some sections of the trail for guided horseback rides.
Special considerations: The Guller Creek valley is popular with hunters during hunting season. Winter access to Guller Creek is via Copper Mountain lifts (fee charged) and ski trails. The trail is located in the Vail Pass Winter Recreation Area and a daily fee is charged in winter.

Finding the trailhead: From I-70 exit 195 (Copper Mountain/Leadville), head south and turn right at the traffic light. In 0.6 mile, turn left onto Ten Mile Circle. In 0.1 mile, turn left and then right into covered parking. Or you can drive another 0.1 mile around the traffic circle and park in the upper parking deck. Walk toward the Center Village and past the first set of buildings, then look to the left for the miniature golf course. The hike starts on the dirt trail to the left of the course. Water and restrooms are located in the building straight ahead. GPS: N39 29.98' / W106 09.30'.

Copper Mountain has seen many changes over the years. Prehistoric Indians and Utes passed by, traveling over Vail Pass in search of the plentiful game that grazed where Dillon Reservoir sits today. After miners found gold near Breckenridge in 1859, hopeful prospectors spread across Summit County. A few men successfully mined the slopes of Copper Mountain. One energetic miner dug a shaft at the summit, finding low-grade copper ore, hence the mountain's name.

In 1879 Judge John S. Wheeler purchased 320 acres, now part of Copper Mountain Resort, and started a hay ranch. As miners arrived, the ranch became a town known by various names: Wheeler's Ranch, Wheeler Station, Wheeler's, Wheeler, and Wheeler Junction. Wheeler Junction prospered, with a hotel,

Colorado Trail and Jacque Ridge

saloons, a post office, and several sawmills. In the 1880s the Colorado & Southern Railroad and the Denver & Rio Grande Railroad reached Wheeler Junction. Mining eventually died out, and by 1937 the railroads had ceased operations. The little town began to return to the earth. Sheepherders tended their flocks on grassy slopes near the abandoned town from 1905 to 1979.

In 1954 USDA Forest Service personnel first recognized that the terrain would provide great skiing. The north-facing slopes would hold snow and offered a variety of angles for all types of skiers. By 1960 investors started to contact the agency about developing a ski area at Copper Mountain. Inquiries came without any follow-up. Finally, in 1968 a group of investors formed Copper Mountain Associates, and Chuck Lewis, a former executive vice president of Vail Associates, became the general partner. He negotiated the purchase of 280 acres at the mountain's base (part of the Wheeler Ranch). The group obtained a ski area permit from the Forest Service, arranged financing, and started construction in 1971. "The most nearly perfect ski mountain in the United States" opened on December 5, 1972, with five ski lifts, twenty trails, and six buildings.

In 1973 Merrill Hastings, in *Colorado Magazine,* suggested a trail that would take hikers from Denver to Durango. Bill Lucas, the USDA Forest Service's Rocky Mountain regional forester at the time, became the advocate of this idea. The route would be called the Colorado Trail. The trail would provide more hiking opportunities and relieve pressure on existing trails in the state. In November 1973 various forest user groups met with Lucas to discuss the possibility of the

Colorado Trail and wildflowers along Guller Creek

long trail. The 470-plus-mile route would use existing trails where possible and build new trails in certain areas. After various starts and stops, Gudy Gaskill from the Colorado Mountain Club and Governor Richard Lamm helped create a two-year plan to finish the long trail. Gaskill created the nonprofit Colorado Trail Foundation (CTF) in 1987 to organize the volunteer crews that would complete the work and to take responsibility for the trail in partnership with the USDA Forest Service. In two summers, about 1,400 volunteers in sixty-six trail crews completed the trail. The CTF sponsors volunteer trail crews each summer to keep the Colorado Trail an experience to enjoy and remember.

The old section of the Colorado Trail followed the paved Vail Pass/Tenmile Canyon National Recreation Trail to a bridge over Tenmile Creek. From there the trail followed Guller Creek to its headwaters and east to Searle Pass. To provide a better backcountry experience, part of this segment was rerouted during the summers of 2000, 2001, and 2002. The CTF and Copper Mountain Resort worked together to plan the new route and obtained USDA Forest Service approval. During those summers, thirteen weeklong trail crews averaging eighteen people each worked creating new tread. The Forest Service and Volunteers for Outdoor Colorado then revegetated the old trail from Jacque Creek down (east) to the paved recreation trail. This hike follows the "new" section of the Colorado Trail to Guller Creek and then 1.4 miles up the valley to the remains of an old cabin. During this hike you'll be walking on the Continental Divide National Scenic Trail as well as the Colorado Trail.

MILES AND DIRECTIONS

0.0 Start to the east of the miniature golf course, to the left of American Eagle Lift (summer chairlift rides). Watch for a rock with the Colorado Trail logo on it and turn right. The trail traverses above the base of American Eagle Lift. It then becomes a road and crosses a little creek above Copper Mountain's Center Village area. Elevation: 9,760 feet.

0.1 Arrive at a service road and continue hiking to the left on the road (uphill).

0.5 The road starts heading downhill to the right. Walk across the road onto the singletrack trail.

0.7 Reach a trail junction. Turn left onto the Colorado Trail.

1.1 Arrive at a trail junction. Turn left and continue uphill on the Colorado Trail.

1.2 Reach a trail junction. Continue straight ahead on the Colorado Trail.

1.6 Come to a trail junction. Turn right onto the Colorado Trail.

2.1 Pass the ski-area boundary sign.

Guller Creek Trail

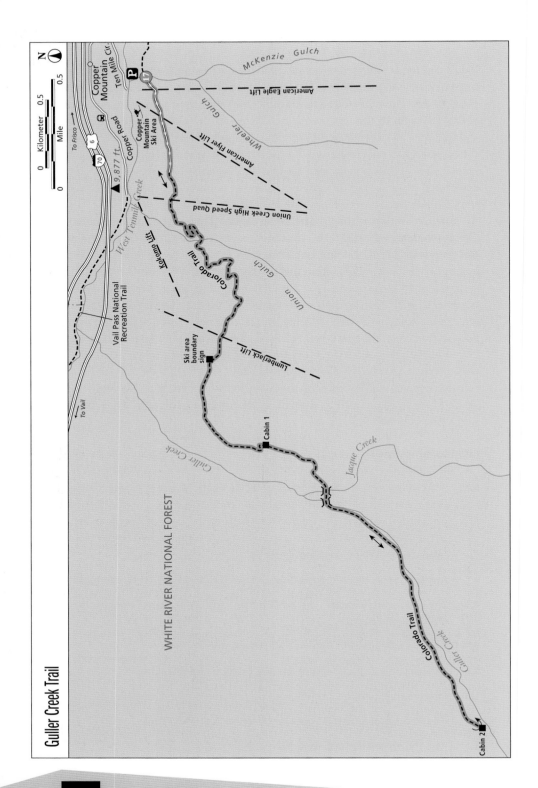

- N
- Copper Mountain Cir.
- Ten Mile Cir.
- To Frisco
- Copper Mountain Ski Area
- Copper Road
- ▲ 9,877 ft.
- West Tenmile Creek
- To Vail
- To Frisco
- 70
- 6
- 0 Kilometer 0.5
- 0 Mile 0.5
- McKenzie Gulch
- American Eagle Lift
- Wheeler Gulch
- American Flyer Lift
- Union Creek High Speed Quad
- Kokomo Lift
- Vail Pass National Recreation Trail
- Colorado Trail
- Union Gulch
- Lumberjack Lift
- Ski area boundary sign
- Guller Creek
- Cabin 1
- Jacque Creek
- WHITE RIVER NATIONAL FOREST
- Colorado Trail
- Guller Creek
- Cabin 2

2.8   Look to your right to see some cabin remains. Take a few minutes to check out the interesting construction. In about 260 feet you'll arrive at the trail junction with Elk Track, the winter access trail. Continue straight ahead on the Colorado Trail.

3.2   Reach Guller Creek. GPS: N39 29.28' / W106 11.43'. Elevation: 10,480 feet. The cabin ruin uphill to the right (northeast) is a great rest spot. (*Option:* For a shorter hike, turn around here for a 6.4-mile hike.) Walk across the bridge and head left on the trail.

4.6   Arrive at a post in a cairn next to the old cabin remains, the end of this featured hike. GPS: N39 28.67' / W106 12.62'. Elevation: 10,740 feet. Enjoy the scenery and lunch, then return the way you came.

9.2   Arrive back at the trailhead.

HIKE INFORMATION

Local Information

Copper Mountain Resort, 209 Ten Mile Circle, Copper Mountain; (866) 841-2481; www.coppercolorado.com

Copper Mountain Resort Association, 0189 Ten Mile Circle, Copper Mountain; (970) 968-6477; www.copperchamber.com

Cabin remains along Guller Creek

Frisco Information Center, 300 Main St., Frisco; (970) 668-5547, (800) 424-1554; www.friscococ.com

Local Events/Attractions

Copper Mountain Resort hosts various events throughout the year, (866) 841-2481; www.coppercolorado.com

Colorado BBQ Challenge, 1 Main St., Frisco; (800) 424-1554; www.townof frisco.com/events/bbq-challenge

Concert in the Park Series, 120 Main St. (Gazebo), Frisco; (800) 424-1554; www.townoffrisco.com/events/concert-in-the-park/

Fall Fest, Main Street event, Frisco; (800) 424-1554; www.townoffrisco.com/events/fallfest/

Hike Tours

Friends of the Dillon Ranger District in partnership with Copper Mountain offers naturalist-guided hikes at the ski area approximately July 1 to Labor Day, (866) 841-2481; www.coppercolorado.com.

Organizations

Colorado Trail Foundation, 710 10th St., #210, Golden; (303) 384-3729; www.coloradotrail.org

Friends of the Dillon Ranger District, PO Box 1648, Silverthorne 80498; (970) 262-3449; www.fdrd.org

Continental Divide Trail Coalition, PO Box 552, Pine 80470; (970) 340-2382; www.continentaldividetrail.org

Public Transportation (free)

Summit Stage, PO Box 2179, Frisco 80443; (970) 668-0999; www.summitstage .com The stage stops at Copper Mountain if you'd prefer to ride a bus.

Wilder Gulch Trail

This gentle trail takes you up a willow-lined subalpine valley, past wonderful wildflowers and old cabin remains to the top of Ptarmigan Pass at 11,765 feet. The last part of the hike is on a dirt road open to motorized vehicles, but the views from the top of the pass are worth the walk. You can see parts of the Sawatch and Gore Ranges as well as Grays and Torreys Peaks in the Front Range. A short hike will take you up Ptarmigan Hill, which offers even better views. Enjoy a day exploring Wilder Gulch.

Start: At the Vail Pass Rest Area lower parking lot

Distance: 7.4 miles out and back

Hiking time: 3 to 4.5 hours

Difficulty: Moderate due to distance and a 1,245-foot elevation gain and 40-foot loss

Trail surface: Dirt trail and dirt road

Best season: Early July through Sept

Other trail users: Mountain bikers and equestrians

Canine compatibility: Dogs must be under voice control

Land status: National forest

Fees and permits: None required in summer. Daily fee required in winter.

Maps: USGS Vail Pass; Nat Geo Trails Illustrated 108 Vail/Frisco/Dillon; Latitude 40° Summit County Trails; USFS White River National Forest map

Trail contact: USDA Forest Service, Dillon Ranger District, 680 Blue River Pkwy., Silverthorne; (970) 468-5400; www.fs.usda.gov/whiteriver; www.dillonranger district.com

Other: Please walk through any muddy spots and avoid trampling trailside vegetation.

Special considerations: Bring your own water; the creek is not always near the trail. Hunters may use this area during hunting season. In winter both snowmobilers and backcountry skiers/snowboarders enjoy this area. Wilder Gulch is groomed in winter for all users and a daily fee is charged.

Finding the trailhead: From I-70 exit 190 (Vail Pass Rest Area), drive toward the rest area (restrooms if open, but water is not potable). Park in the upper parking lot. Walk down the stairs and head to the little building at the southeast end of the lower parking lot. Look for the obvious trail heading south to the right of the wastewater plant. GPS: N39 31.59' / W106 13.09'.

THE HIKE

Initially the trail parallels I-70 then slowly curves to the right as it heads toward Wilder Gulch. In some places grass and plants grow over the trail, but the way is easy to find. Watch for a mucky spot—try to stay on the trail.

Once you've entered Wilder Gulch, enjoy the beautiful wildflowers and open vistas. Ptarmigan Hill rises to the southwest, guarding the little valley at its foot. The buildings on top are part of the emergency communications systems between Summit and Eagle Counties. The trail wanders through beautiful meadows, while willows line the creek to the left. Look for red and yellow paintbrush, pink-purple fireweed, and blue lupine. A few little creeks may cross the trail depending on available moisture. Trees, mainly spruce, grow in small clumps along the trail and on the hill to the north. The south side of the valley, with its north-facing slopes, is more heavily forested. Beaver ponds dot the meandering creek.

Once you're hiking up Wilder Gulch, notice the big stumps to the right. During mining's heyday in the late 1800s, men logged these slopes for lumber for the mines, railroads, buildings, and charcoal for the smelters. In 1885 Wheeler Junction (today's Copper Mountain) boasted six sawmills! Dragging logs over the ground was anything but easy, so loggers cut the trees in winter and horses dragged them over the snow. The stumps reflect the depth of snow when cut. Sometimes trees were burned before cutting to dry them out. Occasionally the trail looks like a cut was taken from the hillside—a road may have once traveled up Wilder Gulch to the old cabin ruins and logging areas.

Cabin remains along Wilder Gulch

Ptarmigan Hill

To find the remains of the old cabin, which perhaps belonged to one of the loggers, notice an orange diamond and a blue diamond nailed to a tree on your right at 1.8 miles. The orange denotes a snowmobile route, while the blue signifies a cross-country skiing trail. You're getting close to the cabin remains. In about 260 feet, notice a large boulder on the right with a couple of trees that appear to grow out of it. The trail then passes by two clumps of trees. After the second clump the area along the trail widens a little more. Look to your left at the beaver ponds. Can you spot the "flat" wooden planks near one of them? Look to your right and at the edge of the trees; see if you can find the cabin ruins with a spruce tree growing out of them. Imagine living in such a small space!

People in Summit County evidently liked naming features after the white-tailed ptarmigan, the smallest member of the grouse family. On the east side along the border between Summit and Grand Counties are Ptarmigan Pass and Ptarmigan Peak in the Ptarmigan Peak Wilderness. This hike ends at Ptarmigan Pass on the border between Eagle and Summit Counties below Ptarmigan Hill.

The chicken-sized white-tailed ptarmigan lives in the alpine and subalpine life zones. In summer their speckled grayish-brown bodies with white tail feathers blend in perfectly with the mottled rocks, making them hard to see. It's possible to almost step on one before noticing it's there.

Ptarmigan mate for life, although after breeding the couple go their separate ways until the next spring. Males live in the alpine tundra all year, while females migrate to habitat around treeline and live in flocks for the winter. Ptarmigan plumage turns white to camouflage them against the winter background. Their feet and legs are heavily feathered for warmth and flotation on the snow.

Willows, which produce next year's buds in the fall, provide nutritious food for the ptarmigan during long, cold winters. They are one of the only wild creatures to gain weight during that time of year. The birds might dive into a snowdrift, especially around willows, to stay warm on cold nights—a ptarmigan version of an igloo.

The birds mate in early to mid-June and the female lays her eggs. After twenty-two to twenty-six days the eggs hatch, and soon tiny chicks line up to follow mom up to the alpine. When threatened, the mother will fake a broken wing to draw predators away from her offspring. Ptarmigans eat buds, stems, seeds, insects, fruits, and flowers.

With the ptarmigan dependent on high alpine habitat, which may be shrinking due to generally warmer temperatures, the Center for Biological Diversity filed a scientific petition with the US Fish & Wildlife Service in 2010 requesting federal protection for ptarmigans in the lower forty-eight states. Presently they are found in alpine areas of Washington, Montana, and Colorado plus Canada and Alaska. The population in Colorado is the largest in the United States outside of Alaska.

Once you reach Wearyman Road, the trail wanders through a spruce forest with colorful wildflowers such as pink Parry's primrose, marsh marigolds, and blue Jacob's ladder. You'll walk through meadows with views of Ptarmigan Hill and blocky red stones formed from sediments eroded from the Ancestral Rockies. At the top of the pass, enjoy the views of the Sawatch and Gore Ranges.

MILES AND DIRECTIONS

0.0 Start at the edge of the pavement on the singletrack trail to the right of the wastewater plant. Elevation: 10,540 feet. After about 200 feet cross Tenmile Creek. The next section may have some wet areas and the trail may be hard to spot. Continue heading south.

0.6 Arrive at the junction with the trail that connects with the paved Vail Pass National Recreation Trail. Turn right and head up Wilder Gulch. GPS: N39 31.11' / W106 13.11'.

2.0 Look to your right to find the cabin ruins with a spruce tree growing out of them. GPS: N39 30.47' / W106 14.30'. Elevation: 10,920 feet.

2.9 Come to the junction with FR 747, Wearyman Road. Turn left and follow the road to the top of Ptarmigan Pass. (*Option:* From here you can return the way you came for a moderate 5.8-mile out-and-back hike.)

3.7 Arrive at the top of Ptarmigan Pass and enjoy the views. GPS: N39 29.58' / W106 15.21'. Elevation: 11,765 feet. Return the way you came.

7.4 Arrive back at the trailhead.

Wilder Gulch Trail

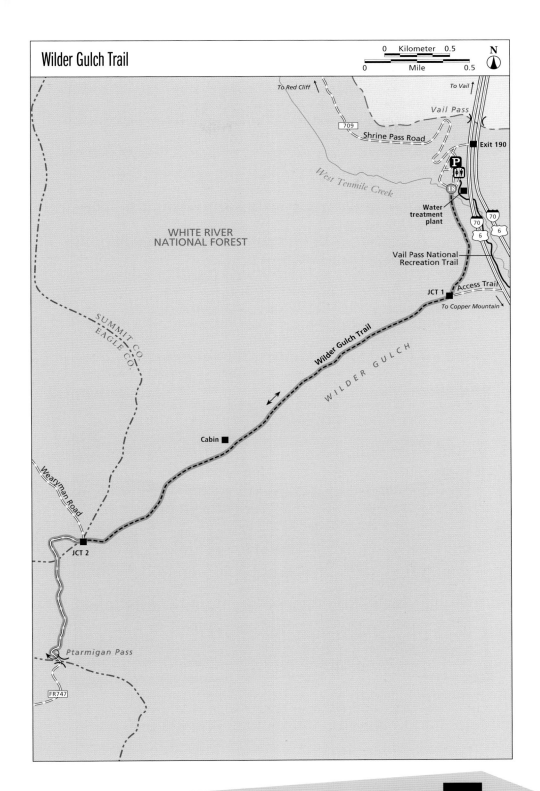

Kilometer 0 0.5

Mile 0 0.5

N

To Red Cliff

To Vail

Vail Pass

709

Shrine Pass Road

Exit 190

WEST Tenmile Creek

P

18

70 70

6 6

WHITE RIVER
NATIONAL FOREST

Water
treatment
plant

Vail Pass National
Recreation Trail

JCT 1

Access Trail

To Copper Mountain

Wilder Gulch Trail

WILDER GULCH

SUMMIT CO.
EAGLE CO.

Cabin

Wearyman Road

JCT 2

Ptarmigan Pass

FR747

Local Information

Copper Mountain Resort Chamber, 0189 Ten Mile Circle, Copper Mountain; (970) 968-6477; www.copperchamber.com

Frisco Information Center, 300 Main St., Frisco; (970) 668-5547, (800) 424-1554; www.friscococ.com

Local Events/Attractions

Colorado BBQ Challenge, 1 Main St., Frisco; (800) 424-1554; www.townoffrisco.com/events/bbq-challenge

Concert in the Park Series, 120 Main St. (Gazebo), Frisco; (800) 424-1554; www.townoffrisco.com/events/concert-in-the-park/

Fall Fest, Main Street event, Frisco; (800) 424-1554; www.townoffrisco.com/events/fallfest/

Copper Mountain Resort hosts various events throughout the year, (866) 841-2481; www.coppercolorado.com

Ptarmigan Pass

Honorable Mentions Summit County

A. Old Dillon Reservoir Trail

This easy and short trek to the town of Dillon's old reservoir (built in 1936) makes a great hike for the whole family. Hikers and mountain bikers use the trail, which has great views of the surrounding area from either the trail or near the reservoir. Anglers also enjoy fishing in the little lake. A joint venture between Summit County and the Towns of Dillon and Silverthorne enlarged the reservoir to 288 acre-feet in 2012. Water from the reservoir comes from the north side of I-70 from Salt Lick Gulch and is used by Dillon for drinking water as well as to provide extra water for downstream flow enhancement.

The trail wiggles up the hill then makes a right switchback for an angled climb to a high point. A bench sits a little down and to the right for a nice 180-degree view from east to southwest. The Front Range with two 14,000-foot peaks rises in the east, Dillon Reservoir lies below, and the spine of the Tenmile Range heads toward Breckenridge. Elevation: 9,180 feet. Return the way you came for a 1-mile out-and-back hike. **Finding the trailhead:** From I-70 exit 203 (Frisco/Breckenridge), turn left (northeast) at the first traffic light and drive past the Holiday Inn for about 1.6 miles to the Old Dillon Reservoir Trail #87 trailhead sign (around the curve past Heaton Bay Campground—watch carefully on the left for the hard-to-see trailhead sign). Turn left (north) into the parking lot. No facilities are available at the trailhead. GPS: N39 36.36' / W106 04.51'. Elevation: 9,075 feet.

For more information, contact the Dillon Ranger District, 680 Blue River Pkwy., Silverthorne; (970) 468-5456; www.dillonrangerdistrict.com.

B. Clinton Gulch Reservoir Trail

Enjoy a 2.3-mile loop stroll around Clinton Gulch Reservoir with its gorgeous backdrop of Fletcher and Wheeler Mountains rising along the ridge of the Tenmile Range. The trail wanders along the eastern lakeshore through meadows and willows while flowers line the trail. A nice bridge crosses the inlet with views north to Jacque Peak and Jacque and Elk Ridges. You'll enter a thick spruce-fir forest on the west side with forest wildflowers blooming under the majestic trees. Keep an eye open for gnomes and fairies for surely they live in this forest wonderland. Make sure to stay on the high trail and not on any of the angler trails close to the lake. The trail exits at the south parking lot, and you can

walk next to the highway on top of the dam (on the lake side of the guardrail) to return to your vehicle. Part of the trail on the west side is on an easement through private property, so please stay on the trail. **Finding the trailhead:** From I-70 exit 195 (Copper Mountain/Leadville), head south on CO 91 for 7.2 miles (just before mile marker 15) to a parking lot on the left on the east side of Clinton Gulch Reservoir (not marked as such). Turn left and park. A portable toilet may be available, but no potable water. The trailhead is at the south end of the parking lot. GPS: N39 24.93' / W106 10.27'. Elevation: 11,080 feet.

For more information, contact Summit County Open Space & Trails, County Commons, 0037 Peak One Dr., SCR 1005, Frisco; (970) 668-4060; www.co.summit .co.us/index.aspx?NID=105.

C. Hallelujah Self-Guided Nature Trail

Enjoy a moderate 0.35-mile lollipop interpretive loop through spruce-fir forest along the edge of Copper Mountain's ski runs while learning about area history and life in the subalpine. Watch for cute little pikas scurrying around the boulder field, mouths full of grass and flowers to store for the winter. You'll pass an old cabin ruins and enjoy a view of Vail Pass, not to mention colorful wildflowers. To access the trailhead, first obtain a lift ticket from Copper's Guest Services then ride up the American Eagle Chair (dogs not allowed). Besides being an easy way to reach the trail, you're rewarded with a bird's-eye view of the scenery around Copper Mountain. **Finding the trailhead:** From I-70 exit 195 (Copper Mountain/ Leadville), head south and turn right at the traffic light. In 0.6 mile, turn left onto Ten Mile Circle. In 0.1 mile, turn left and then right into covered parking. Or you

can drive another 0.1 mile around the traffic circle and park in the upper parking deck. Walk into the Center Village and look straight ahead for the sign directing you to Guest Services, where you need to obtain a lift ticket. Water and restrooms are located in this building. When you get off American Eagle Chair, walk straight ahead and a tad left to the path lined with wood. Food and restrooms are also located in Solitude Station near the top of the chair. GPS: N39 28.98' / W106 09.39'. Elevation: 11,250 feet.

For more information, contact Copper Mountain Resort, 209 Ten Mile Circle, Copper Mountain 80443; (866) 841-2481; www.coppermountaincolorado.com.

Vail and Eagle County

Hikers head down the Notch Mountain Trail (hike 30).

If you think of world-class skiing and a swank resort for the rich and famous when you hear the word "Vail," the eighteen hikes in this section will show you another side to this beautiful section of Colorado. For your first hint, stand in the middle of Vail Village and look northeast to the craggy 13,000-foot peaks that tower over the Gore Valley. The west side of the Gore Range tends to be lusher than the east side because storms hit the mountains and drop much of their moisture. Not all the mountains are as steep and craggy as those in the Gore Range. To the west of Vail Pass, the terrain rolls in gentle ridges.

Miners discovered gold and silver to the south of the Vail area, but not to the same extent as in Summit County. Vail and Eagle County became the breadbasket of the area. After World War II snow became the new gold with the development of the Vail and Beaver Creek ski resorts. Snow melts into water, and several hikes take you past water diversions and give you a history of water wars. The eastern slope siphons many acre-feet of water from this water-rich part of Colorado for city dwellers and agriculture on the dry plains.

A variety of scenic trails leads hikers to beautiful lakes, frothy creeks, and dancing waterfalls nestled high in wildflower-filled meadows and cirques in the Eagles Nest and Holy Cross Wildernesses. Other trails explore narrow valleys at the base of which ranchers grew crops and livestock. Several trails pass through slowly recovering lodgepole forest killed by pine beetles. South of Eagle lies a beautiful high alpine lake, reached by a hike through lush forest. Another trail takes you along the ridge of Red Table Mountain for an incredible view of the famous Maroon Bells and nearby peaks from the summit of Mount Thomas.

With the variety of terrain, hikers have endless possibilities to explore this beautiful area.

Gore Range framed by the line shack porch (hike 25)

Shrine Ridge Trail

Colorful, gorgeous, never-ending wildflowers and views make this trail a very popular hike. Mid-July to early August is typically the best time for the flower show. You may even enjoy a snowball fight at the drift just below Shrine Ridge. The views of the craggy Gore Range, Tenmile Range, and the Sawatch Range with the famous Mount of the Holy Cross are always spectacular. Remember the camera!

Start: At the Shrine Ridge parking lot at the top of Shrine Pass by the bulletin board
Distance: 4.6 miles out and back
Hiking time: 1.7 to 3 hours
Difficulty: Moderate due to distance and an 800-foot elevation gain
Trail surface: Dirt road and dirt trail
Best season: Early July to early Oct
Other trail users: Equestrians
Canine compatibility: Dogs must be under control
Land status: National forest
Fees and permits: None required in summer. Daily fee required in winter.
Maps: USGS Vail Pass and Red Cliff; Nat Geo Trails Illustrated 108 Vail/Frisco/Dillon; Latitude 40° Vail and Eagle Trails; USFS White River National Forest map
Trail contact: USDA Forest Service, Eagle-Holy Cross Ranger District, 24747 US 24, Minturn; (970) 827-5715; www.fs.usda.gov/whiteriver
Other: Please walk through any muddy spots and avoid trampling trailside vegetation. Staying on the trail also avoids spread of noxious weeds and prevents the trail from widening. In winter the Shrine Pass area is a favorite with both snowmobilers and backcountry skiers/snowboarders. The winter trailhead is the Vail Pass Rest Area, and a daily fee is charged. A separate ski trail takes off from the first switchback on Shrine Pass Road. For more information on winter travel, log onto www.huts.org (huts and routes, Shrine Mountain Inn), call (970) 827-5715, or visit www.fs.usda.gov/whiteriver.
Special considerations: Water is not plentiful along this trail. Hunters use this area in the fall.

Finding the trailhead: From I-70 exit 190 (Vail Pass Rest Area), turn left and drive over the bridge and basically straight ahead onto the sometimes rough dirt road marked "Shrine Pass and Red Cliff (FR 709)." Drive approximately 2.3 miles to the top of Shrine Pass. Park in the parking lot on the south (left) side of the road. Vault toilets are available. GPS: N39 32.76' / W106 14.49'.

THE HIKE

The trail to Shrine Mountain and Wingle Ridge once was known to only a few people and sheepherders. Word of the colorful wildflowers and beautiful vistas made the rounds, and soon more and more people wandered along the trail. Part of the trail crosses fragile alpine wetlands and willows. Unfortunately, people trampled the area, widening the bogs, and the little singletrack trail became a muddy mess. In September 2002 a weekend crew of about 175 volunteers with Volunteers for Outdoor Colorado worked on 2 miles of trail, building erosion controls to prevent further damage.

About 300 million years ago, long before modern humans wandered the area, the Frontrangia part of the Ancestral Rockies rose a little west of where today's Front Range lies. Colorado was situated near the equator in a tropical climate. As Frontrangia eroded, gray to red sediments came to rest in the shallow seas that surrounded the mountain range. By the time the current Rockies rose, the shallow sea sediments had metamorphosed into sandstone, shale, conglomerate, and marine limestone, called the Minturn Formation. Above it sits the reddish conglomerate and sandstone of the Maroon Formation, which can be seen along the hike to Shrine Mountain.

Many moons ago, Native Americans traveled across Vail Pass following game that summered in the Blue River valley (in today's Summit County). The Utes called the area Nah-oon-kara, meaning "where the river of the blue rises." When excavation started for the I-70 rest area in 1974, evidence that was uncovered

View of Gore Range from Shrine Ridge

showed use by native peoples over 7,000 years. Campfire remains, butchered animal bones, scrapers, and projectile points led archaeologists to believe at least seven different waves of native occupation occurred there, probably as a summer hunting camp. About 200 years ago evidence of occupation stopped, probably because with horses, the Utes no longer camped on the pass.

The Shrine Ridge Trail leaves from the road going to the Shrine Mountain Inn. The privately owned facility consists of three cabins, all with hot and cold running potable water and flush toilets. Reservations can be made through the 10th Mountain Division Hut Association. The inn is open year-round and is located on private property. Please do not visit unless you have reservations.

Today you can enjoy subalpine wildflowers in all their glory. Varieties of daisies, bistort, willows, Jacob's ladder, monkshood, chiming bells, and little red elephants bloom along the first part of the trail. After crossing a little creek, the trail starts to climb through forest with blackened stumps and tall stumps, a reminder of a large fire and logging activity in the late 1800s. Meadows painted in hues of yellow, red, and purple dazzle the eye. The little creek at about 1 mile is often bordered by rosy paintbrush, little red elephants, and Parry's primrose, in shades of pink to purple.

Just below the final ascent to the ridge, a dense field of blue lupine blooms below the snowbanks. Watch for flying snowballs, as hikers enjoy snowball fights in midsummer. Up on the left side of the ridge heading to Shrine Mountain are fields of red paintbrush and blue lupine with the Sawatch Range and Mount of the Holy Cross for a backdrop. To the right of the ridge are interesting red rock formations, which with some imagination could be shrines of some sort. Rock gardens abound in the area. Watch for marmots and chipmunks scurrying around and crows flying overhead.

Shrine Mountain probably received its name from the fantastic view of Mount of the Holy Cross, once a national monument to which people made pilgrimages. The interesting red rock outcrops that remind people of shrines may be another source for its name.

MILES AND DIRECTIONS

0.0 Start at the bulletin board near the vault toilets in the parking lot (elevation 11,089 feet). Walk southwest on the dirt road. After about 350 feet turn left onto the singletrack trail at the Shrine Ridge Trail sign.

0.9 Arrive at the trail junction with the trail from the Shrine Mountain Inn. Continue straight ahead.

1.5 Look for a big flat rock along the right side of the trail as it climbs to the ridge. It offers a nice view of the Gore Range and is a good picture spot.

Shrine Ridge Trail

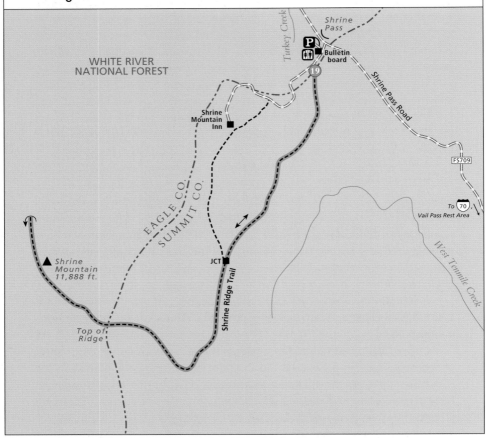

1.75 You may find a snowbank here just below the ridge. Enjoy! Climb a few more feet to the top of the ridge. GPS: N39 31.91' / W106 15.36'. Elevation: 11,840 feet. Turn right to continue toward Shrine Mountain.

1.9 Pass a social trail coming in from the left. Continue straight ahead and enjoy the wildflowers and the view of Mount of the Holy Cross to the west.

> *Shrine Ridge was officially named Wingle Ridge in November 2003 in memory of Pete Wingle. Pete, a longtime USDA Forest Service employee, administered recreation on national forest lands and assisted in the development of Copper Mountain Ski Resort. He also served on the boards of the 10th Mountain Division Hut Association and the Summit Huts Association.*

2.3 Arrive on a rock outcrop with great views. GPS: N39 32.25' / W106 15.61'. Return the way you came.

4.6 Arrive back at the parking lot.

HIKE INFORMATION

Local Information

Copper Mountain Resort Chamber, 0189 Ten Mile Circle, Copper Mountain; (970) 968-6477; www.copperchamber.com

Frisco Information Center, 300 Main St., Frisco; (970) 668-5547, (800) 424-1554; www.friscococ.com

Vail Valley Partnership,101 Fawcett Rd., Ste. 240, Avon 81620; (970) 476-1000; www.visitvailvalley.com

Local Events/Attractions

Colorado BBQ Challenge, 1 Main St., Frisco; (800) 424-1554; www.townoffrisco .com/events/bbq-challenge/

Concert in the Park Series, 120 Main St. (Gazebo), Frisco; (800) 424-1554; www.townoffrisco.com/events/concert-in-the-park/

Fall Fest, Main Street event, Frisco; (800) 424-1554; www.townoffrisco.com/ events/fallfest/

Copper Mountain Resort hosts various events throughout the year, (888) 219-2441; www.coppercolorado.com

Bravo! Vail Valley Music Festival, 2271 N. Frontage Rd. W., Ste. C, Vail; (877) 812-5700; www.vailmusicfestival.org

Bud Light Hot Summer Nights Concert Series, Gerald R. Ford Amphitheater, 530 S. Frontage Rd. E., Vail; (970) 845-TIXS [8497], (888) 920-ARTS [2797]; www .vvf.org/vvf/info/events.entertainment.hotsummernights.aspx

Volunteers for Outdoor Colorado (VOC) is a nonprofit organization established in 1984 that sponsors outdoor work projects throughout Colorado from April through October, partnering with various land management agencies. Youth programs and crew leadership training are also offered. Contact VOC at 600 S. Marion Pkwy., Denver 80209; call (303) 715-1010 or log onto www.voc.org.

Upon reaching the top of Bowman's Shortcut, you may start singing the Sound of Music. *Great views of Mount of the Holy Cross and the Sawatch Range to the south-west, the Gore Range to the east, and the Tenmile Range to the south uplift the spirit. Colorful wildflowers fill the meadows in July. Bowman's Shortcut Trail is often gently interspersed with a few steep stretches. The trail winds through lodgepole and spruce-fir forest then crosses several open meadows on a gentle ridge. In winter this trail is part of the Commando Run of the US Army's 10th Mountain Division fame.*

Start: At the Bowman's Shortcut Trail trailhead

Distance: 5.4 miles out and back

Hiking time: 2.2 to 3.7 hours

Difficulty: Moderate due to an 880-foot elevation gain

Trail surface: Dirt trail

Best season: July to early Oct

Other trail users: Equestrians and mountain bikers

Canine compatibility: Dogs must be under control

Land status: National forest

Fees and permits: None required in summer. Daily fee required in winter.

Maps: USGS Vail Pass and Red Cliff; Nat Geo Trails Illustrated 108 Vail/Frisco/Dillon; Latitude 40° Vail and Eagle Trails; USFS White River National Forest map

Trail contact: USDA Forest Service, Eagle-Holy Cross Ranger District, 24747 US 24, Minturn; (970) 827-5715; www.fs.usda.gov/whiteriver

Other: In winter the Shrine Pass area is a favorite with both snowmobilers and backcountry skiers/snowboarders. The winter trailhead is near the Vail Pass Rest Area, and a daily fee is charged. A separate ski trail takes off from the first switchback on the Shrine Pass Road. For more information on winter travel, log onto www.huts.org (huts and routes, Shrine Mountain Inn), call (970) 827-5715, or visit www.fs.usda.gov/whiteriver.

Special considerations: No water is available along the trail. Hunters use this area in the fall.

Finding the trailhead: From I-70 exit 190 (Vail Pass Rest Area), turn left and drive across the bridge and basically straight ahead onto the sometimes rough dirt road marked "Shrine Pass and Red Cliff (FR 709)." Drive approximately 3.9 miles over Shrine Pass and past the viewpoint for the Mount of the Holy Cross. Turn right onto Lime Creek Road (FR 728). Turn left in 0.5 mile when the road splits. The trailhead is another 0.1 mile on the right. Parking is available on the left. No facilities are available at the trailhead. Vault toilets are available at the top of Shrine Pass and the Mount of the Holy Cross viewpoint known as Julia's Deck. Restrooms are available at the rest area if it is open. GPS: N39 33.81' / W106 16.12'.

THE HIKE

The best part of Bowman's Shortcut Trail comes along the high, gentle ridge—the great views cover a large section of the central mountains. You can see at least three 14,000-foot peaks: Mount Elbert and Mount Massive near Leadville and Mount of the Holy Cross. What appears to be a high meadow above a headwall is really Homestake Reservoir. To the east the craggy peaks of the Gore Range treat the eye. In July the wildflowers bloom spectacularly in the high meadows as well. A sampling of flowers includes rosy paintbrush, yellow lousewort, little pink lewisia (bitterroot), little blue-purple violets, blue-white lupine, purple daisies, and white bistort.

In winter Bowman's Shortcut is part of the backcountry ski route called Commando Run, named in honor of the US Army's famous 10th Mountain Division. The troops trained at Camp Hale north of Leadville and in areas surrounding Minturn and Vail, including Bowman's Shortcut, for high-altitude missions on skis and commando raids during World War II.

Bowman's Shortcut post and Gore Range from the top

In 1940 both the American Alpine Club and Charles Minot (Minnie) Dole, founder of the National Ski Patrol, encouraged the War Department and the US Army to offer mountain warfare training. The German military already had trained mountain division troops. Such experience would be useful in northern Europe and in winter in the mountains. Dole "contend[ed] that it is more reasonable to make soldiers out of skiers than skiers out of soldiers." By late 1940 both organizations were advising the Army on winter and mountain warfare equipment. New designs developed and tested included nylon climbing ropes, down sleeping bags, and dehydrated food. Training started in six army divisions at Lake Placid, New York. The following year a larger division from Fort Lewis, Washington, trained on Mount Rainier. By November 1941 the National Ski Patrol came under contract with the War Department to recruit civilian volunteers, each of whom had to provide three letters of recommendation about his competence in skiing or mountaineering. Over 7,000 men were recruited by mid-1944.

Construction of Camp Hale started in April 1942, and by the end of the year, part of the 87th Regiment and the Mountain Training Group command moved in. The 10th Light Division (Alpine) was activated at Camp Hale in 1943, including a rock climbing school at Homestake Creek and ski runs and lifts at Cooper Hill near Camp Hale. In November 1944 the division was renamed the 10th Mountain Division and contained three infantry regiments.

German lines in the northern Italian Alps had proved nearly impossible to penetrate. Mount Belvedere was a key German position, from which they controlled access to the Po Valley. To protect Mount Belvedere, the German artillery

Gore Range from the top of Bowman's Shortcut

entrenched themselves on nearby Riva Ridge. In February 1945 the 10th Mountain Division troops, 700 men strong, made a bold night climb of Riva Ridge, gaining as much as 2,000 feet in elevation via five climbing routes, one to each of Riva's five peaks. Two routes required fixed ropes. They captured the German position with only one casualty. Counterattacks began, but a week later Riva Ridge was in the hands of the Allies. For the fierce week of fighting, the division suffered twenty-one men killed, fifty-two wounded, and three prisoners of war. Within two weeks, troops gained control of Mount Belvedere and other important peaks in the area. The cost: 192 killed, 730 wounded, and 1 prisoner of war. By late April the 10th Mountain Division entered the Po Valley. On May 2, 1945, the German Army in Italy surrendered. A total of 19,780 men served in the 10th Mountain Division in Italy. In July 1945 the troops were sent back for more training to prepare to attack positions in Japan. After the atomic bomb was dropped and Japan surrendered, the 10th Mountain Division was deactivated.

In 1985 the US Army reactivated the 10th Mountain Division as a light infantry division based at Fort Drum, New York.

At least thirteen men with the surname Bowman served in the 10th Mountain Division. Perhaps one of them lent his name to the Bowman's Shortcut Trail.

The trail starts out gently switchbacking through thick spruce-fir forest. A steep section starts at about 0.9 mile and continues for about 0.2 mile. Several viewpoints give you an excuse to catch your breath if necessary. The trail crosses a saddle at 1.7 miles then climbs a little more through scenic meadows to a cairn holding a post (in which "Bowman's Shortcut" has been carved) at 2.8 miles. This trail is popular with mountain bikers who continue farther along the trail, dropping down to Two Elk Pass and continuing to Minturn on the Two Elk National Recreation Trail.

Enjoy the view and the flowers from the post!

MILES AND DIRECTIONS

0.0 Start at the Bowman's Shortcut Trail trailhead. Elevation: 10,820 feet.

0.5 The trail appears to split. Continue to the right and drop down a tad before heading uphill again.

1.2 Enjoy a nice view of the Tenmile Range to the south.

1.7 Arrive at a saddle between two little hills.

2.7 Stop at the cairn at the top of Bowman's Shortcut. Enjoy the views of many ranges in central Colorado. GPS: N39 34.30' / W106 17.77'. Elevation: 11,700 feet. Return the way you came.

5.4 Arrive back at the trailhead.

Bowman's Shortcut Trail

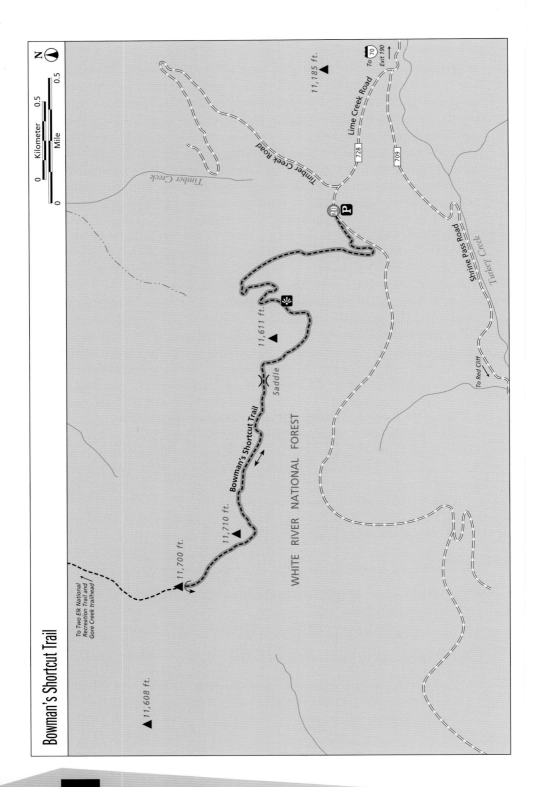

Local Information

Copper Mountain Resort Chamber, 0189 Ten Mile Circle, Copper Mountain; (970) 968-6477; www.copperchamber.com

Frisco Information Center, 300 Main St., Frisco; (970) 668-5547, (800) 424-1554; www.friscococ.com

Vail Valley Partnership, 101 Fawcett Rd., Ste. 240, Avon 81620; (970) 476-1000; www.visitvailvalley.com

Local Events/Attractions

Colorado BBQ Challenge, 1 Main St., Frisco; (800) 424-1554; www.townoffrisco .com/events/bbq-challenge/

Copper Mountain Resort hosts various events throughout the year, (888) 219-2441; www.coppercolorado.com

Bravo! Vail Valley Music Festival, 2271 N. Frontage Rd. W., Ste. C, Vail; (877) 812-5700; www.vailmusicfestival.org

Bud Light Hot Summer Nights Concert Series, Gerald R. Ford Amphitheater, 530 S. Frontage Rd. E., Vail; (970) 845-TIXS [8497], (888) 920-ARTS [2797]; www.vvf .org/vvf/info/events.entertainment.hotsummernights.aspx

The US Army's 10th Mountain Division suffered heavily in routing the Germans—4,866 casualties including 975 deaths. For more details on the 10th Mountain Division, check out the chronology at www.10thmtndivassoc.org/chronology.pdf

Bowman's Shortcut Trail and Mount of the Holy Cross

21

Gore Lake

The Gore Creek Trail climbs steeply at first then undulates above or along rough-and-tumble Gore Creek. Ascending the drainage, you roam through coniferous forest and open meadows, past aspen trees, lush bushes, and colorful wildflowers—a new scene around each bend. After 4.4 miles the trail to Gore Lake passes the Recen brothers' graves, climbing very steeply for a while, then winds through a gorgeous area until reaching the lake, nestled in a cirque beneath craggy peaks. Many nice lunch spots can be found to enjoy the lake and ridges.

Start: At the Deluge Lake Trail/Gore Creek Trail bulletin board

Distance: 12.4 miles out and back

Hiking time: 6.5 to 8.5 hours

Difficulty: Most difficult due to steep spots, rocky terrain, distance, and a 2,679-foot elevation gain

Trail surface: Dirt trail with some rocky sections

Best season: July to early Oct

Other trail users: Equestrians

Canine compatibility: Dogs must be on leash in the Eagles Nest Wilderness; under voice control elsewhere

Land status: National forest and wilderness

Fees and permits: None required. Limit of 15 people per group.

Maps: USGS Vail East and Willow Lakes; Nat Geo Trails Illustrated 108 Vail/Frisco/Dillon; Latitude 40° Vail and Eagle Trails; USFS White River National Forest map

Trail contact: USDA Forest Service, Eagle-Holy Cross Ranger District, 24747 US 24, Minturn; (970) 827-5715; www.fs.usda.gov/whiteriver

Other: The trail is mainly within the Eagles Nest Wilderness area. Please comply with wilderness regulations.

Special considerations: Bring your own water; the creek is not always near the trail. Hunters may use this area during hunting season. The trail is neither marked nor maintained for winter use, and it crosses several avalanche paths.

Finding the trailhead: From I-70 exit 180 (Vail East Entrance), drive on Bighorn Road, just south of I-70, for 2.1 miles to the trailhead parking (a wide dirt area) on the left side of the road, just before Gore Creek Campground. No facilities are located at the trailhead. GPS: N39 37.66' / W106 16.49'.

Gore Creek, the Gore Range, and various other entities are named for Sir St. George Gore, the Eighth Baronet of Manor Gore. His vast estate was located in northwest Ireland, but he lived south of London. In 1854 the 43-year-old bachelor organized a hunting trip leaving from St. Louis and heading west to New and Old Parks in Colorado and the lower Yellowstone Valley. His entourage and equipment were quite the show. England's most skilled gunsmiths created his gun collection, adorning every square inch of each weapon. Jim Bridger of mountain-man fame became Gore's head guide.

Gore Creek was once called Piney Creek.

Recen brothers' graves on Gore Creek Trail

Gore's convoy included forty men plus two valets and a dog handler, one hundred horses, twenty yoke of oxen, fifty hunting hounds, and twenty-eight vehicles, including his fancy yellow-wheeled carriage.

Gore slept and ate in a green and white tent with a French carpet laid over a rubber pad. The tent contained a camp stove, chests and trunks, the ornate guns in their racks, an ornamental brass bed, and a fur-lined commode. Servants brought him gourmet-style meals. Every morning Gore's valet would build a fire in the stove and boil water. An hour later Gore took a bath in his oval bathtub, shaved, and then ate breakfast before heading out for the day's adventures.

Indians and whites alike despised Gore for his wanton killing of wildlife. Over three years he reportedly killed more than 2,000 bison, 1,600 elk and deer, and 100 bears, mostly for sport.

The Gore Creek Trail climbs fairly steeply at first, but occasionally levels out. Wildflowers bloom in a rainbow of colors. When storms come from the west, they drop more moisture on the west side of the Gore Range, resulting in lush vegetation and many berry bushes. Aspen trees turn golden in the fall, while spruce, fir, and skinny lodgepole pines remain green (or red if mountain pine beetles or spruce budworm have killed the trees). The trail wanders high above the creek before meeting it after about a mile. Just before Deluge Creek you enter a lush "jungle" then scramble up a hunk of sloping rock with good places for feet. A sturdy bridge crosses Deluge Creek's wide bed. The trail continues up valley, crossing over several avalanche paths on both sides after mile 2.0.

Trail to Gore Lake

At the junction of the Gore Creek Trail and the trail to Gore Lake, look to the left for the big sign on a tree over the graves of Andrew and Daniel Recen. Henry Recen, a Swedish immigrant, built the first cabin in Frisco at the mouth of Tenmile Canyon. He returned to Sweden and in 1876 brought his brothers Daniel and Andrew back with him. In 1878 Daniel discovered the Queen of the West mine on the southeast side of Jacque Peak near today's Copper Mountain, later selling it for $80,000. Andrew meanwhile found silver at the Enterprise Lode nearby. Daniel's next discovery was the Excelsior near today's I-70 exit 201. The two brothers lived the high life until the silver crash of 1893, which broke their fortunes. They hunted and trapped, building a cabin along Gore Creek. The Gore Creek Trail ends at the top of Red-Buffalo Pass, a ridge that you can see while hiking. From the pass a hiker can either head south to Frisco over Eccles Pass or continue east to Silverthorne along South Willow Creek.

From the graves the trail climbs very steeply. Watch for a view of the creek cascading down its rocky bed through the thick forest. The trail mellows after

Mound Fire How-To

Many people enjoy an evening campfire for camaraderie, warmth, storytelling, and even security. From other perspectives, fires can damage the vegetation underneath as well as leave ugly scars on ground and rock. However, there are ways to "have your fire and prevent damage, too."

A mound fire is an ecological and aesthetic way to build a fire and prevent both environmental damage and ugly scars. First, make sure no fire bans are in effect and that you are below treeline. Next, find either a big level rock embedded in the ground, make a rock base out of "flat" rocks, or find exposed soil with less than 3 inches of plant remains. Be sure not to build your fire under tree branches. Find some "mineral soil" along a creek or by an uprooted tree. Mineral soil is dirt and/or sand that has a minimum of pine needles, leaves, or twigs in it. Put enough soil on a large plastic garbage bag to make a flat-topped mound about 6 to 8 inches thick and about 18 inches or less in diameter. Carry the garbage bag and soil to your chosen spot and shape the mound.

To gather firewood, spread out and pick up downed and dead wood that's no larger than your wrist. Gather the wood from various places on the ground so you don't remove all dead wood in an area. Birds use dead branches on trees, so please don't break any off. Build your fire on the mound within 1 inch of the edges. Enjoy!

When finished, let the fire cool to white ash. Scatter the cold ash and any unused wood over a large area. That way no one will see that you had a fire. Return the soil to where you found it. If the garbage bag has no burn holes, you passed the mound fire test!

Gore Lake

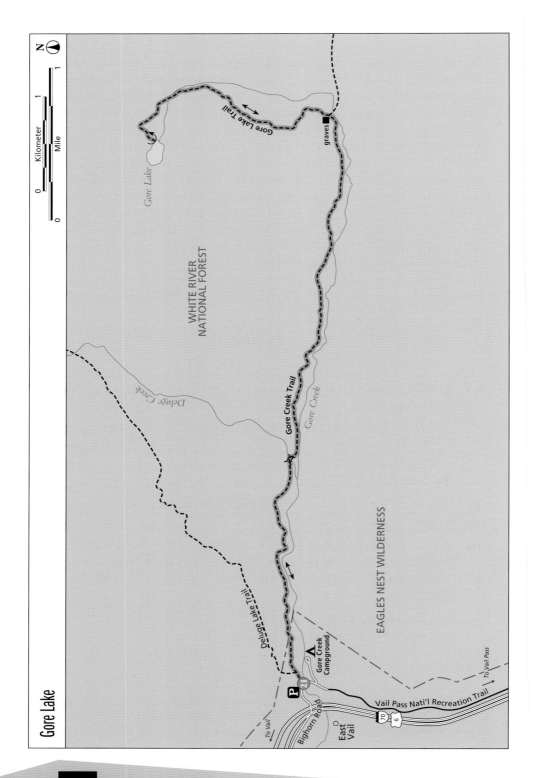

0.5 mile, crossing meadows and patches of forest with craggy peaks nearby. A final push brings you to a little pond with a view of Gore Lake. Wander around and find a good place to enjoy lunch and the scenery next to this high alpine lake.

MILES AND DIRECTIONS

0.0 Start at the Deluge Lake Trail/Gore Creek Trail bulletin board. Elevation: 8,711 feet. Please sign the register a few steps up the trail.

0.1 Arrive at the Deluge Creek Trail junction. Continue straight ahead on the Gore Creek Trail.

0.4 Reach the Eagles Nest Wilderness boundary.

1.2 Continue straight ahead on the main trail past a couple of side trails that head to the right.

1.85 Arrive at Deluge Creek and a nice bridge. Good rest stop. GPS: N39 37.74' / W106 14.80'. Elevation: 9,480 feet. (*Option:* You can return from here for a 3.7-mile out-and-back hike.)

3.3 Cross a huge avalanche path where the snow roars down from the left (north) of the trail.

4.4 Arrive at the junction with the Gore Lake Trail. GPS: N39 37.50' / W106 12.30'. Elevation: 10,200 feet. Enjoy a break and snack here before the last steep climb to the lake. Turn left, walk past the Recen brothers' graves, and head uphill.

4.9 You've finished the steepest stretch of trail. Beautiful meadows and craggy peaks treat your eyes along the next stretch.

6.2 Get your first glimpse of Gore Lake. The inlet is a few feet farther. GPS: N39 38.47' / W106 12.46'. Elevation: 11,390 feet. Take some time to wander around the lakeshore in different directions and enjoy the beautiful setting. Return the way you came.

12.4 Arrive back at the trailhead.

> *Eagles Nest Wilderness regulation on campfires: "Campfires must be at least 100 feet from all streams or trails. Campfires are prohibited within ¼ mile of all lakes and within ¼ mile of treeline. Campfires are prohibited above treeline."*

Local Information

Vail Valley Partnership, 101 Fawcett Rd., Ste. 240, Avon 81620; (970) 476-1000; www.visitvailvalley.com

Local Events/Attractions

Bravo! Vail Valley Music Festival, 2271 N. Frontage Rd. W., Ste. C, Vail; (877) 812-5700; www.vailmusicfestival.org

Bud Light Hot Summer Nights Concert Series, Gerald R. Ford Amphitheater, 530 S. Frontage Rd. E., Vail; (970) 845-TIXS [8497], (888) 920-ARTS [2797]; www.vvf .org/vvf/info/events.entertainment.hotsummernights.aspx

Betty Ford Alpine Gardens, 500 S. Frontage Rd., Vail; (970) 476-0103; www .bettyfordalpinegardens.org

Colorado Ski and Snowboard Hall of Fame, 231 S. Frontage Rd. E., Vail; (970) 476-1876; www.skimuseum.net

Clubs and Organizations

Friends of the Eagles Nest Wilderness, www.fenw.org, or call the Dillon Ranger District, (970) 468-5400, for the current contact.

Colorado Mountain Club-Gore Range Group; www.cmc.org/About/CMC Groups/GoreRange.aspx

Gore Lake

Booth Lake

Beautiful Booth Lake with its little island is tucked in an alpine cirque with fantastic wildflowers. The trail climbs through forest and meadows past Booth Falls, a 60-foot waterfall. It continues to ascend like a giant staircase to fields of wildflowers that dazzle the eyes. Little waterfalls add their sparkle. One last climb up the side of the cirque brings you to the lake, a piece of paradise tucked up in the Gore Range. A backpack to the meadows below the lake may be the best way to enjoy this special place. You can also turn around at the falls for a 4-mile out-and-back hike.

Start: At the gate at the end of the small parking lot on Booth Falls Road
Distance: 9.8 miles out and back
Hiking time: 6 to 8 hours
Difficulty: Most difficult due to steep sections, distance, and a 3,040-foot elevation gain
Trail surface: Dirt trail with some rocky sections
Best season: July to early Oct
Other trail users: Equestrians
Canine compatibility: Dogs must be on leash
Land status: National forest and wilderness
Fees and permits: None required. Limit of 15 people per group.
Maps: USGS Vail East; Nat Geo Trails Illustrated 108 Vail/Frisco/Dillon; Latitude 40° Vail and Eagle Trails

Trail contact: USDA Forest Service, Eagle-Holy Cross Ranger District, 24747 US 24, Minturn; (970) 827-5715; www.fs.usda.gov/whiteriver
Other: The trail is mainly within the Eagles Nest Wilderness area. Please comply with wilderness regulations.
Special considerations: Bring your own water; the creek is not always near the trail. The lake is near treeline. Be sure to leave early so you can arrive at the lake and enjoy it before afternoon thunderstorms (lightning) start. Hunters may use this area during hunting season. The trail is neither marked nor maintained for winter use, and it crosses several avalanche paths.

Finding the trailhead: From I-70 exit 180 (Vail East Entrance), drive left (west) on the North Frontage Road for 0.8 mile to Booth Falls Road (by Vail Mountain School). Turn right and drive 0.3 mile to a very small parking lot. If the parking lot is full, head back to the North Frontage Road and watch for the signs that direct you to overflow parking. (Or you can ride the free Vail bus to the stop by Vail Mountain School.) No facilities are located at the trailhead. GPS: N39 39.04' / W106 19.26'.

Booth Falls is an extremely popular hike near Vail. The trail switchbacks steeply to the Eagles Nest Wilderness boundary, crossing over limestone that formed in a shallow sea about 300 million years ago. It then mellows, climbs, and mellows again while passing through aspen and spruce-fir forests. Meadows are frequent, filled with thimbleberries, raspberries, white yarrow, pink Woods' rose, various yellow members of the sunflower family, strawberries, red paintbrush, and many others. Notice the red cliffs above the trail. The Minturn Formation is the result of the rise of the Ancestral Rockies between 320 and 270 million years ago and their subsequent erosion. In one meadow you may think the vegetation is winning out over the trail because large green thimbleberry leaves almost hide it. Looking off to the northwest you can catch a glimpse of 60-foot Booth Falls, which tumbles over hard Precambrian basement rock (over 540 million years old). The trail climbs steeply up a rocky and sometimes wet section as it crosses the Gore Fault where Precambrian rock has pushed the Minturn Formation into a vertical position.

A trampled area under spruce trees on the left is the clue that Booth Falls is close. You're above the falls, so you can watch the water tumbling over the cliff. Most hikers turn around here, but the best part is yet to come. A little snack break at this point makes for easier hiking. The trail climbs steeply through thick forest for the next 0.25 mile then drops a little to Booth Creek. Blue chiming bells, Colorado blue columbine, white bistort, yellow paintbrush, and cow parsnip

Flower-lined trail by Booth Lake

22

grace your way. In wetter areas, purple monkshood is prevalent. By 2.9 miles the trail has climbed, flattened, then climbed again numerous times. Some big boulders provide nice seats for another snack before ascending a steep headwall with water bars for steps. You're now in the upper meadows punctuated with dashes of forest. Engelmann spruce and subalpine fir are the dominant tree species at this elevation. Spruce can grow as tall as 120 feet and live 450 years in this harsh environment where summer lasts less than three months, mean annual temperatures range around 35°F, and frost is possible even in summer. Snow collects among the trees, falling from the sky and blowing off the ridgetops on the fierce winter winds. Notice the spire shape of the trees. Wider tops would catch snow and break. The upside-down conical shape works better for survival. As summer progresses, purplish cones hang from the tops of spruce trees. Seeds ripen inside the cones, which open in autumn to release their seeds (but the cones remain). Fir cones actually point up, and when the bracts fall off in autumn to release the seeds, the inner core sticks up like a candle. Successful ingredients for seed germination include shade, cool temperatures, and moist soil. As you hike along, take a moment to identify the trees. Spruce needles are sharp and square—you can roll a needle between your fingers. Fir needles are flat and friendly, soft to the touch.

When the trail crosses a big rock slab, make sure to turn around and look south for a spectacular view of Vail's ski runs and Mount of the Holy Cross towering over it all. William Henry Jackson's photos and Thomas Moran's paintings of the mountain with the snowy cross back in the 1870s provided people with a view of the wonders of the West. People felt the cross was a sign from God. In 1929 President Herbert Hoover established Mount of the Holy Cross National Monument to protect the area. Unfortunately World War II intervened, the area became a training ground for the US Army's 10th Mountain Division, and national monument status was removed in 1950.

Wildflowers bloom profusely in the upper meadows in July and early August. A waterfall plunges off a little cliff as the trail curves west. One last grunt up the side of a cirque past beautiful natural rock gardens brings you to a view of Booth Lake. Wander along the trail to find a nice spot to sit and enjoy your lunch amid this beautiful setting in the wild Gore Range.

🌿 Green Tip:
If you choose to backpack up Booth Creek, camp below the lake where you can find a good campsite. Water is easily obtained in the creeks in the upper meadows; be sure to treat it. Please refrain from building campfires, which leave unsightly scars on the ground. Spend the evening instead enjoying the multitude of stars visible in the dark night sky.

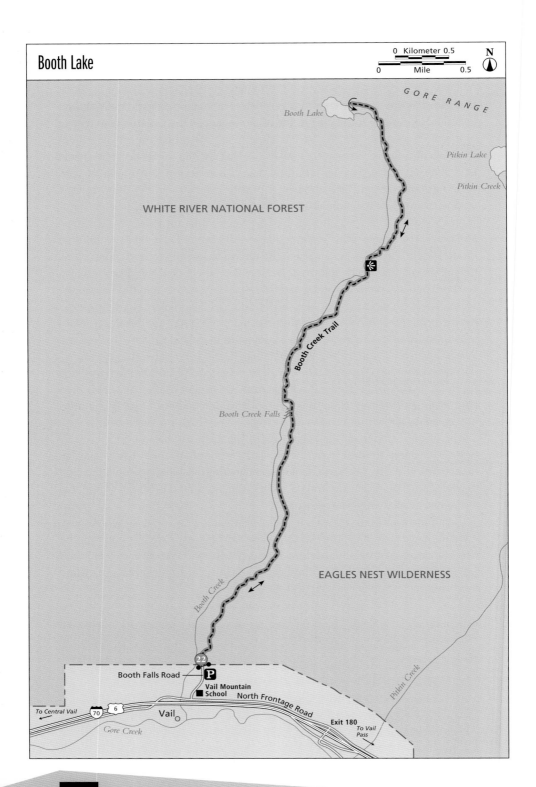

Booth Lake

0 Kilometer 0.5
0 Mile 0.5
N

GORE RANGE

Booth Lake

Pitkin Lake

Pitkin Creek

WHITE RIVER NATIONAL FOREST

Booth Creek Trail

Booth Creek Falls

EAGLES NEST WILDERNESS

Booth Creek

Pitkin Creek

22

Booth Falls Road

P

Vail Mountain School

North Frontage Road

To Central Vail

70 6

Vail

Gore Creek

Exit 180
To Vail Pass

0.0   Start at the gate at the end of the little parking lot. Elevation: 8,440 feet. Please sign the register a few steps up the trail by the bulletin board.

0.25   Arrive at the Eagles Nest Wilderness boundary.

1.4   A social trail leads to the creek to the left. Continue straight ahead on the main trail, which climbs steeply.

2.0   Come to a trampled spot along the trail. Booth Falls is to the left. GPS: N39 40.36' / W106 18.68'. Elevation: 9,800 feet. (*Option:* Return the way you came for a difficult 4-mile out-and-back hike.)

2.4   The trail drops to travel along the creek for a short distance.

2.8   Arrive at a meadow with wildflowers and views of craggy peaks.

3.2   Come to the top of a steep headwall.

3.4   The trail crosses a rock slab. Stop and look back for a great view of Mount of the Holy Cross above the ski runs at Vail. GPS: N39 41.15' / W106 18.16'. Elevation: 10,620 feet.

4.4   The trail wanders through beautiful subalpine meadows and past a little waterfall.

Booth Lake with its island

4.8 Cross the top of the cirque and descend a few feet to Booth Lake. GPS: N39 41.97' / W106 18.28'. Elevation: 11,480 feet.

4.9 The trail fades. Nice lunch spots can be found around here. Return the way you came.

9.8 Arrive back at the trailhead.

HIKE INFORMATION

Local Information
Vail Valley Partnership, 101 Fawcett Rd., Ste. 240, Avon 81620; (970) 476-1000; www.visitvailvalley.com

Local Events/Attractions
Bravo! Vail Valley Music Festival, 2271 N. Frontage Rd. W., Ste. C, Vail; (877) 812-5700; www.vailmusicfestival.org

Bud Light Hot Summer Nights Concert Series, Gerald R. Ford Amphitheater, 530 S. Frontage Rd. E., Vail; (970) 845-TIXS [8497], (888) 920-ARTS [2797]; www.vvf.org/vvf/info/events.entertainment.hotsummernights.aspx

Betty Ford Alpine Gardens, 500 S. Frontage Rd., Vail; (970) 476-0103; www.bettyfordalpinegardens.org

Colorado Ski and Snowboard Hall of Fame, 231 S. Frontage Rd. E., Vail; (970) 476-1876; www.skimuseum.net

Clubs and Organizations
Friends of the Eagles Nest Wilderness, www.fenw.org, or call the Dillon Ranger District, (970) 468-5400, for the current contact.

Colorado Mountain Club-Gore Range Group; www.cmc.org/About/CMC Groups/GoreRange.aspx

Public Transportation (free)
Vail Bus, Vail Transportation Center, 241 E. Meadow Dr., Vail; (970) 479-2178; www.vailgov.com

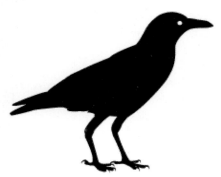

Upper Piney River Falls

The Piney River, fed by snow that cloaks the spectacular peaks of the Gore Range, flows through a beautiful valley edged by aspen on the north and spruce-fir on the south. The first 1.3 miles of the Upper Piney River Trail undulate gently through meadows with good spots for lunch, relaxation, and great views. The trail climbs through aspen and mixed conifer forest, crossing numerous little creeks before switchbacking downhill about 280 feet past house-size boulders. The river falls where it has carved a channel through rock slabs. Enjoy your lunch along this cascading creek.

Start: At the Upper Piney River Trail bulletin board to the north of the parking lot

Distance: 6.0 miles out and back

Hiking time: 2.5 to 4 hours

Difficulty: Moderate due to distance and a 540-foot elevation gain and 140-foot loss

Trail surface: Dirt trail

Best season: June through Oct

Other trail users: Equestrians

Canine compatibility: Dogs must be on leash

Land status: Private property (easement), national forest, and wilderness

Fees and permits: None required. Limit of 15 people per group.

Maps: USGS Vail East and Vail West; Nat Geo Trails Illustrated 108 Vail/Frisco/Dillon; Latitude 40° Vail and Eagle Trails; USFS White River National Forest map

Trail contact: USDA Forest Service, Eagle-Holy Cross Ranger District, 24747 US 24, Minturn; (970) 827-5715; www.fs.usda.gov/whiteriver

Other: Until you reach the wilderness boundary, the trail passes through the private Piney River Ranch on an easement. Please stay on the trail. The ranch offers accommodations and camping; for more information go to www.pineyriverranch.com. The trail is mainly within the Eagles Nest Wilderness area. Please comply with wilderness regulations.

Special considerations: Bring water because the creek is far from the trail along this hike. Hunters use this area during hunting season. The road is closed for the winter 10.5 miles from the trailhead—snowmobilers, cross-country skiers, and snowshoers recreate on Red Sandstone Road.

Finding the trailhead: From I-70 exit 176 (Vail), go north to North Frontage Road and turn left. Continue 0.9 mile to Red Sandstone Road and turn right. At the third switchback at 0.7 mile, head a little left onto the dirt Red Sandstone Road (FR 700). Passenger cars can easily navigate the road, although it can be quite bumpy with washboards. Follow the signs to Piney River Ranch and Piney Lake. From where the road turns to dirt, it's a 10.5-mile drive to the trailhead. The parking lot is on the right before the ranch gate. No public facilities are available. The trail starts across the road. GPS at the trailhead bulletin board: N39 43.24' / W106 24.30'.

THE HIKE

As early as 1910 the Denver Water Board (DWB) took to heart its mission to provide water to Denver residents, and looked to Colorado's western slope for sources. DWB started buying water rights there. In 1927, plans showed a dam across the Blue River creating Dillon Reservoir. The 23.3-mile Roberts Tunnel would transport the water to the South Platte River and on to Denver.

In 1956 the DWB claimed water in the Piney River drainage on the west side of the Gore, and a year later filed a plan with the state engineer showing an additional diversion of 100,000 acre-feet from that drainage and from the Eagle River, hence known as the Eagle-Piney Diversion Project. Piney Lake would be enlarged to a 40,000 acre-foot reservoir, about 3 miles long, and a gravity-fed

Upper Piney River Trail and Gore Range

> *Frank and Al Marugg first homesteaded the Piney Lake area. At the time, silver fox furs sold for a decent amount of money, and the brothers started a fox farm. Avid fishermen, they also built a summer resort at the lake. By the 1930s brook trout were stocked in the lake, and it became a favorite fishing place of people living in Minturn and along Gore Creek (where Vail is today). Access was mainly by horse.*

tunnel would carry the water under the Gore Range to Dillon Reservoir. The DWB had purchased 72 acres of land at Piney Lake, but not enough for the envisioned reservoir. Meanwhile in 1932 and 1933, the Gore Range-Eagles Nest Primitive Area had been established along both sides of the Gore Range, including land near Piney Lake.

In the early 1970s Colorado's congressional delegation introduced bills to create the Eagles Nest Wilderness from the primitive area. The Eagle-Piney diversion created a big stir. People and groups questioned the need for the water in Denver and the impact of reduced water flows on Gore Creek and the Eagle and Colorado Rivers. Arizona, California, and Mexico were already dealing with the salinity of the Colorado due to other water diversions, not to mention that various intergovernmental agreements require that a certain amount of Colorado River water needs to flow to those states. Western slope folks felt new water diversions would seriously hurt their economic future—fertile valleys would be lost under reservoirs and prime recreation areas would suffer. In addition, the DWB planned to build the Gore Range Canal along the eastern side of the Gore Range to capture an additional 70,000 acre-feet of water to put in Dillon Reservoir to transport to Denver. Water wars raged regularly between the dry eastern slope with a large and growing population and the sparsely populated, water-rich western slope.

The DWB fought valiantly to have the Piney Valley eliminated from the proposed wilderness, but lost the battle partially because it could still use about 80 percent of its water claims for the additional cost of pumping water instead of the proposed gravity-fed tunnel. To make matters worse, in September 1975 a court-appointed water referee denied the DWB's water claims in the Piney area. The referee ruled that DWB had failed to meet state requirements for securing the actual water rights on the Piney River. Plus the DWB had been granted only a conditional water decree to Eagle River water, not water rights. He also ruled that the DWB had neither claims nor rights to the water on the east side of the Gore Range.

Congress officially designated the 133,910-acre Eagles Nest Wilderness in Public Law 94-352, which the president signed on July 12, 1976.

The Eagle-Piney collection system project never happened, but Denver Water still owns the land at Piney Lake. Hansen Development Company, LLC first leased the property for recreational purposes. In 2010 the business interests were sold to Piney River Ranch, LLC, which now holds a long-term lease with Denver Water to use the area where its buildings are located. The Upper Piney River Trail contours along a sloping meadow to the north of the ranch buildings and lake, beneath red cliffs and aspen groves. An abundance of wildflowers graces the trail.

The Piney River lazily snakes its way through willows and meadows south of the trail where the reservoir would have been. After 1.3 miles the trail starts climbing, entering thick coniferous forest and crossing numerous little creeks. Just when you may wonder why the trail is going up when waterfalls should be in the river below, the trail heads downhill. After twisting past a house-sized boulder, you'll arrive in a lush area then at the rock slabs through which the river has carved a drop, creating waterfalls. Smaller cascades jump and sparkle a little upstream. Many possible lunch spots invite you to stay awhile and relax.

MILES AND DIRECTIONS

0.0 Start at the Upper Piney Trail 1885 bulletin board to the north of the parking lot. Elevation: 9,360 feet. The trail heads right along Piney Lake's north shore.

0.5 Reach the Eagles Nest Wilderness boundary.

0.7 Arrive at the junction with the Marugg Creek Trail. Continue straight ahead.

1.3 Look for a side trail heading to the right to a slab of rock by some aspen trees. GPS: N39 43.80' / W106 23.09'. Elevation: 9,400 feet. The rock slab is a great place for relaxing. The trail climbs steadily through aspen forest beyond this point.

2.6 The trail starts to switchback downhill toward the Piney River. Elevation: 9,760 feet.

3.0 Arrive at the river. The falls are to the right, plunging between slabs of rocks. Several nice lunch spots are available. GPS: N39 44.16' / W106 21.69'. Elevation: 9,620 feet. Return the way you came.

6.0 Arrive back at the trailhead.

HIKE INFORMATION

Local Information
Vail Valley Partnership,101 Fawcett Rd., Ste. 240, Avon; (970) 476-1000; www.visit vailvalley.com

Upper Piney River Falls

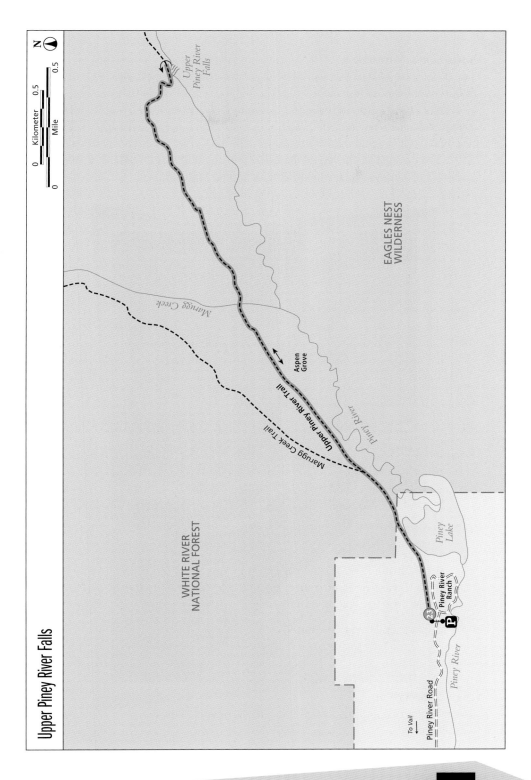

Local Events/Attractions

Bravo! Vail Valley Music Festival, 2271 N. Frontage Rd. W., Suite C, Vail; (877) 812-5700; www.vailmusicfestival.org

Betty Ford Alpine Gardens, 500 S. Frontage Rd., Vail; (970) 476-0103; www.bettyfordalpinegardens.org

Bud Light Hot Summer Nights Concert Series, Gerald R. Ford Amphitheater, 530 S. Frontage Rd. E., Vail; (970) 845-TIXS [8497], (888) 920-ARTS [2797]; www.vvf.org/vvf/info/events.entertainment.hotsummernights.aspx

Upper Piney River Falls

North Trail

This pleasant hike traverses a hillside through various types of vegetation on the north side of Vail. This trail is popular with mountain bikers and hikers. You can enjoy views of Vail and the ski area along the first part of the trail, which passes through bushes and sagebrush meadow. After several switchbacks, Mount of the Holy Cross and Mount Jackson poke above the hills to the southwest. The trail wanders through aspen forest, especially beautiful in autumn when the leaves are golden. The featured hike reaches its turnaround at the junction with the Buffehr Creek Trail, but directions are included for a shorter point-to-point hike.

Start: At the North Trail System bulletin board
Distance: 4.4 miles out and back
Hiking time: 2 to 3 hours
Difficulty: Moderate due to a 700-foot elevation gain
Trail surface: Dirt trail
Best season: Mid-June through Oct. (North Trail closed Apr 15 to June 15 for elk calving season.)
Other trail users: Mountain bikers and equestrians
Canine compatibility: Dogs must be on leash
Land status: National forest

Fees and permits: None required
Maps: USGS Vail West; Nat Geo Trails Illustrated 108 Vail/Frisco/Dillon; Latitude 40° Vail and Eagle Valley Trails; USFS White River National Forest map
Trail contact: USDA Forest Service, Eagle-Holy Cross Ranger District, 24747 US 24, Minturn; (970) 827-5715; www.fs.usda.gov/whiteriver
Special considerations: Bring water because none is available along the trail. Watch for mountain bikers.

Finding the trailhead: From I-70 exit 176 (Vail), head north to North Frontage Road and turn left. In 0.9 mile, turn right onto Red Sandstone Road. Drive 0.4 mile to the parking lot (straight ahead) where Red Sandstone Road curves right. No facilities are available at the trailhead. GPS: N39 38.90′ / W106 23.78′

THE HIKE

Try to imagine people farming and ranching here, long before the town of Vail and the ski area began. By the 1880s homesteaders had wandered into the Gore Creek valley, establishing ranches and hoping for a better life. John Wesley Phillips headed one such family. With several mines around nearby Red Cliff, he found a ready market for spring lambs and potatoes. With fourteen children to feed, he hunted deer, elk, bear, grouse, and rabbit. His children attended school only in the summer in a sod-roofed building at a nearby ranch. In winter Phillips taught his sons to make skis from barnwood. They used leather straps for bindings and goose oil on the bottoms instead of today's ski wax.

The Denver & Rio Grande (D&RG) Railroad established a station named Minturn in June 1887. Located near the confluence of Gore Creek and the Eagle River, it was surrounded by many farms and ranches. The station had a roundhouse and shipping yards, and many men came to work the railroad. Jacob Buffehr worked for the D&RG for fifteen years and was an alderman in Minturn in 1911. About 1916 Jacob and his wife, Mary, decided to try dairy farming and purchased the ranch at the confluence of a creek and Gore Creek. Some accounts say the creek was originally called Willow; today the creek bears the name of the Buffehr family.

By the early 1900s several ranches lined Gore Creek, connected by one dirt road. When fall arrived, families readied themselves for the long winter by pickling and preserving food they had grown during the short summer; the men split and stacked firewood. During winter, new clothes and quilts were sewn, while woodworking projects, reading, and games filled the cold days. Loggers found it easier to cut trees in winter when teams of horses could drag the wood down on sleds. One rancher used an A-drag pulled by horses to pack down the snow in the road. In heavy snow years the packed road rose as high as the fence tops! People loved a good party and turned out for dances, music, and drama held at neighbors' homes.

Mount of the Holy Cross and Notch Mountain from the trail

After World War II, veterans of the US Army's 10th Mountain Division realized that Vail Mountain offered ideal skiing terrain. They envisioned a ski community and proceeded to design it and obtain approvals from the USDA Forest Service. Vail Ski Area opened in December 1962, and the town of Vail was incorporated in 1966.

Fast forward about thirty years. The Eagles Nest Wilderness had been designated by Congress in 1976. Trails leading into the area are fairly steep and are open only to foot travel and equestrians. With mountain biking a fast-growing sport, and some existing trails and roads contouring along the hills above town to the north, the idea grew to develop a trail system from West Vail to East Vail. Hikers could also access it from their neighborhoods for easier walks than the wilderness area offered. In 1996 the Town of Vail partnered with the USDA Forest Service to design and build new tread and to improve existing trails. The town funded the construction, including financing a Forest Service trail crew. Volunteers for Outdoor Colorado built one section of tread. The trail from Arosa Drive in West Vail to the Son of Middle Creek trailhead near East Vail was completed in 1999.

The fairly smooth trail switchbacks its way up a hill with several nice viewpoints along the way. You can find raspberry plants and currant bushes, holly grape, yellow sulphur flowers, and sagebrush, among others. The aspen forest is lush and especially beautiful in fall. At about 1.4 miles a huge Douglas fir shades the trail. The Sawatch Range rises to the southwest, while the pointy peaks of the Gore Range poke above the Gore Valley. The views are great both going and coming.

MILES AND DIRECTIONS

0.0 Start at the North Trail System bulletin board. Elevation: 8,300 feet. The trail splits almost immediately. Turn right.

1.1 At the left switchback, walk a little to the right for a nice view.

1.2 Enjoy the view to the southwest of Mount of the Holy Cross and Mount Jackson.

2.2 Arrive at the junction with the Buffehr Creek Trail, which heads uphill to the right. GPS: N39 38.62' / W106 24.81'. Elevation: 9,000 feet. Return the way you came. (See option below for a point-to-point hike.)

4.4 Arrive back at the trailhead.

Option
For a 3.75-mile point-to-point hike, before going to the trailhead off Red Sandstone Road, leave another vehicle at the Buffehr Creek Trail trailhead.

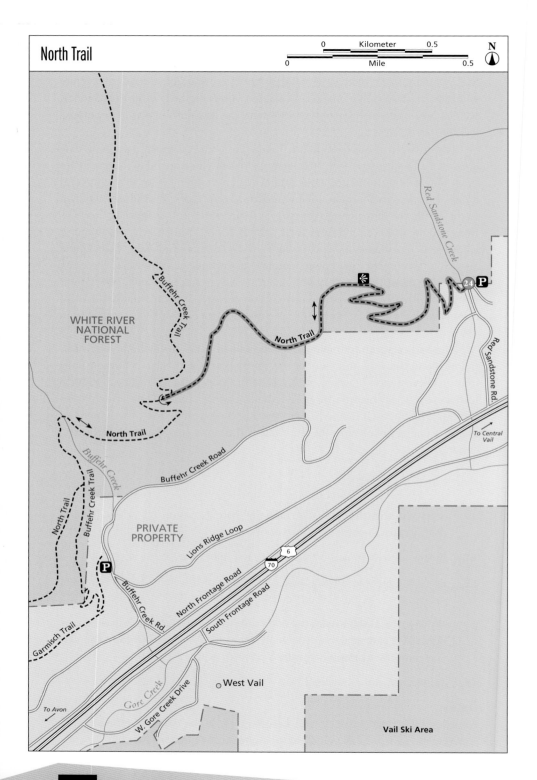

0   Kilometer   0.5

0   Mile   0.5

N

Red Sandstone Creek

Buffehr Creek Trail

WHITE RIVER
NATIONAL
FOREST

North Trail

24 P

Red Sandstone Rd.

To Central
Vail

North Trail

Buffehr Creek Road

Buffehr Creek

Buffehr Creek Trail

North Trail

PRIVATE
PROPERTY

Lions Ridge Loop

6

70

North Frontage Road

South Frontage Road

P

Buffehr Creek Rd.

Garmisch Trail

To Avon

Gore Creek

West Vail

W Gore Creek Drive

Vail Ski Area

To leave a shuttle car, from I-70 exit 173 (West Vail), drive east on the North Frontage Road past Safeway, City Market, and other stores and restaurants. At 0.6 mile, by mile marker 174, turn left onto Buffehr Creek Road. Drive 0.25 mile to the trailhead and parking area on the left. No facilities are available. GPS: N39 38.22' / W106 24.93'.

0.0 Follow the Finding the trailhead directions to start at the trailhead off Red Sandstone Road.

2.2 Arrive at the junction with the Buffehr Creek Trail; continue westward as the trail switchbacks steeply down a rocky trail.

2.6 The trail splits. Turn right and head down into the drainage. You're on both the North Trail and the Buffehr Creek Trail.

2.75 Cross Buffehr Creek. GPS: N39 38.57' / W106 25.07'. Elevation: 8,400 feet.

3.0 Arrive at the junction of North and Buffehr Creek Trails. Continue basically straight ahead and downhill on Buffehr Creek Trail.

3.5 Come to the junction with the Garmisch Trail. Turn left and continue downhill.

3.75 Arrive at the Buffehr Creek Trail trailhead and your waiting vehicle. Elevation: 8,160 feet.

HIKE INFORMATION

Local Information

Vail Valley Partnership, 101 Fawcett Rd., Ste. 240, Avon; (970) 476-1000; www.visit vailvalley.com

Vail Pass

Back in 1887, English naturalist Theodore Dru Alison Cockerell camped at the top of a pass (Vail Pass), finding arrowheads and pottery shards. He named it Pottery Pass. Locals later called it Black Gore Pass because Black Gore Creek's headwaters started there. In the 1930s Charles D. Vail became the chief engineer for the Colorado highway department. At that time the state had only 500 miles of paved roads. By 1945, under his leadership, about 4,500 miles of highway had been paved. Some of Vail's plans did not sit well with Salida's residents. He wanted to build a road where Monarch Pass is today. Locals wanted it farther south over Marshall Pass. Vail prevailed, but locals wanted to call it Monarch-Agate Pass. Instead signs with Vail Pass appeared. The governor interceded, and Monarch Pass became the official name. In 1940 Black Gore Pass officially became Vail Pass.

North Trail through the aspen

Local Events/Attractions

Bravo! Vail Valley Music Festival, 2271 N. Frontage Rd. W., Ste. C, Vail; (877) 812-5700; www.vailmusicfestival.org

Bud Light Hot Summer Nights Concert Series, Gerald R. Ford Amphitheater, 530 S. Frontage Rd. E., Vail; (970) 845-TIXS [8497], (888) 920-ARTS [2797]; www.vvf.org/vvf/info/events.entertainment.hotsummernights.aspx

Betty Ford Alpine Gardens, 500 S. Frontage Rd., Vail; (970) 476-0103; www.bettyfordalpinegardens.org

Colorado Ski and Snowboard Hall of Fame, 231 S. Frontage Rd. E., Vail; (970) 476-1876; www.skimuseum.net

Clubs and Organizations

Colorado Mountain Club-Gore Range Group; www.cmc.org/About/CMCGroups/GoreRange.aspx

Walking Mountains Science Center, 318 Walking Mountains Ln., Avon; (970) 827-9725; www.walkingmountains.org

Meadow Mountain

Wander up the trail on the aptly named Meadow Mountain through green meadows and cool aspen forests to a line shack on a wide ridge just south of Eagle-Vail. The meadows harbor the remains of the Nelson ranch buildings, great views of the Gore Range, tall grasses, and wildflowers. Enjoy your lunch on the line shack's shady porch. The easy runs at the Beaver Creek Ski Area lie to the southwest, while ski trails on Vail's Game Creek Bowl can be seen to the east. From lettuce farm and ranch to ski area, Meadow Mountain offers an interesting and beautiful hike.

Start: At the Meadow Mountain trailhead bulletin board
Distance: 9.7 miles out and back
Hiking time: 4.5 to 6.5 hours
Difficulty: Difficult due to distance and a 2,006-foot elevation gain
Trail surface: Dirt road (closed to public motorized use in summer) and dirt trail
Best season: June to early Oct
Other trail users: Equestrians and mountain bikers
Canine compatibility: Dogs must be under control
Land status: National forest
Fees and permits: None required

Maps: USGS Minturn; Nat Geo Trails Illustrated 108 Vail/Frisco/Dillon; Latitude 40° Vail and Eagle Trails; USFS White River National Forest map
Trail contact: USDA Forest Service, Eagle-Holy Cross Ranger District, 24747 US 24, Minturn; (970) 827-5715; www.fs.usda.gov/whiteriver
Other: In winter the trail is open to snowshoers, cross-country skiers, and snowmobilers.
Special considerations: Bring your own water, as little is available along the trail. Hunters may use this area during hunting season.

Finding the trailhead: From I-70 exit 171 (West US 6/East US 24 Minturn/Leadville), turn right and head south on US 24 for 0.3 mile then turn right toward the USDA Forest Service's Holy Cross Ranger District office and Park 'n Ride. Park in the Park 'n Ride lot at the first left turn. (The ECO bus stops at this Park 'n Ride.) The trailhead is near the white house. No facilities are available at the trailhead, but restrooms and water are available at the district office when it's open. GPS: N39 36.38' / W106 26.67'.

The Utes spent summers hunting in the Eagle River valley and surrounding high country. Their lives changed as miners swarmed the area around Leadville after Abe Lee discovered gold there in 1860. Silver became king in the late 1870s. Miners wandered over the hills, staking claims along the upper Eagle River. Some became discouraged with mining and homesteaded nearby, producing food for their families and hungry miners. More newcomers arrived in the early 1880s, setting down roots along the Eagle River. They grew hay, potatoes, peas, and oats, and raised cattle. Originally Minturn was named Booco after local homesteader George C. Booco, who owned the land on which he platted the town. Peter Nelson and his wife, Johanna, homesteaded near Booco on Meadow Mountain in 1888. Their land crossed the Eagle River and continued up the lower slopes to the east. The Nelsons raised horses, cattle, and sheep on their property, which some people had thought to be very barren land. But with much work and irrigation, Nelson grew timothy for hay for both his stock as well as to sell to others. The family also raised hogs, chickens and turkeys. At some time the Nelson ranch house burned, and they purchased a new one from Sears, Roebuck, and Company, according to Bill Burnett in *Minturn, A Memoir*. The white house near the trailhead is that house.

In the late 1880s the Denver & Rio Grande (D&RG) Railroad extended their line from Leadville to Glenwood Springs and on to the Aspen mining areas. The railroad arrived in Booco in 1887 complete with a station, which the D&RG renamed Minturn in honor of Robert H. Minturn, who helped finance the railroad expansion.

Nelson Ranch buildings along the Meadow Mountain Trail

An interesting book about the Minturn area including Meadow Mountain is **Minturn, A Memoir** *by Bill Burnett, published in 2007.*

During the 1920s, lettuce became a popular and profitable crop to grow in the Eagle River valley. The Nelson ranch became famous for its Evercrisp lettuce. Peter Nelson's brother, Ben, homesteaded a ranch to the south, just west of where Minturn is today. In order to water their crops, the brothers constructed a high ditch and a low ditch to bring water from Grouse Creek to their land. The ranchers had to dig the ditches by hand or with horse-drawn plows and scrapers. Dynamite split large rocks into smaller chunks. Japanese sharecroppers lived in buildings near the low ditch. They arrived each spring, planted lettuce, and raised chickens.

Refrigerated railcars didn't exist at the time, so farmers shipped their crispy crop as far as the East Coast in train cars chilled with ice from the Minturn icehouse. During winter, crews chopped 18 x 20 x 24-inch blocks of ice out of a pond near Pando, south on the Eagle River near Tennessee Pass. After the water froze again, they cut more blocks, which could each weigh up to 200 pounds. The ice train carried the precious cargo to the icehouse in Minturn for storage. When the farmers harvested their lettuce crop, they packed about four dozen head of lettuce in wooden crates and loaded them on wagons that measured 15 feet wide by 20 feet long. A loaded lettuce wagon weighed a lot, and six horses held it going down the hill. The wagon had wooden brake shoes on the wheels, and Ben Nelson put pressure on them with a long wooden shaft. He often made three to four trips per day during lettuce harvesting. Once at the lettuce shed by the railroad, people cleaned the lettuce, put it into wax paper–lined crates and added chipped ice to each layer. The crates were loaded onto insulated railcars that contained a bunker filled with ice blocks on each end.

The lettuce boom didn't last forever. Deer enjoyed the tasty lettuce, too. Diseases such as California tip burn could ruin an entire crop. Eventually, lack of soil knowledge and crop rotation depleted the soil. The lettuce boom went bust. The Nelsons continued to grow some lettuce and trucked it to Denver for about five years via Vail Pass after the highway was completed in 1941.

Jack Oleson bought many homesteads around Minturn including the Nelson ranch in 1962. He proceeded to build a ski area on Meadow Mountain, which operated from 1966 to 1969. He installed a Poma lift and a double chairlift—2,250 feet long—to an elevation of 8,800 feet. A warming house and restaurant sat at the base. Unfortunately the snow melted too fast and the 900-foot vertical wasn't challenging enough for most skiers.

In August 1972, Willis Nottingham, who owned a large ranch around Beaver Creek and Bachelor Gulch near Avon, sold his property to Vail Associates to become the Beaver Creek Ski Resort. A year earlier Vail Associates had purchased Pete Nelson's ranch from Oleson. Pete Siebert, one of Vail's founders, thought Meadow Mountain would be an important part of skiing near Vail, but the purchase of Nottingham's property postponed any development of Meadow Mountain. The USDA Forest Service acquired the land from Vail Associates in 1979.

The first ranch remnant you pass is an old corral and cabin to the north. At about 1.9 miles, look to your left (east) and downhill to see an old house and collapsed barn from the Nelson ranch. For about 2.5 miles the road carries you up through green meadows—keep an eye open for deer. Purple larkspur and blue columbine bloom happily in the lush aspen forest. At 4.6 miles the trail mellows when it attains an aspen-lined ridge. The line shack sits in an open meadow a little farther. The porch timbers frame the craggy Gore Range to the northeast. The Flat Tops rise in the northwest. The line shack may have been used by ranch hands herding sheep or cattle. Enjoy your hike back through ranching history!

MILES AND DIRECTIONS

0.0   Start at the Meadow Mountain trailhead bulletin board. Elevation: 7,750 feet. Walk up the road behind the white house.

1.0   Come to the junction with a trail that heads south to Grouse Creek. Continue straight ahead on the road.

1.9   To your left lies an old house and barn. GPS: N39 35.57' / W106 26.74'.

2.6   The road splits. GPS: N39 35.49' / W106 27.3'. Keep walking straight ahead on the road. The left trail goes to West Grouse Creek.

4.25 Enjoy the view of the Gore Range and some of the ski runs at Vail.

4.85 Arrive at the Meadow Mountain line shack. GPS: N39 35.34' / W106 28.49'. Elevation: 9,756 feet. Return the way you came.

9.7   Arrive back at the trailhead.

HIKE INFORMATION

Local Information
Town of Minturn, 302 Pine St., Minturn; (970) 827-5645; www.minturn.org
Vail Valley Partnership,101 Fawcett Rd., Ste. 240, Avon 81620; (970) 476-1000; www.visitvailvalley.com

Local Events/Attractions
Bravo! Vail Valley Music Festival, 2271 N. Frontage Rd. W., Ste. C, Vail; (877) 812-5700; www.vailmusicfestival.org

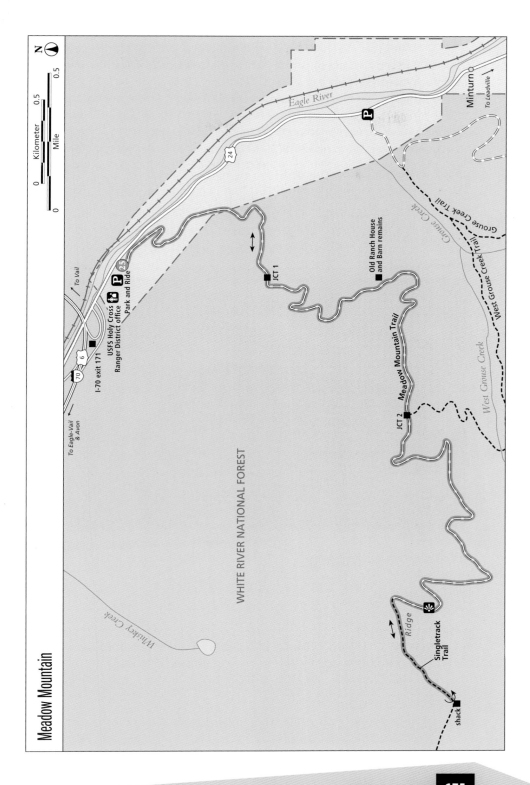

Meadow Mountain

N

Kilometer
0   0.5

0   0.5
Mile

To Vail

To Eagle-Vail
& Avon

I-70 exit 171

USFS Holy Cross
Ranger District office

Park and Ride

70

6

24

25

P

P

Eagle River

Minturn

To Leadville

Whiskey Creek

WHITE RIVER NATIONAL FOREST

JCT 1

Old Ranch House
and Barn remains

Meadow Mountain Trail

JCT 2

Grouse Creek

Grouse Creek Trail

West Grouse Creek Trail

West Grouse Creek

Ridge

Singletrack
Trail

shack

Betty Ford Alpine Gardens, 500 S. Frontage Rd., Vail; (970) 476-0103; www
.bettyfordalpinegardens.org

Bud Light Hot Summer Nights Concert Series, Gerald R. Ford Amphitheater,
530 S. Frontage Rd. E., Vail; (970) 845-TIXS [8497], (888) 920-ARTS [2797]; www
.vvf.org/vvf/info/events.entertainment.hotsummernights.aspx

Minturn Market, Minturn; (970) 827-5645; www.minturnmarket.org

Public Transportation (fee charged)

Eagle County Regional Transportation (ECO Transit) provides bus service around
Eagle County, PO Box 1070, 3289 Cooley Mesa Rd., Gypsum 81637; (970) 328-
3520; www.eaglecounty.us/Transit/.

Line shack on the Meadow Mountain Trail

Grouse Lake

The hike to Grouse Lake follows Grouse Creek, which could be more aptly named Berry Bush Creek—especially the first section. The trail climbs steadily through spruce-fir forest interspersed with aspen. A few flatter sections provide ample time to catch your breath. Moss-covered rocks punctuate little creeks, and flowers border the trail. Pointy Grouse Peak overlooks a long valley that holds grass-lined Grouse Lake. The lake lies just within the Holy Cross Wilderness.

Start: At the Grouse Creek Trail trailhead

Distance: 9.2 miles out and back

Hiking time: 4 to 7.7 hours

Difficulty: Most difficult due to distance and a 2,865-foot elevation gain

Trail surface: Dirt road (closed to motorized use) and dirt trail

Best season: July to early Oct

Other trail users: Equestrians

Canine compatibility: Dogs must be under control; uncontrolled dogs must be on leash at Grouse Lake

Land status: National forest and wilderness

Fees and permits: No fees required. In the Holy Cross Wilderness, group size limit is 15 people. One person in each group of overnight users must carry a free self-issued wilderness use permit.

Maps: USGS Vail East and Willow Lakes; Nat Geo Trails Illustrated 108 Vail/Frisco/Dillon; Latitude 40° Vail and Eagle Trails; USFS White River National Forest map

Trail contact: USDA Forest Service, Eagle-Holy Cross Ranger District, 24747 US 24, Minturn; (970) 827-5715; www.fs.usda.gov/whiteriver

Other: Grouse Lake is in the Holy Cross Wilderness. Please comply with wilderness regulations.

Special considerations: Water is sometimes available along the trail. Grouse Creek Trail travels through a narrow valley in places, and satellite reception for GPS receivers is often poor, as is cell phone coverage. This area is popular with hunters in the fall. Snowshoers and people walking their dogs frequently utilize the first couple of miles in the winter. The trail is neither marked nor maintained for winter use.

Finding the trailhead: From I-70 exit 171 (West US 6/East US 24 Minturn/Leadville), turn right and head south on US 24 for approximately 1.4 miles to the Grouse Creek Trail trailhead parking lot on the right (west) side of US 24. No facilities are available at the trailhead, but the USDA Forest Service's Holy Cross Ranger District office (restrooms and water when the office is open) is 0.3 mile south of I-70, and Minturn is south of the trailhead. GPS: N39 35.63' / W106 26.05'.

THE HIKE

The trail to Grouse Lake is lined with innumerable berry bushes of several varieties, including twinberry, elderberry, gooseberry, currant, and thimbleberry. Little creeks run clear and cold, with moss-covered rocks and logs creating exquisite aquatic gardens.

Grouse Lake is in the Holy Cross Wilderness. This special area was designated by Congress in the Colorado Wilderness Act of 1980 on December 22. Sometimes referred to as a water wilderness, this area contains the headwaters of the Eagle River. Streams, snowmelt, and many alpine lakes provide an abundance of water.

The Grouse Creek Trail starts up a dirt road (closed to motorized use) through sagebrush and rabbitbrush. When the trail becomes singletrack and enters the forest, it winds back and forth over Grouse Creek and other little creeks.

Grouse Lake

Grouse Creek Trail

The thimbleberry shrub with its huge leaves is a member of the rose family and grows profusely along the lower trail. Its large white flowers (similar to strawberry blooms) develop into large raspberry-like berries. The fruit is edible and rich in vitamin C. If you do pick any fruit to eat, please only pick a few because the local wildlife, especially bears, relies on the berries to fatten up for the winter. Be careful if you hike this trail in late August and September, when black bears are bulking up on as many as 20,000 calories a day! Bears are mainly vegetarians, but will eat insects and carcasses. When hiking in bear country, keep your dog leashed to prevent it from surprising a bear. If you do see a bear, stand still and stay calm, making sure the bear has room to leave. For other useful tips, check out www.wildlife.state.co.us/WildlifeSpecies/ (click on Living with Wildlife).

After mile 2.5, watch for trees with patches of bark missing. Porcupines like to eat the outer bark and inner cambium layer. If they get carried away and strip the bark entirely around the tree, the tree will die. These large rodents come back to the same tree, eating above their last dinner because sugar-rich sap collects there. Porcupines like to munch on evergreen trees at night. They also eat berries, nuts, seeds, and flowers. These spiny critters enjoy siestas during the day, snuggled high in tree branches. One porcupine may have as many as 30,000 quills. The slow-moving animal does not throw its quills, but will swing its tail into an enemy's face, leaving quills in its victim's face and maybe mouth—a painful experience indeed. If you see a porcupine, enjoy it from a distance and make sure to keep any pets leashed and away from its tail!

After a short climb Grouse Lake comes into view. Grasses are slowly filling it in. A large rock near the shore sat mostly in the lake in 2007, but six years later grasses encircled it. Looking around and across the lake, you can see where patches of grass are popping up in the lake. Looking toward pointy Grouse Peak, notice an area full of willows where perhaps water once stood.

If you eat lunch at the lake, a gray jay or two may pay you a visit. Commonly called camp robbers, they love to beg for handouts, eyeing your lunch from nearby trees. They cache food for winter, gluing small pieces of food to tree branches that will be above snow level. Enjoy watching their antics, but please don't feed them. They can become pests, and they need to forage on their own instead of depending on human food. The lifelong mates nest, lay, and incubate their eggs during late winter when temperatures can still plunge below zero.

The hike to Grouse Lake takes you past various different sights—you may even see a grouse!

MILES AND DIRECTIONS

0.0 Start at the Grouse Creek Trail trailhead. Elevation: 7,835 feet. The first part of the trail is a dirt road.

0.15 The Meadow Mountain Cutoff Trail comes in from the right. Continue straight ahead on the road.

0.3 The road goes left and the trail to Grouse Lake goes straight ahead. Continue southwest on the singletrack to Grouse Lake. GPS: N39 35.51' / W106 26.27'.

0.5 Arrive at the junction of West Grouse Creek and Grouse Lake Trails. Take the left fork to Grouse Lake.

1.0 Cross Grouse Creek.

1.5 Cross Grouse Creek and head uphill into the thick forest.

1.7 Cross a ditch with a culvert.

2.4 The trail crosses the creek.

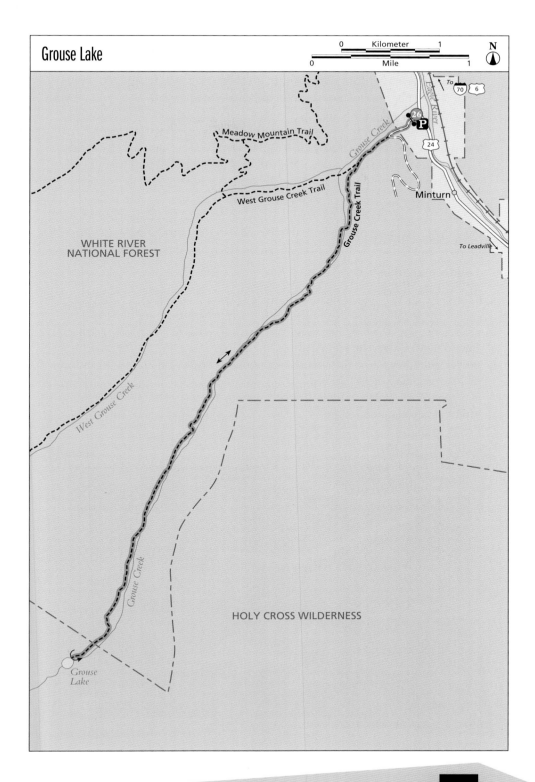

Grouse Lake

0 Kilometer 1
0 Mile 1

N

Meadow Mountain Trail

Grouse Creek

To 70 6

26
P

24

West Grouse Creek Trail

Minturn

Grouse Creek Trail

To Leadville

WHITE RIVER
NATIONAL FOREST

West Grouse Creek

HOLY CROSS WILDERNESS

Grouse Creek

Grouse
Lake

3.5 The trail crosses a mucky area where a puncheon bridge disintegrated. A few spikes still stick up from logs, so be careful. GPS: N39 33.35′ / W106 27.99′. Just beyond the muck the trail curves to the right.

4.1 Cross a little creek and start the final climb to the lake.

4.6 Arrive at Grouse Lake. GPS: N39 32.54′ / W106 28.51′. Elevation: 10,700 feet. A good lunch spot is down the side trail to the left. Return the way you came.

9.2 Arrive back at the trailhead.

HIKE INFORMATION

Local Information
Town of Minturn, 302 Pine St., Minturn; (970) 827-5645; www.minturn.org

Vail Valley Partnership, 101 Fawcett Rd., Ste. 240, Avon 81620; (970) 476-1000; www.visitvailvalley.com

Local Events/Attractions
Bravo! Vail Valley Music Festival, 2271 N. Frontage Rd. W., Ste. C, Vail; (877) 812-5700; www.vailmusicfestival.org

Betty Ford Alpine Gardens, 500 S. Frontage Rd., Vail; (970) 476-0103; www.bettyfordalpinegardens.org

Mini-falls in Grouse Creek

Bud Light Hot Summer Nights Concert Series, Gerald R. Ford Amphitheater, 530 S. Frontage Rd. E., Vail; (970) 845-TIXS [8497], (888) 920-ARTS [2797]; www .vvf.org/vvf/info/events.entertainment.hotsummernights.aspx
Minturn Market, Minturn; (970) 827-5645; www.minturnmarket.org

Colorado Outdoor Recreation Search and Rescue (CORSAR) Card

Every year in Colorado over 1,000 search-and-rescue (SAR) missions are conducted for hikers, hunters, and other outdoor enthusiasts who run into problems in the backcountry. Colorado has many well-trained volunteer SAR groups. They devote numerous hours to training and to actual rescues. Each county sheriff is responsible for search and rescue, yet often lacks a sufficient budget to pay for costs incurred for search helicopters, equipment, and SAR training. Sheriffs seldom charge for rescue efforts except in cases of extreme negligence.

In 1987 the Colorado legislature created the Colorado Search and Rescue Fund (CSRF). Twenty-five cents from each hunting license, fishing license, plus boat, snowmobile, and off-road vehicle registration finances this fund. The fund's purpose is to help sheriffs recover costs of SAR operations and to provide funding for SAR equipment and training.

As more hikers, mountain bikers, climbers, and backcountry skiers required rescue, the Colorado legislature created the Colorado Outdoor Recreation Search and Rescue (CORSAR) card. The CORSAR card costs only $3 per year ($12 for five years) with $2 going to the CSRF and $1 to the vendor.

If you need rescue in the backcountry, a SAR team will come (depending on where you are), whether you have a CORSAR card or not. The card is *not* insurance and does not pay for medical helicopter evacuation. SAR missions typically incur costs for fuel, equipment repair, and other items necessary for the search and rescue, including helicopters used in the effort. Having a CORSAR card or other license mentioned above means certain expenses the SAR group or sheriff accrued during the rescue can be quickly refunded from the CSRF. If you don't have a CORSAR card or other license, sheriffs must wait until the end of the year, apply for operational expense reimbursement, and hopefully receive some money.

So before starting on your first Colorado hike, buy a CORSAR card and help our volunteer SAR groups stay equipped and prepared!

For more information, log onto www.colorado.gov then search for "search and rescue card." You can buy the CORSAR card online or find a vendor via the website.

The trail up West Grouse Creek wanders through lodgepole forest, meadows, and aspen forest then enters thicker spruce and fir forest the higher you hike. About 2 miles up the trail, lodgepole pines killed by mountain pine beetles have been cut to prevent trees from falling on hikers on the trail. West Grouse Creek occasionally appears along the trail, a small but pretty creek with mossy rocks and little cascades, lined with wildflowers and bushes. The hike has two suggested turnarounds: one at the ruins of a cabin and the other near a boulder field where you can enjoy lunch next to the creek.

Start: At the Grouse Creek Trail trailhead

Distance: 7.8 miles out and back

Hiking time: 4 to 5.5 hours

Difficulty: Difficult due to distance and a 2,365-foot elevation gain

Trail surface: Dirt road (closed to motorized use) and dirt trail

Best season: Mid-June to early Oct

Other trail users: Equestrians on the entire trail, mountain bikers on the first 1.5 miles

Canine compatibility: Dogs must be under control

Land status: National forest

Fees and permits: None required

Maps: USGS Vail East and Willow Lakes; Nat Geo Trails Illustrated 108 Vail/Frisco/Dillon; Latitude 40° Vail and Eagle Trails; USFS White River National Forest map

Trail contact: USDA Forest Service, Eagle-Holy Cross Ranger District, 24747 US 24, Minturn; (970) 827-5715; www.fs.usda.gov/whiteriver.

Special considerations: Bring your own water; the creek is not always near the trail. Hunters use this area during hunting season. Snowshoers and people walking their dogs frequently utilize the first couple of miles in the winter. The trail is neither marked nor maintained for winter use.

Finding the trailhead: From I-70 exit 171 (West US 6/East US 24 Minturn/Leadville), turn right and head south on US 24 approximately 1.4 miles to the Grouse Creek Trail trailhead parking lot on the right (west) side of US 24. No facilities are available at the trailhead, but the USDA Forest Service's Holy Cross Ranger District Office (restrooms and water when the office is open) is 0.3 mile south of I-70, and Minturn is south of the trailhead. GPS: N39 35.63' / W106 26.05'.

THE HIKE

West Grouse and Grouse Creeks are evidently named for the chicken-like bird of the same name, specifically the dusky grouse, a subspecies of blue grouse. This species is the second-largest grouse in North America, with males weighing in around 3 pounds and females a pound less. They mate near the aspen-sagebrush interface, but also in subalpine meadows. Females lay up to nine eggs in ground nests hidden by shrubs or trees. Good grouse feeding grounds include plants such as clover, dandelion, flower buds, and grouse whortleberry along with plenty of insects for growing young. Males move to spruce-fir forest in midsummer while females stay in breeding grounds until early fall. Both sexes winter in lodgepole or Douglas fir forests where needles provide nutrition during long cold periods. Keep your eyes open while hiking, and maybe you can spot a grouse or two walking along the ground. They blend in quite well with their surroundings, so you may pass them without seeing them. When they fly, their wings make a loud flapping noise.

The Grouse Creek Trail starts up a dirt road (closed to motorized use) through sagebrush and rabbitbrush. Not long after the trail becomes singletrack and enters the forest, it splits in two: Left goes to Grouse Lake and right goes up along West Grouse Creek. At about 1.5 miles the trail crosses an old logging road. Mountain pine beetles killed many of the lodgepole pine trees here, and the dead trees were removed to prevent them from falling onto the trail, especially during high winds. Living lodgepole pines are still standing—notice how

West Grouse Creek Trail

> *Native Americans used the trunks of the lodgepole for tepee poles (thus the name "lodgepole").*

tall and skinny these trees are with branches and needles at the top of the tree. On the way down, the lack of trees opens a nice view of the Gore Range to the northwest.

Lodgepole pine is typically called the tree of fire. Most trees produce serotinous cones that are sealed shut by resin until a very hot fire opens them and releases the seed. As lodgepole age, they become more susceptible to fires and pine beetles, nature's method of making way for new tree life. Drought in Summit and Eagle Counties during the 2000s weakened the trees, and the beetles found a feast of old and unhealthy trees to infect.

Mountain pine beetles have a one-year life cycle. Adults bore into a live tree under the bark. If the tree cannot repel them with its sap, the beetles mate and the female lays about seventy-five eggs in a vertical tunnel. When the eggs hatch, the larvae tunnel through the tree, feeding as they go, until they become pupae in June and July. The insects transmit bluestain fungi, which help kill the tree by preventing the necessary flow of sap. As adults the beetles fly from the dead tree to a live tree in late July to start the cycle again.

The trail climbs steeply at times with some mellow spots in between. In one flatter spot the remains of a cabin lie forlornly next to the trail. A metal box (perhaps part of a stove), niched logs with nails, and a rock wall are all that remain. Who lived in the cabin and why are unknown. On the next steep stretch, you'll cross a ditch that flows through a culvert under the trail. Ranchers probably dug the ditch years ago to take water north to the meadows on aptly named Meadow Mountain. A good lunch spot is along the creek near the next boulder field. The trail continues another 5 miles or so beyond here, entering the Holy Cross Wilderness at mile 4.8. Enjoy a day exploring the West Grouse Creek Trail!

MILES AND DIRECTIONS

0.0   Start at the Grouse Creek Trail trailhead. Elevation: 7,835 feet. The first part of the trail is a dirt road.

0.15   The Meadow Mountain Cutoff Trail comes in from the right. Continue straight ahead on the road.

0.3   The road goes left and the trail to Grouse Lake goes straight ahead. Continue southwest on the singletrack to Grouse Lake. GPS: N39 35.51' / W106 26.27'.

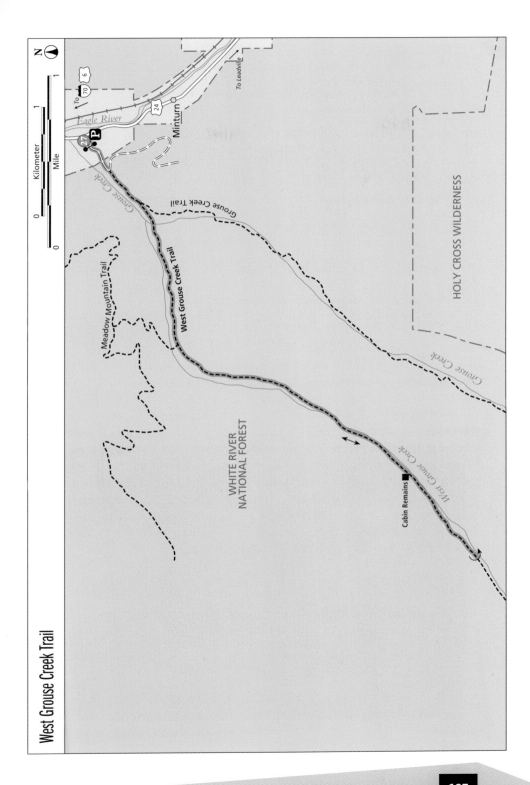

West Grouse Creek Trail

0.5 Arrive at the junction of West Grouse Creek and Grouse Lake Trails. Take the right fork to West Grouse Creek.

0.6 Cross West Grouse Creek.

0.9 The trail appears to split. Follow the main trail to the left.

1.5 Cross a road that comes across from the Meadow Mountain Trail to the north.

2.6 Cross West Grouse Creek.

3.1 Arrive at a little wide spot on the right. Look carefully for a metal box, niched logs, some nails, and a rock wall. GPS: N39 34.06' / W106 28.25'. Elevation: 9,760 feet. (*Option:* Turn around here for a 6.2-mile out-and-back hike.)

3.4 Cross a culvert carrying water under the trail.

3.9 Arrive at a boulder field. To the left are some nice lunch spots along West Grouse Creek. GPS: N39 33.71' / W106 28.83'. Elevation: 10,200 feet. Return the way you came.

7.8 Arrive back at the trailhead.

Cabin remains along West Grouse Creek

Little red elephants

HIKE INFORMATION

Local Information

Town of Minturn, 302 Pine St., Minturn; (970) 827-5645; www.minturn.org

Vail Valley Partnership,101 Fawcett Rd., Ste. 240, Avon 81620; (970) 476-1000; www.visitvailvalley.com

Local Events/Attractions

Bravo! Vail Valley Music Festival, 2271 N. Frontage Rd. W., Ste. C, Vail; (877) 812-5700; www.vailmusicfestival.org

Betty Ford Alpine Gardens, 500 S. Frontage Rd., Vail; (970) 476-0103; www.bettyfordalpinegardens.org

Bud Light Hot Summer Nights Concert Series, Gerald R. Ford Amphitheater, 530 S. Frontage Rd. E., Vail; (970) 845-TIXS [8497], (888) 920-ARTS [2797]; www.vvf.org/vvf/info/events.entertainment.hotsummernights.aspx

Minturn Market, Minturn; (970) 827-5645; www.minturnmarket.org

Mountain Pine Beetles

The lodgepole pine forests of Summit and Eagle Counties have turned red and brown in many places. No, the USDA Forest Service is not growing red trees for Christmas. During the mining years of the late 1800s and early 1900s, loggers deforested much of the two counties, harvesting wood for mines, railroads, buildings, smelting, and heating. Fire suppression became the law of the land, but the lodgepole pine forest ecosystem depends on fire to stay healthy.

Lodgepole pine forest is typically called the forest of fire. Most trees produce serotinous cones that are sealed shut by resin until a very hot fire opens them and releases the seed. Some lodgepole have nonserotinous cones, so they can also regenerate without fire. An interesting statistic from studies after the 1988 Yellowstone fire: From 50,000 to 970,000 seeds per acre covered burned areas. Lodgepole stands may have lower-intensity fires that clear undergrowth and fuel build-up (intervals of 25 to 50 years) or high-intensity crown stand-replacement fires (intervals of perhaps 300 years). As lodgepole age, they become more susceptible to fires and pine beetles, nature's method of making way for new tree life.

The forests in Summit and Eagle Counties today contain many same-age lodgepole pines that are more than one hundred years old. Colorado has experienced several years of drought, which stressed high-country forests. Temperatures have also been slightly warmer than average. Mix all the ingredients together, and the time was ripe for a mountain pine beetle epidemic. The little insects have been around for thousands of years helping to recycle forests. Usually outbreaks occur in unhealthy and over-mature stands of pines.

Mountain pine beetles have a one-year life cycle. Adults leave their birth tree in late summer to find a home for the next generation. They bore into a live tree under the bark. If the tree cannot repel them with its sap, the beetles mate and the female lays about seventy-five eggs in a vertical tunnel. When the eggs hatch, the larvae tunnel through the tree, feeding as they go, until they become pupae in June and July. The insects transmit bluestain fungi, which help kill the tree by preventing the necessary flow of sap. As adults the beetles fly from the dead tree to a live tree in late July to start the cycle again. They may number enough to attack two or three trees. The needles of dead trees turn red and eventually fall off. The dead tree dries out and becomes fuel for any fire that comes along.

If the forest is left alone, the natural cycle could take a couple of different paths. Fire might destroy the dead trees, while the heat opens lodgepole cones and releases the seeds. A new lodgepole pine forest would start the cycle again as in Yellowstone National Park. Depending on the fire and location, aspen trees might be the first tree species to appear, sprouting from underground roots. If an extremely intense and hot fire occurs, the soil may be sterilized. The area may remain open, colonized in time by grasses and plants. Eventually the soil will recover enough nutrients to support tree growth.

In some areas, lodgepole pines would naturally be replaced by spruce-fir forest. If spruce and fir seedlings are growing in a lodgepole pine forest infested with mountain pine beetles and no fire occurs, the young seedlings will continue to grow amid the dead lodgepole. Spruce and fir both need the shade and shelter provided by the dead trees to grow and thrive. In this case the lodgepole pine ecosystem would be replaced by the spruce-fir ecosystem.

The beetles started attacking trees in Summit County in earnest in about 2003, and before that in the Vail area. By 2013 the beetle infestation had slowed.

The USDA Forest Service and Congress as well as the State of Colorado have been trying to figure out how best to deal with this recent pine beetle problem. As more people move to the high country and build homes in the forest, using fire to keep the lodgepole ecosystem healthy is unpopular and dangerous. Homeowners are learning to use fire mitigation techniques around their homes, and many are treating their private forests for mountain pine beetles with advice from the Colorado State Forest Service. The USDA Forest Service is thinning some forests, but does not have ample funding to treat everywhere. If trees can be cut and treated before the beetles fly, the number of newly infected trees can be minimized. In wilderness areas, nature is typically allowed to take its course.

For more information, see these resources:

mountain pine beetle: www.ext.colostate.edu/pubs/insect/05528.html

mountain pine beetle life cycle: www.for.gov.bc.ca/hfp/publications/00133/cycle.htm

lodgepole pine ecology: www.fs.fed.us/database/feis/plants/tree/pinconl/all.html

Two Elk National Recreation Trail

Follow a crystal clear little creek up a narrow valley to the base of Vail Ski Area's Tea Cup Bowl and Blue Sky Basin on the Two Elk National Recreation Trail, which crosses a ridge over Two Elk Pass connecting Minturn to I-70 near East Vail. This hike explores part of the trail on the west side, a pleasant journey through thick forest, past rocky outcrops, amid lush aspen forests, and across fields of colorful wildflowers. Options for a shorter 1.6-mile or medium 5.8-mile out-and-back hike are mentioned.

Start: At the Two Elk Trailhead bulletin board
Distance: 8.4 miles out and back
Hiking time: 3.5 to 5.5 hours
Difficulty: Difficult due to distance and a 1,530-foot elevation gain
Trail surface: Dirt trail
Best season: July to mid-Oct (After first 2 miles trail is closed across Vail's Back Bowls from May 6 to July 1 for elk calving. Access road closed 1.3 miles from trailhead Dec 1 to Apr 14.)
Other trail users: Mountain bikers and equestrians
Canine compatibility: Dogs must be under control
Land status: National forest
Fees and permits: None required

Maps: USGS Minturn and Red Cliff; Nat Geo Trails Illustrated 108 Vail/Frisco/Dillon; Latitude 40° Vail and Eagle Trails; USFS White River National Forest map
Trail contact: USDA Forest Service, Eagle-Holy Cross Ranger District, 24747 US 24, Minturn; (970) 827-5715; www.fs.usda.gov/whiteriver
Special considerations: Bring your own water; the creek is not always near the trail. Numerous berry bushes line the trail at the west end. Be bear aware, especially in late August and September as bears fatten up for the winter. Hunters may use this area during hunting season. The trail is neither marked nor maintained for winter use.

Finding the trailhead: From I-70 exit 171 (West US 6/East US 24 Minturn/Leadville), drive south on US 24 through Minturn 2.5 miles to Cemetery Road. Turn left then stay left and cross the railroad tracks. Turn right at the next intersection and drive past the cemetery. Turn right at the next junction to Two Elk Trail and the shooting range. The road gets narrow and bumpy here. At the next junction, turn left. Drive past the shooting range. Total mileage from US 24 is 1.8 miles. The road dead-ends at the trailhead. No facilities are available. GPS: N39 33.95' / W106 24.07'.

THE HIKE

In September 1979 the White River National Forest submitted an application to the US Secretary of Agriculture to designate the Two Elk Trail (#2005) as a National Recreation Trail (NRT). Congress passed the National Trail System Act in 1968, which recognizes special trails in different regions. They can be designated as National Scenic, National Historic, or National Recreation Trails. The first two require an act of Congress, but either the Secretary of Interior or Secretary of Agriculture can approve NRTs. The agency that manages the trail must submit an application for designation.

The Two Elk Trail application noted the closeness to I-70, Vail, the metropolitan Denver area, and Glenwood Springs. The scenic views from the top of Two Elk Pass were described, including Mount of the Holy Cross. The trail crosses the bottom of the back bowls of Vail Ski Area: Sundown, Sunup, Teacup, and China. These areas provide wildlife habitat for deer, elk, chipmunks, gray jays, snowshoe hares, and other wildlife. The application was approved December 13, 1979.

When you enter the forest around mile 0.2, look around at the various bushes and flowers. Those with large leaves and big white flowers or large raspberry-like fruits are thimbleberries. Humans have long used the thimbleberry for both food and medicinal purposes. The pretty pink flower with five large petals is the Woods' rose, commonly found in aspen forests.

The trail travels high above the creek to a bridge. Creek-side vegetation is fairly thick, containing many bushes and cottonwood trees. To the south of the trail, conifer trees and occasional aspen cover the hillside.

View down the valley of Two Elk National Recreation Trail

Beyond the bridge the trail comes close to the creek and the plants grow thick, almost hiding the trail. The valley widens with meadows of wildflowers of all shapes and colors. A type of mint grows among purple daisies; white yarrow with its fern-like leaves punctuates yellow sulphur flowers while red paintbrush, purple harebells, fireweed, and geraniums add their color.

At mile 2.9 a huge sign appears after you cross a little creek. The reddish sign states that Minturn is 3 miles back the way you came and Chair 5 (High Noon Express) is a 30-minute hike to the north. Imagine trudging up the valley in ski boots with skis over your shoulder! The meadow here is a nice lunch spot and an optional turnaround for a 5.8-mile out-and-back hike. Vail Ski Area's Sundown Bowl lies up the slope a bit. Chair 5 started operating in 1962 when the ski area opened.

World War II brought young men to Camp Hale, south of Two Elk Creek, to train in the US Army's 10th Mountain Division. After the war ended, one of the veterans, Peter W. Seibert, became a ski instructor at Aspen and later managed Loveland Basin Ski Area. Another war veteran, Earl Eaton, worked in Aspen and at Loveland Basin Ski Area and became Pete's friend. They dreamed of finding the perfect ski mountain and searched for it in various western states. In the mid-1950s Eaton found the open bowls above Two Elk Creek. He took Seibert up the mountain, and they realized this mountain was the place. Seibert and Eaton envisioned not only a ski area but also a base village, similar to those in Europe. They created a company that purchased the 500-acre Hanson Ranch, which straddled US 6 along Gore Creek. In 1959 they applied to the USDA Forest Service for the permit to build their dream. They obtained the permits in 1961, enticed investors, and secured loans for their project. The Vail Corporation

Two Elk Creek

The October 11, 1973, *Eagle Valley Enterprise* contained a story by Pinky Fahey about the naming of Two Elk Creek. For many years Native Americans used the narrow valley where they found rocks to make their arrowheads and plentiful elk for food. As white settlers arrived, Ben Bolt and Ernie Evans wandered up the same valley hunting for meat. They came across several Indians making arrowheads. After passing the industrious rock chippers, they heard grunts and other weird noises. Just ahead they saw two bull elks fighting, presumably battling for a harem. While both white men and Indians watched, one elk jabbed an antler tine (point) into the other's chest, killing it. Ben and Ernie gathered the dead elk for meat and carried it back downstream. Ernie later told Ben that after he started his homestead near this valley, he'd return east for his family and bring them west to Two Elk Creek.

began clearing ski runs and installing a gondola and chairlifts on the mountain while building shops, restaurants, and hotels in the valley. Interested homeowners purchased 121 residential lots.

The ski area opened in December 1962 with a dearth of snow, but the white gold fell by Christmas. Vail has since evolved into a world-renowned destination.

Turnaround for this hike is the base of Chairs 36 (Tea Cup Express Lift) and 37 (SkyLine Express Lift). Chair 36 accesses several of Vail's Back Bowls. Chair 37 heads up Blue Sky Basin, which opened in 2002. The trail continues to the top of Two Elk Pass where you can drop down to the Vail Pass National Recreation Trail and then to the parking area by the Gore Creek Campground. The trail travels about 11 miles from the trailhead near Minturn to the Gore Creek Campground. Mountain bikers tend to ride from east to west for a long downhill run, so keep an ear and eye open for them. Enjoy the varying scenery, including views of Grouse Mountain on the way back.

MILES AND DIRECTIONS

0.0 Start at the Two Elk Trailhead bulletin board. Elevation: 8,030 feet. At the first trail junction, go right and cross a bridge. At the next junction, turn left and head upstream.

0.2 Pass a cairn supporting a post that says "Two Elk Trail."

0.8 Arrive at the bridge over Two Elk Creek. GPS: N39 34.02' / W106 23.40'. Elevation: 8,280 feet. (*Option:* For a short 1.6-mile out-and-back hike, turn around here.)

2.9 Look for a big ski area directional sign on the left after you cross a little creek. The meadow is a nice place for lunch. GPS: N39 35.03' / W106 21.75'. Elevation: 9,040 feet. (*Option:* You can turn around here for a 5.8-mile out-and-back hike.)

4.2 Arrive at the junction with the singletrack Two Elk Trail near the bases of Chair 36 and Chair 37. GPS: N39 35.04' / W106 20.46'. Elevation: 9,560 feet. Return the way you came.

8.4 Arrive back at the trailhead.

🌿 **Green Tip:**
For rest stops, go off-trail so others won't have to walk around you. Head for resilient surfaces to avoid trampling too much vegetation.

Two Elk National Recreation Trail

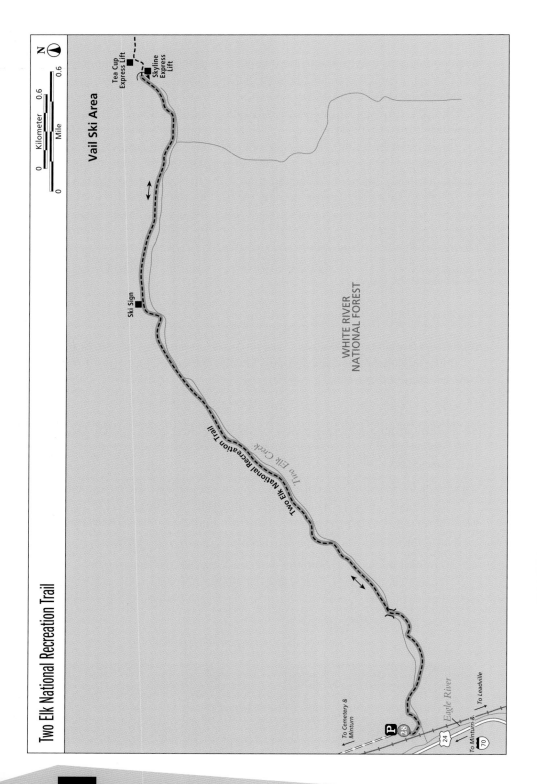

Vail Ski Area

Tea Cup Express Lift

Skyline Express Lift

Ski Sign

WHITE RIVER NATIONAL FOREST

Two Elk National Recreation Trail

Two Elk Creek

Eagle River

To Cemetery & Minturn

To Minturn & To Leadville

24

70

28

P

N

Kilometer
0   0.6

Mile
0   0.6

Local Information

Vail Valley Partnership,101 Fawcett Rd., Ste. 240, Avon; (970) 476-1000; www.visit vailvalley.com

Vail Ski Resort; PO Box 7, Vail 81658; (800) 805-2457; www.vail.com

Local Events/Attractions

Bravo! Vail Valley Music Festival, 2271 N. Frontage Road W., Ste. C, Vail; (877) 812-5700; www.vailmusicfestival.org

Betty Ford Alpine Gardens, 500 S. Frontage Rd., Vail; (970) 476-0103; www .bettyfordalpinegardens.org

Bud Light Hot Summer Nights Concert Series, Gerald R. Ford Amphitheater, 530 S. Frontage Rd. E., Vail; (970) 845-TIXS [8497], (888) 920-ARTS [2797]; www .vvf.org/vvf/info/events.entertainment.hotsummernights.aspx

Colorado Ski and Snowboard Hall of Fame, 231 S. Frontage Rd. E., Vail; (970) 476-1876; www.skimuseum.net

Clubs and Organizations

Colorado Mountain Club-Gore Range Group; www.cmc.org/groups/groups _gorerange.aspx

Two Elk National Recreation Trail along Two Elk Creek

29

Cross Creek Trail

Hike along an undulating, rocky trail through a forest lush with wildflowers and berry bushes. Spruce, fir, lodgepole pine, and aspen grow amid house-sized boulders draped in moss and lichen. Cross Creek tumbles where the land drops steeply and slows into pools where fish tease anglers. Past the bridge over Cross Creek, the trail winds through a lush forest to rocky terrain with views of the tip of Mount of the Holy Cross. Ferns almost hide the trail through an aspen forest. Enjoy your lunch next to a grass-lined little lake that momma and baby ducks enjoy.

Start: At the Cross Creek Trail bulletin board
Distance: 5.2 miles out and back
Hiking time: 2.5 to 3.5 hours
Difficulty: Moderate due to distance and a 580-foot elevation gain
Trail surface: Rocky dirt trail
Best season: June 20 through Sept (Access road closed by snow about 7.5 miles from trailhead until June 20. Check website or call for closure dates.)
Other trail users: Equestrians
Canine compatibility: Uncontrolled dogs must be on leash
Land status: National forest and wilderness
Fees and permits: No fees required. Limit of 15 people per group. One person in each group of overnight users must carry a free self-issued wilderness use permit.
Maps: USGS Minturn; Nat Geo Trails Illustrated 108 Vail/Frisco/Dillon; Latitude 40° Vail and Eagle Trails; USFS White River National Forest map
Trail contact: USDA Forest Service, Eagle-Holy Cross Ranger District, 24747 US 24, Minturn; (970) 827-5715; www.fs.usda.gov/whiteriver
Other: The trail is mainly within the Holy Cross Wilderness. Please comply with wilderness regulations.
Special considerations: Bring water with you as the trail is not always near the creek. Hunters may use this area during hunting season.

Finding the trailhead: From I-70 exit 171 (West US 6/East US 24 Minturn/Leadville), drive south on US 24 through Minturn for 4.9 miles to Tigiwon Road (FR 707), just past mile marker 148. Turn right and drive 1.7 miles to the Cross Creek Trail trailhead, on the right side of the road. Except for the first section, the road is narrow. Parking is available on the left as well. No facilities are available at the trailhead. GPS: N39 32.93' / W106 25.11'.

29

THE HIKE

The trail along Cross Creek takes you past humongous boulders, across rock slabs, and through a mixed conifer and aspen forest. Thimbleberries, with huge raspberry-like leaves and flowers, line part of the way. The scenery changes with every twist, turn, and undulation. By 0.9 mile, you can see Cross Creek, and a couple of side trails lead you to the creek.

Congress designated the Holy Cross Wilderness in the Colorado Wilderness Act of 1980. Sometimes referred to as a water wilderness, this area boasts many alpine lakes and streams, which flow into the Eagle River.

Designation of the Holy Cross Wilderness was full of conflict. Colorado Springs and Aurora owned water rights in the area. The Homestake Project, which includes Homestake Reservoir and a water-collection system along Homestake Creek south of Cross Creek, had been built in the 1960s to divert about 27,000 acre-feet of water to the two cities on the east slope of Colorado. The 1980 Act even specified that nothing in the Act would interfere with the construction, maintenance,

Cross Creek bridge

or repair of the Homestake Water Development Project. Homestake Project Phase II planned to divert water from Cross Creek and Fall Creek. Four small dams would be built in the wilderness area along with a 13-mile underground tunnel to divert about 22,000 acre-feet annually. Concerns arose about the extensive meadows and high-altitude wetlands. In 1982 the Holy Cross Wilderness Defense Fund organized to fight the project. Eagle County became involved and denied the permits for the project. Lawsuits were filed, won, lost, and overturned for several years. In 1994 the Colorado Court of Appeals upheld Eagle County's decision to deny the construction permits for Homestake II. Both the Colorado Supreme Court and the US Supreme Court declined to hear the case.

During spring runoff in 2010, Cross Creek flowed so deeply and quickly that it washed out the bridge. To avoid a future washout, the Forest Service moved the bridge upstream and built a very sturdy bridge the next year. Across the bridge are a few lunch spots; the bridge makes a good turnaround point for a 2.5-mile out-and-back hike. Beyond here the trail climbs steeply next to a big boulder then enters a lush forest with huge moss-laden boulders. Coming out of the little canyon, the terrain opens up, and at a rocky viewpoint you can see the tip of Mount of the Holy Cross ahead and to the left. An unofficial side trail drops steeply to the creek to a little waterfall and some wide pools with ample places to sit. Continuing on, the trail passes a viewpoint down into the area just described then enters a thick aspen forest where you may wish you had a machete for the tall ferns growing along and over the trail. A few marshy ponds appear downhill to the left, but the best pond is yet to come. After dropping down a tad on the trail where a boulder field lies to your right, look to your left for a little lake through the trees. A nice big rock provides a great lunch spot. With some luck you may see momma duck swimming around with her little ones chasing each other across the lake.

The Cross Creek Trail continues another 11 miles or so up through beautiful meadows, past high alpine lakes, to the junction with the Missouri Lakes Trail and Fancy Pass Trail. You can backpack for several days virtually circumnavigating the Mount of the Holy Cross and ending up at the Fall Creek Trail trailhead, which is at the end of Tigiwon Road.

MILES AND DIRECTIONS

0.0 Start at the Cross Creek Trail bulletin board. The wilderness boundary sign is in 150 feet. Elevation: 8,514 feet.

0.1 Pass a flat slab of rock. The trail drops about 80 feet, only to start climbing again.

0.8 Arrive at a big mossy rock wall on the left and a trail that descends to the creek on the right. Some flat rocks and a nice cascade make this side trip worthwhile. About 320 feet out and back.

Cross Creek Trail

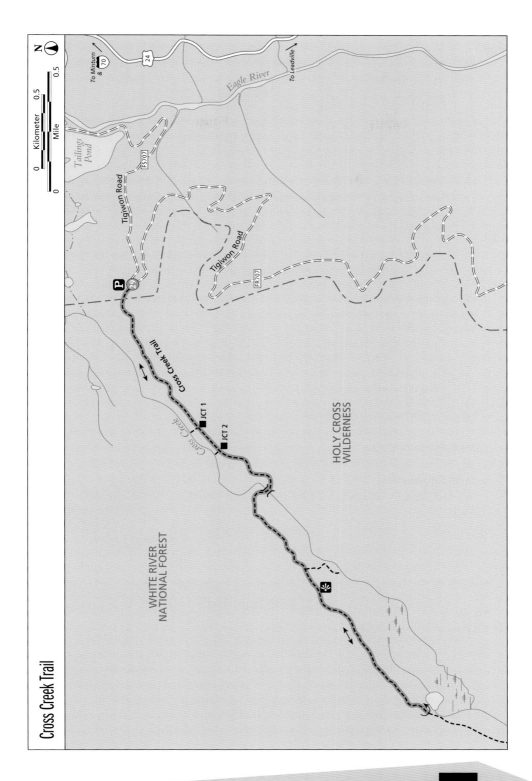

N

| 0 | Kilometer | 0.5 |
| 0 | Mile | 0.5 |

To Minturn & 70

24

Eagle River

To Leadville

Tailings Pond

FS707

Tigiwon Road

Tigiwon Road

FR707

P

Cross Creek Trail

JCT 1

JCT 2

Cross Creek

WHITE RIVER NATIONAL FOREST

HOLY CROSS WILDERNESS

0.9 After crossing a flat rock slab, look to your right for a trail heading toward the creek. Flat rocks make a great lunch spot next to the creek. Fish jump and swim in the quiet pools. About 160 feet out and back.

1.25 Arrive at the bridge over Cross Creek. Some lunch spots are available on the north side of the bridge. GPS: N39 32.45' / W106 26.03'. Elevation: 8,720 feet. (*Option:* Turn around here for a 2.5-mile out-and-back hike.)

1.8 The trail splits. The Cross Creek Trail continues straight ahead and uphill. The wider trail that heads downhill goes to a nice area along the creek complete with pools, a waterfall, and rocks to sit on. GPS: N39 32.32' / W106 26.41'.

1.9 A rock slab to the left provides great views both up and down the Cross Creek valley. Enter a beautiful aspen forest.

2.25 Some marshy ponds lie downhill to the left. Continue heading up the trail.

2.6 A boulder field lies above and to the right (north) of the trail. When you see a truck-sized boulder on the left, look for a little trail between two smaller boulders. The trail takes you to a nice rock for lunch with a good view of the pond. GPS (lunch rock): N39 31.90' / W106 27.07'. Elevation: 9,020 feet. Return the way you came.

5.2 Arrive back at the trailhead.

HIKE INFORMATION

Local Information
Town of Minturn, 302 Pine St., Minturn; (970) 827-5645; www.minturn.org

Vail Valley Partnership, 101 Fawcett Rd., Ste. 240, Avon; (970) 476-1000; www.visitvailvalley.com

Why Leash Your Dog?

Keeping dogs leashed on the trail benefits you, your pet, other visitors, and wildlife. Dogs will surely come out the losers in a bout with the porcupines and mountain lions that live in these areas. Bears have also been known to chase dogs back to their owners. Freely roaming dogs can cause serious damage to delicate ecosystems. A leashed dog can also help you become more aware of wildlife, as dogs can easily detect smells and movement that would go unnoticed by humans.

Cross Creek Trail

Local Events/Attractions

Bravo! Vail Valley Music Festival, 2271 N. Frontage Rd. W., Ste. C, Vail; (877) 812-5700; www.vailmusicfestival.org

Betty Ford Alpine Gardens, 500 S. Frontage Rd., Vail; (970) 476-0103; www.bettyfordalpinegardens.org

Bud Light Hot Summer Nights Concert Series, Gerald R. Ford Amphitheater, 530 S. Frontage Rd. E., Vail; (970) 845-TIXS [8497], (888) 920-ARTS [2797]; www.vvf.org/vvf/info/events.entertainment.hotsummernights.aspx

Minturn Market, Minturn; (970) 827-5645; www.minturnmarket.org

Restaurants

The Minturn Saloon, 146 N. Main St., Minturn; (970) 827-5954; www.minturnsaloon.com

Kirby Cosmo's BBQ Bar, 474 Main St., Minturn; (970) 827-9027; www.kirbycosmos.com

Clubs and Organizations

Colorado Mountain Club-Gore Range Group; www.cmc.org/groups/groups_gorerange.aspx

Notch Mountain

This hike takes you to the historic stone shelter on Notch Mountain for a fantastic view of Mount of the Holy Cross. The trail starts gently, passing through spruce-fir forest with occasional glimpses of the notch in Notch Mountain. Eventually the trail climbs to treeline, then through tundra and boulder fields via switchbacks. Watch for pikas, white-tailed ptarmigans, marmots, and beautiful alpine wildflowers. The switchbacks make the hike easier than most trails up 13,000-foot peaks. Remember to leave early to reach the summit by 11 a.m. so you can head back by noon and avoid thunderstorms.

Start: At the Fall Creek Trail trailhead bulletin board
Distance: 10.5 miles out and back
Hiking time: 5 to 7 hours
Difficulty: Most difficult due to distance and a 2,763-foot elevation gain, plus about 120 feet in undulations
Trail surface: Dirt trail, very rocky in spots
Best season: June 20 to mid-Oct (Access road closed by snow about 7.5 miles from trailhead until June 20. Check website or call for closure dates.)
Other trail users: Equestrians
Canine compatibility: Uncontrolled dogs must be on leash
Land status: National forest and wilderness
Fees and permits: No fees required. Limit of 15 people per group. One person in each group of overnight users must carry a free self-issued wilderness use permit.
Maps: USGS Mount of the Holy Cross and Minturn; Nat Geo Trails Illustrated 126 Holy Cross/Ruedi Reservoir; Latitude 40° Vail and Eagle Trails; USFS White River National Forest map
Trail contact: USDA Forest Service, Eagle-Holy Cross Ranger District, 24747 US 24, Minturn; (970) 827-5715; www.fs.usda.gov/whiteriver
Other: The dirt access road may be bumpy with rocks and potholes. Most passenger cars can make the trip with care. The road is narrow so be careful when rounding curves. The parking lot gets crowded early, as the trailhead for Mount of the Holy Cross is also here. The trail is mainly within the Holy Cross Wilderness. Please comply with wilderness regulations. Overnight camping is prohibited in the Notch Mountain shelter.
Special considerations: Bring plenty of water with you, as it is scarce along the trail. Hunters may use this area during hunting season. The Tigiwon Road is used by snowmobilers and cross-country skiers. The trail is neither maintained nor marked for winter use.

THE HIKE

In the 1800s various stories about a mountain with a "snowy cross" circulated around Colorado. In 1869 William H. Brewer reported seeing Mount of the Holy Cross (14,005 feet) from the summit of Grays Peak (14,269 feet). As part of the Hayden Survey in the 1870s, William Henry Jackson photographed various areas of Colorado. The Hayden Survey was one of four great surveys of the West sponsored by the US government between 1867 and 1878. From 1873 to 1875, leader Ferdinand V. Hayden concentrated on Colorado.

Mount of the Holy Cross from Notch Mountain

President Herbert Hoover proclaimed 1,392 acres around Mount of the Holy Cross as a national monument in 1929. Survey crews laid out an automobile route from US 24 to Tigiwon, and a road was completed in 1932. In 1950 President Harry Truman retracted national monument status and returned the land to the USDA Forest Service.

The 1873 survey set a goal to find this mysterious peak. Jackson climbed Grays Peak and also spotted the cross from the summit. By August the survey group arrived near present-day Minturn. For three days they attempted in vain to find a route on Notch Mountain (13,237 feet) from which to view and photograph the "cross." Fallen trees and thick willows made the going too rough for pack animals, and the group ended up carrying Jackson's 100 pounds of photography gear on foot. Jackson used a wet glass plate camera. Not only was the "film" made of glass, which had to be handled carefully, but it needed to be developed soon after exposure. Jackson carried a portable darkroom tent and all necessary chemicals and supplies with him. Finally finding an approach, the men spent two days on the still-difficult hike, with little food and no shelter. (The surveyors thought they could do it in one day.) Finally atop Notch Mountain, fog decreased visibility to a few feet. Luckily, the fog broke briefly, giving Jackson a glimpse of the infamous cross across the valley. The next morning dawned clear and still,

Notch Mountain shelter and Mount of the Holy Cross

giving him a beautiful shot of the cross. He took several pictures, which caused a sensation across the country as people believed the snow-filled cross to be a sign from God.

The devout began to make annual pilgrimages to Mount of the Holy Cross in 1927. The Civilian Conservation Corps (CCC) constructed the Notch Mountain Trail, the large community house at Tigiwon, and the stone shelter on Notch Mountain. This trail was originally used by packhorses as well as hikers. Pilgrimages ceased in the early 1940s, presumably because of World War II.

The cross is created by a 1,500-foot vertical gully and a 750-foot horizontal rock bench on the mountain's eastern face. Collected snow causes the formation to stand out against the mountainside. The right arm deteriorated due to rockslides, and access remained difficult even after the CCC's work. Even slightly damaged, a cross of snow still forms today. The USDA Forest Service maintains the historic Notch Mountain stone shelter and its lightning rods to provide protection for hikers in case a thunderstorm moves in. Overnight camping is prohibited in the Notch Mountain shelter.

Make sure to start on the Fall Creek Trail, not the Half Moon Pass Trail. The first mile is fairly gentle, but rocky. The trail then climbs, with occasional small elevation drops. The terrain drops steeply to the left, to Fall Creek below. After 2.3 miles the trail widens where a scattering of boulders provide a perfect spot for a break before turning right up the Notch Mountain Trail.

The Pika

Notch Mountain is a good area to see alpine animals and birds, particularly marmots, pikas, and white-tailed ptarmigan.

The pika lives in the alpine and subalpine zones year-round, abiding in rock piles. The pika alert reverberates through the rocks. Active during winter as well as summer, the pika eats hay piles it busily collects during the summer. The small, mouse-like creature with the short tail belongs to the rabbit order. Look closely or you might miss the busy critter as it scurries among the rocks. A mouthful of grass and flowers whizzes by as the pika stores its hay. Researchers have discovered that pikas will steal each other's piles. Watch for big white splotches on boulders along the trail. The splotches indicate pika restrooms. Bright orange lichen often grows near the splotches, energized by the nitrogen-rich fertilizer.

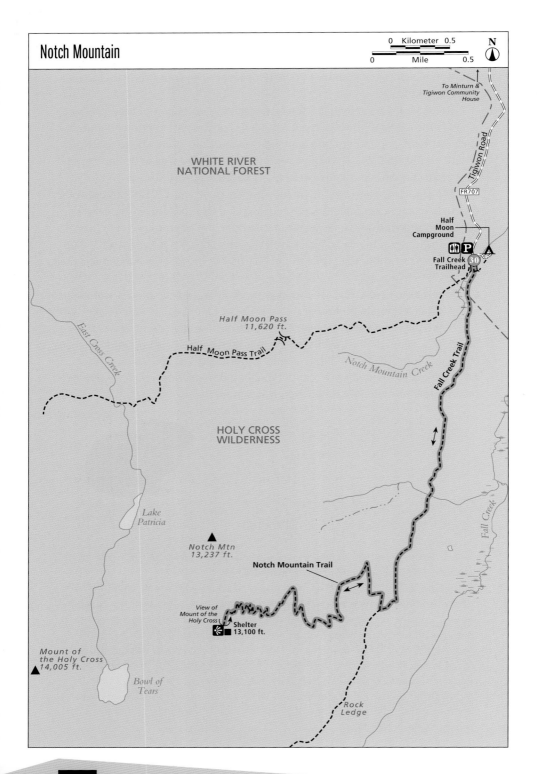

Notch Mountain

0   Kilometer   0.5

0   Mile   0.5

N

WHITE RIVER
NATIONAL FOREST

To Minturn &
Tigiwon Community
House

Tigiwon Road

FR707

Half
Moon
Campground

Fall Creek
Trailhead

30

Half Moon Pass
11,620 ft.

Half Moon Pass Trail

Notch Mountain Creek

Fall Creek Trail

HOLY CROSS
WILDERNESS

East Cross Creek

Lake
Patricia

Notch Mtn
13,237 ft.

Notch Mountain Trail

Fall Creek

View of
Mount of the
Holy Cross

Shelter
13,100 ft.

Mount of
the Holy Cross
14,005 ft.

Bowl of
Tears

Rock
Ledge

From the rest spot it's another 2.9 miles to the shelter and viewpoint. After a few switchbacks the trail begins to pass through treeline and zigzags across the slope to the summit. More than twenty switchbacks help you ascend the last 780 feet. Avoid the temptation to shortcut the switchbacks, as they keep the trail at a reasonable grade (which makes for easier hiking in the thinning air) and protect the terrain.

Once you reach the ridge and stone shelter, Mount of the Holy Cross looms large directly ahead. The alpine wildflowers grow thick and beautiful in July and early August. White arctic gentians signal summer's end. Please walk carefully on the fragile tundra, using rocks for steps as much as possible. And if you must spend the night, camp below treeline.

MILES AND DIRECTIONS

0.0 Start at the Fall Creek Trail trailhead bulletin board (versus the Half Moon Pass Trail trailhead). Elevation: 10,314 feet. Cross a creek on a bridge and take the right fork in the trail (head south).

1.4 The trail traverses a landslide area.

1.5 Cross a wide creek on boulders. (*Note:* The crossing may be easier or harder depending on water volume. Be careful.)

2.3 Reach the trail intersection with Notch Mountain Trail. GPS: N39 28.26' / W106 26.56'. This is a good place for a break. Turn right (north) onto Notch Mountain Trail.

3.5 Start to enter the land above the trees. (*Note:* Turn back if thunderstorms are imminent.)

4.2 Switchbacks increase in number up to the ridge. Depending on where you start counting, you'll zigzag up more than twenty switchbacks in 780 feet. (*Note:* Please do not shortcut the switchbacks. Shortcutting causes environmental damage and erosion that does not heal quickly at this elevation. Also, don't attempt this trail during whiteouts or low visibility. If you miss any of four particular switchbacks, you'll be freefalling over a cliff.)

5.25 Reach the stone shelter on Notch Mountain, with a breathtaking view of Mount of the Holy Cross. GPS: N39 28.17' / W106 27.56'. Elevation: 13,100 feet. (*Note:* The shelter is meant for protection from lightning. Overnight camping is prohibited.) Return the way you came.

10.5 Arrive back at the trailhead.

Local Information
Town of Minturn, 302 Pine St., Minturn; (970) 827-5645; www.minturn.org

Vail Valley Partnership, 101 Fawcett Rd., Ste. 240, Avon; (970) 476-1000; www.visitvailvalley.com

Local Events/Attractions
Camp Hale (WWII training ground of the 10th Mountain Division), between Leadville and Minturn; (970) 527-8715; www.camphale.org; www.fs.usda.gov/whiteriver

Bravo! Vail Valley Music Festival, 2271 N. Frontage Rd. W., Ste. C, Vail; (877) 812-5700; www.vailmusicfestival.org

Betty Ford Alpine Gardens, 500 S. Frontage Rd., Vail; (970) 476-0103; www.bettyfordalpinegardens.org

Bud Light Hot Summer Nights Concert Series, Gerald R. Ford Amphitheater, 530 S. Frontage Rd. E., Vail; (970) 845-TIXS {8497}, (888) 920-ARTS [2797]; www.vvf.org/vvf/info/events.entertainment.hotsummernights.aspx

Minturn Market, Minturn; (970) 827-5645; www.minturnmarket.org

Heartleaf arnica

Lake Constantine

Long Lake Constantine lies nestled in a high valley beneath the elongated ridge of 13,271-foot Whitney Peak and the ridge running south of Notch Mountain. The sights along the trail constantly change as it contours high above Fall Creek. After the Notch Mountain Trail junction, the trail climbs and descends numerous times before reaching the lake. At one point a rock ledge comes across the trail. The trail first winds through thick spruce-fir forest, but later crosses beautiful meadows before arriving at the picturesque lake.

Start: At the Fall Creek Trail trailhead bulletin board
Distance: 8.0 miles out and back
Hiking time: 4.5 to 6 hours
Difficulty: Moderate due to distance and a 1,126-foot elevation gain, plus numerous undulations
Trail surface: Dirt trail, very rocky in spots
Best season: June 20 to mid-Oct (Access road closed by snow about 7.5 miles from trailhead until June 20. Check website or call for closure dates.)
Other trail users: Equestrians
Canine compatibility: Uncontrolled dogs must be on leash
Land status: National forest and wilderness
Fees and permits: No fees required. Limit of 15 people per group. One person in each group of overnight users must carry a free self-issued wilderness use permit.
Maps: USGS Mount of the Holy Cross and Minturn; Nat Geo Trails Illustrated 126 Holy Cross/Ruedi Reservoir; Latitude 40° Vail and Eagle Trails; USFS White River National Forest map
Trail contact: USDA Forest Service, Eagle-Holy Cross Ranger District, 24747 US 24, Minturn; (970) 827-5715; www.fs.usda.gov/whiteriver
Other: The dirt access road may be bumpy with rocks and potholes. Most passenger cars can make the trip with care. The road is narrow so be careful when rounding curves. The parking lot gets crowded early, as the trailhead for Mount of the Holy Cross is also here. Half Moon Campground near the trailhead has seven campsites. The trail is within the Holy Cross Wilderness. Please comply with wilderness regulations.
Special considerations: Water is not easily available along most of the trail. Hunters may use this area during hunting season. Snowmobilers and cross-country skiers use the Tigiwon Road in winter. The trail is neither marked nor maintained for winter use.

THE HIKE

Make sure to start on the Fall Creek Trail, not the Half Moon Pass Trail. The first mile is fairly gentle, but rocky. The trail then climbs, with occasional small elevation drops. The terrain drops steeply to the left to Fall Creek below. At 2.3 miles the trail widens, with a scattering of boulders providing a perfect spot for a break at the junction with the Notch Mountain Trail. You're basically at the same elevation as Lake Constantine, and from here the trail goes up and down and up and down. One tricky short section crosses a rock ledge as it traverses a hillside. The trail wanders through thick spruce-fir forest where gnomes and fairies surely must live. Grouse whortleberry, heartleaf arnica, rosy paintbrush, and lousewort grow under the trees. Then it crosses some marshy areas and meadows where little pink elephants, ruby-red king's crowns, rose crowns, white cow parsnip, and blue harebells bloom.

The north end of Lake Constantine

Fall Creek Trail

In the July 23, 1921, issue of the *Eagle County News,* one writer described a trip to Mount of the Holy Cross where they crossed Fall Creek Pass and looked down on Lake Constantine. "Unless one can see this sight with his own eyes he cannot imagine the beauty of the spot. Why go to see the lakes of Scotland and Switzerland when there are even more beautiful scenes within a few hours walk of our own homes." The hikers lived in nearby Red Cliff. Two years later an article in the April 23, 1923, *Eagle County News* reported that the Forest Service was planning to develop recreational areas around the Mount of the Holy Cross during the following three years. Part of the plan included reconstruction of the Fall Creek Trail past Lake Constantine. Other trails mentioned for reconstruction were the path up Cross Creek to connect with Missouri Creek and the trail past Lake Constantine to French Creek (probably over Fall Creek Pass). A new horse trail to the top of Notch Mountain made the list. The Holy Cross "region abounds in natural attractions for tourists, campers, fishermen, mountain climbers, and all lovers of the great outdoors." Tourism was just starting to grow in the Minturn and Red Cliff area, and the Forest Service wanted to lay a good foundation for the anticipated visitors. In 1929 President Herbert Hoover proclaimed 1,392 acres around Mount of the Holy Cross as a national monument, which remained until 1950.

Before the attack on Pearl Harbor, Charles Minot (Minnie) Dole, the founder of the National Ski Patrol (1938), had suggested to the US Army that troops needed training in winter survival and skiing because both Germany and Italy had ski troops. The US Army built Camp Hale in 1942 at 9,300 feet along the Eagle River north of Leadville and created a ski area on nearby Cooper Hill for training. The 12,000 men received lessons from 600 ski instructors, walking up a run or riding on the T-bar lift then skiing down with packs and rifles on their backs. In addition they learned how to bivouac during cold winters. The troops did find time for leisure. One article in a 1943 issue of the Camp Hale *Ski-zette* reported an interesting rock climbing exercise after which the company hiked to Lake Constantine where they caught numerous fish for dinner. A year later a reporter wrote about a weekend fishing excursion to Lake Constantine where they lost their way until one party member slipped on a snowbank, sliding "hundreds of feet on a drift only to fall right on the trail."

Enjoy your visit to Lake Constantine as people have done for almost one hundred years.

MILES AND DIRECTIONS

0.0 Start at the Fall Creek Trail trailhead bulletin board (versus the Half Moon Pass Trail trailhead). Elevation: 10,314 feet. Cross a creek on a bridge and take the right fork in the trail (head south).

1.4 The trail traverses a landslide area.

1.5 Cross a wide creek on boulders. (*Note:* The crossing may be easier or harder depending on water volume. Be careful.)

2.3 Reach the trail intersection with the Notch Mountain Trail. GPS: N39 28.26' / W106 26.56'. This is a good place for a break. Continue straight ahead on the Fall Creek Trail.

3.0 The trail traverses a rock ledge.

4.0 Come to Lake Constantine. GPS: N39 27.16' / W106 27.37'. Elevation: 11,371 feet. Return the way you came.

8.0 Arrive back at the trailhead.

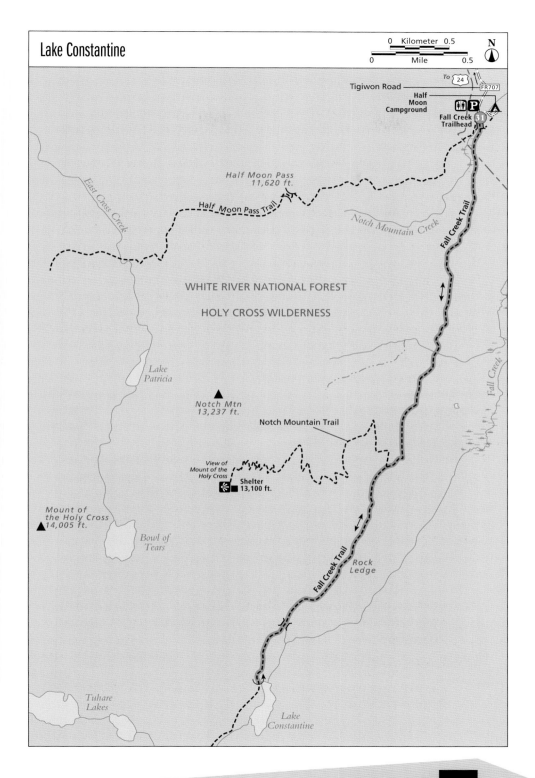

Lake Constantine

Local Information

Town of Minturn, 302 Pine St., Minturn; (970) 827-5645; www.minturn.org

Vail Valley Partnership,101 Fawcett Rd., Ste. 240, Avon; (970) 476-1000; www.visitvailvalley.com

Local Events/Attractions

Camp Hale (WWII training ground of the 10th Mountain Division), between Leadville and Minturn; (970) 527-8715; www.camphale.org; www.fs.usda.gov/whiteriver

Bravo! Vail Valley Music Festival, 2271 N. Frontage Rd. W., Ste. C, Vail; (877) 812-5700; www.vailmusicfestival.org

Betty Ford Alpine Gardens, 500 S. Frontage Rd., Vail; (970) 476-0103; www.bettyfordalpinegardens.org

Bud Light Hot Summer Nights Concert Series, Gerald R. Ford Amphitheater, 530 S. Frontage Rd. E., Vail; (970) 845-TIXS [8497], (888) 920-ARTS [2797]; www.vvf.org/vvf/info/events.entertainment.hotsummernights.aspx

Minturn Market, Minturn; (970) 827-5645; www.minturnmarket.org

Fall Creek Trail approaching Lake Constantine

Missouri Lakes

Beautiful Missouri Lakes are nestled high in a valley in the Holy Cross Wilderness beneath Savage Peak and Missouri Pass. The sights along the trail change constantly as it wanders through forest, over slabs of rocks, across crystal clear streams, along meadows of colorful wildflowers, past waterfalls, and near some interesting mini-canyons. The journey to the lakes makes a good day hike or an overnight backpack. Because the first lake you come to along the trail is only 3.1 miles in, the Missouri Lakes are a popular destination with four lakes and smaller tarns to explore. Two shorter options are also included here.

Start: At the Missouri Lakes Trailhead bulletin board
Distance: 6.8 miles out and back
Hiking time: 3 to 4.5 hours
Difficulty: Difficult due to a 1,495-foot elevation gain
Trail surface: Dirt trail and rock slabs
Best season: Late June through Sept
Other trail users: Equestrians
Canine compatibility: Uncontrolled dogs must be on leash in the Holy Cross Wilderness; under control elsewhere
Land status: National forest and wilderness
Fees and permits: No fees required. Limit of 15 people per group. One person in each group of overnight users must carry a free self-issued wilderness use permit.
Maps: USGS Mount of the Holy Cross and Mount Jackson; Nat Geo Trails Illustrated 126 Holy Cross/Ruedi Reservoir; Latitude 40° Vail and Eagle Trails; USFS White River National Forest map

Trail contact: USDA Forest Service, Eagle-Holy Cross Ranger District, 24747 US 24, Minturn; (970) 827-5715; www.fs.usda.gov/whiteriver
Other: Most of this trail is in the Holy Cross Wilderness. Please comply with wilderness regulations. Campfires are not permitted within the Missouri Creek drainage or near Missouri Lakes.
Special considerations: Bring your own water; the creek is not always near the trail. Hunters may use this area during hunting season. Homestake Road/FR703 is closed by snow during winter—ski or snowshoe!

32

Finding the trailhead: From I-70 exit 171 (West US 6/East US 24 Minturn/Leadville), drive south on US 24 through Minturn for 12.9 miles to Homestake Road (FR 703), just past mile marker 156. Make a sharp right turn onto FR 703, which is dirt and narrow in spots. The road can be rough with washboards, but passable by passenger cars. At 7.8 miles the road splits. Turn right here onto the road to Missouri Creek Trail and drive 2.2 miles to the trailhead parking lot for both Missouri Lakes and Fancy Pass. Missouri Lakes Trail is to the left. A vault toilet is available; bring your own water. GPS: N39 23.40' / W106 28.25'.

THE HIKE

In 1878 miners headed north from Leadville to Battle Mountain along the Eagle River. Some headed west up Homestake Creek to seek their fortunes. The camps and towns of Gold Park, Holy Cross City, Missouri Camp, and Camp Fancy sprang up almost overnight. Miners formed the Holy Cross Mining District. Gold Park started in 1880 and a year later boasted a population of 400 people. A post office, general store, and two hotels plus saloons supported the miners and workers of the Gold Park Mining and Milling Company and its nearby stamp mill. A stage ran daily between Red Cliff and Gold Park. Holy Cross City emerged on the east slopes of French Mountain (unofficial name) with a general store, assayer, justice of the peace, post office, boardinghouse, and scattered cabins. A cast-iron-bottomed flume connected the stamp mill at Holy Cross City to the one at Gold Park. The top mill crushed the ores small enough to wash them down to the lower mill for further processing. Unfortunately the gold that miners found near the surface did not result in a mother lode below the surface as they had predicted. While surface ore assayed at $100 per ton in gold, at 4 feet deep its value dropped to $9 per ton. By 1883 Gold Park had been abandoned. Miners tried to resurrect their dreams from 1896 to 1899 at Holy Cross City by drilling deep into French Mountain. When they did intersect veins at 3,000 feet, the ore was very low grade and milling it proved too expensive. Miners left the towns to find richer diggings, and the buildings have slowly decayed back into the earth.

In the 1940s the US Army's 10th Mountain Division troops from Camp Hale bivouacked and trained in Gold Park, Homestake Creek, and on nearby peaks. Almost 100 years later Congress designated the Holy Cross Wilderness in the Colorado Wilderness Act of 1980. Part of the water from its many alpine lakes and streams flows into the Eagle River and on to the Colorado River, while the remaining water is diverted to cities on Colorado's east slope.

At mile 0.9 of this hike, you pass a diversion dam and little pond just before the Holy Cross Wilderness boundary sign. The dam is part of the Homestake Project, which includes a water-collection system along Homestake Creek and its

Little gorge along Missouri Lakes Trail

tributaries and Homestake Reservoir, which was completed in 1968. The project diverts about 27,000 acre-feet of water to Colorado Springs and Aurora, east-slope cities that own the water rights. Water is more abundant on the less populated west slope than the drier, heavily populated east slope, and diverting water from west to east started in the late 1800s. The water travels from Homestake Reservoir through the 5.2-mile-long Homestake Tunnel under the Continental Divide to Turquoise Reservoir near Leadville. The water flows through another conduit to Twin Lakes Reservoir and into the Arkansas River. The Otero Pump Station moves water from the Arkansas River to the South Platte River Basin. From there, Aurora's share of the water goes to Spinney Reservoir in South Park, and Colorado Springs' water heads to Rampart Reservoir in the foothills west of that city.

The first 0.5 mile is quite gentle, traveling through lodgepole and spruce-fir forest. Strawberries, raspberries, geraniums, cinquefoil, pearly everlasting, and other wonderful wildflowers line the path. After climbing a hill, enjoy the nice waterfall dropping down rocky ledges to the left. The trail climbs more steeply past the wilderness boundary sign, sometimes crossing over big slabs of rock. Notice the white veins and swirls of quartz running through the rocks. You'll pass a cool little gorge then wander along gently flowing Missouri Creek. You're in the mountains and the trail must go up, following the cascading creek in a half gorge. From here the trail alternates gentle with steep, through spruce-fir forest and flower-filled meadows. Suddenly, at 3.1 miles you've arrived at the easiest-to-reach lake. Enjoy the scene with pointy Savage Peak to the south. Some nice rock slabs make a great lunch spot. Continue up the flower-lined trail to the largest lake, where more rocks provide good places to sit and enjoy the scenery. Have fun exploring the numerous lakes and nature's beauty.

MILES AND DIRECTIONS

0.0   Start at the Missouri Lakes Trailhead bulletin board. Elevation: 10,010 feet.

0.85 Enjoy the waterfall to the left of the trail. (*Option:* Turn around here for an easy 1.7-mile out-and-back hike.)

0.9   Arrive at a diversion dam and the Holy Cross Wilderness boundary. GPS: N39 23.15' / W109 29.07'. The trail starts to climb more steeply and sometimes up rock slabs.

1.3   Cross a bridge over Missouri Creek by a narrow little gorge.

1.5   The creek is close to the trail with some nice views of peaks ahead.

1.75 The trail climbs along the creek in a half gorge by a pretty little waterfall.

2.9   Arrive at an unmarked trail junction on the left. This trail heads to the lowest lake. Continue right and up the main trail. GPS: N39 23.39' / W106 30.64'.

3.1   Arrive at one of the Missouri Lakes. GPS: N39 23.49' / W106 30.84'. Elevation: 10,410 feet. (*Option:* Return the way you came for a difficult 6.2-mile out-and-back hike.)

3.4   Come to the largest of the Missouri Lakes. GPS: N39 23.69' / W106 30.74'. Elevation: 11,502 feet. Return the way you came. (*Option:* You can continue about 1 mile to the top of Missouri Pass at 11,986 feet for a view into the beautiful Cross Creek valley and Treasure Vault Lake. Return the way you came for a difficult 8.8-mile out-and-back hike.)

6.8   Arrive back at the trailhead.

Miners ran their extracted ore through stamp mills, which crushed the ore into smaller pieces for further processing. Powered by water, a crankshaft lifted and dropped heavy metal weights (stamps) on the material.

Missouri Lakes

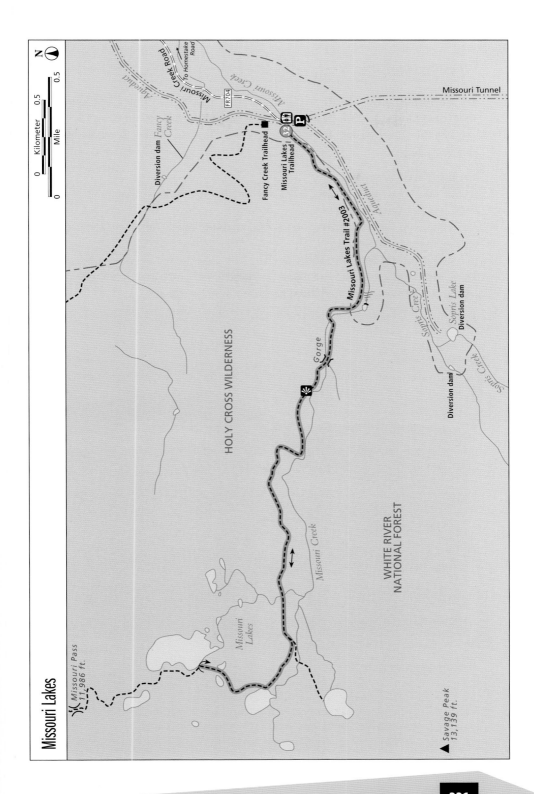

Missouri Pass
11,986 ft.

HOLY CROSS WILDERNESS

WHITE RIVER
NATIONAL FOREST

Savage Peak
13,139 ft.

Missouri Creek

Missouri Lakes

Gorge

Missouri Lakes Trail #2003

Aqueduct

Sopris Creek

Sopris Lake

Diversion dam

Sopris Creek

Diversion dam

Fancy Creek Trailhead

Missouri Lakes
Trailhead

Diversion dam

Aqueduct

Fancy Creek

Missouri Creek Road

To Homestake
Road

FR 704

Missouri Creek

Missouri Tunnel

N

0   Kilometer   0.5

0   Mile   0.5

Local Information

Town of Minturn, 302 Pine St., Minturn; (970) 827-5645; www.minturn.org

Vail Valley Partnership, 101 Fawcett Rd., Ste. 240, Avon; (970) 476-1000; www.visitvailvalley.com

Local Events/Attractions

Bravo! Vail Valley Music Festival, 2271 N. Frontage Rd. W., Ste. C, Vail; (877) 812-5700; www.vailmusicfestival.org

Betty Ford Alpine Gardens, 500 S. Frontage Rd., Vail; (970) 476-0103; www.bettyfordalpinegardens.org

Bud Light Hot Summer Nights Concert Series, Gerald R. Ford Amphitheater, 530 S. Frontage Rd. E., Vail; (970) 845-TIXS [8497], (888) 920-ARTS [2797]; www.vvf.org/vvf/info/events.entertainment.hotsummernights.aspx

Minturn Market, Minturn; (970) 827-5645; www.minturnmarket.org

Missouri Lake and Savage Peak

Beaver Lake

Beaver Lake is a small gem tucked between forested hills just inside the Holy Cross Wilderness. The hike starts near the base of the Centennial Lift at the Beaver Creek Ski Area, follows a nature trail with interpretive signs, then joins the Beaver Lake Trail. It wanders along Beaver Creek, passing various ski area buildings and under chairlifts, providing a summer view of the ski area. Colorful wildflowers and bushes line the trail. While steep in places, the trail has some mellow spots that provide a place to catch your breath. Little fish swim in Beaver Lake, a great place to relax. An option to go or return a different way, including a chairlift ride, is also given.

Start: At the 5 Senses Trail sign next to the Beaver Creek Club

Distance: 6.2 miles out and back

Hiking time: 3 to 4.5 hours

Difficulty: Difficult due to a 1,666-foot elevation gain

Trail surface: Sidewalk, paved road, dirt road, and dirt trail

Best season: June through Oct

Other trail users: Equestrians

Canine compatibility: Dogs must be on leash in Beaver Creek; uncontrolled dogs must be on leash in the Holy Cross Wilderness

Land status: Beaver Creek Village, national forest, wilderness

Fees and permits: No fees required. Limit of 15 people per group in Holy Cross Wilderness. One person in each group of overnight users must carry a free self-issued wilderness use permit.

Maps: USGS Grouse Mountain; Nat Geo Trails Illustrated 121 Eagle/Avon; Latitude 40° Vail and Eagle

Valley Trails; USFS White River National Forest map

Trail contact: USDA Forest Service, Eagle-Holy Cross Ranger District, 24747 US 24, Minturn; (970) 827-5715; www.fs.usda.gov/whiteriver

Other: Part of this trail is within the Holy Cross Wilderness. Please comply with wilderness regulations.

Special considerations: Bring water because little is available along the trail. Hunters may use this area during hunting season. The trail is neither marked nor maintained for winter use.

THE HIKE

Abe Lee discovered gold near Leadville in 1860, and silver became king in the late 1870s. Miners wandered over the hills, staking claims along the upper Eagle River. Some became discouraged with mining and homesteaded nearby, producing food for their families and hungry miners. More newcomers arrived in the early 1880s, setting down roots along the Eagle River. One homesteader, George A. Townsend, settled at the confluence of the Eagle River and Beaver Creek. He called the area Avondale, perhaps after an English town. Settlers named Beaver Creek after the numerous industrious rodents (beavers) that lived along the creek. In the late 1880s the Denver & Rio Grande Railroad extended their line from Leadville to Glenwood Springs and on to the Aspen mining areas. Their depot near Townsend's land became known as Avon.

In 1887 William and Angeline Nottingham homesteaded at Avon. Many other families, including the Holdens, Taylors, Harts, Robertsons, and Smiths, settled along Beaver Creek. The farmers grew hay, potatoes, peas, and oats and raised cattle. Many worked in nearby mines to make ends meet. A little sawmill on the shore of Beaver Lake provided lumber. During the 1920s lettuce became a popular and profitable crop. Farmers shipped their crispy crop in train cars chilled with ice from the Minturn icehouse. During winter, crews chopped 18 x 20 x 24-inch blocks of ice out of a pond near Pando, south on the Eagle River near Tennessee Pass. After the water froze again, they cut more blocks. The ice train carried the precious cargo to the icehouse in Minturn for storage. Deer enjoyed the tasty lettuce, too. Eventually, lack of soil knowledge and crop rotation depleted the soil. The lettuce boom went bust.

By the 1950s the Nottinghams had enlarged their property by buying six more homesteads. Their profitable operation included part of today's Avon, the

Beaver Creek valley, and the upper portion of Bachelor Gulch. Their three sons inherited different sections of the ranch. One of Vail's founders, Peter Seibert, had offered to buy the Nottingham ranch for a ski resort around 1956. The family refused his offer, and Seibert instead helped create what is now Vail. In 1970 the International Olympic Organizing Committee (IOOC) selected Denver for the 1972 Winter Olympics, and the Beaver Creek area was one of their choices. Willis Nottingham realized times had changed and sold 2,200 acres of his ranch to Vail Associates for the Beaver Creek resort. Seibert, others, and the Forest Service worked with the IOOC to plan a ski mountain and international Olympic village. Colorado voters soon rejected the Olympics, and Colorado politics interfered for several years. The USDA Forest Service granted the special-use permit in 1976. Beaver Creek opened in 1980 and has since grown from 425 to 1,832 skiable acres.

The Beaver Lake Trail is fairly steep in places, but flatter sections in between the grunts give you a chance to catch your breath. The ski area boundary ends near the wilderness boundary. Once you're at the lake, take the middle path to a nice area for lunch. You can continue up the trail a ways, then follow one of the little trails down toward the lake. The farther up the main trail you go, the steeper the descent to the lake. On a still day the lake reflects the surrounding forest and sky. Enjoy the peace and quiet before returning to civilization.

Beaver Lake

MILES AND DIRECTIONS

0.0   Start at the 5 Senses Trail sign next to the Beaver Creek Club. Elevation: 8,080 feet. Follow the path across the bridge over Beaver Creek, then turn left and follow the sidewalk to the Beaver Creek Chapel. On the other side of the chapel, find the 5 Senses Trail beyond the electrical box. If you find yourself confused trying to follow the trail, which becomes multiple trails in places, you can walk along the road to the right.

0.6   Reach the Beaver Lake Trail bulletin board. GPS: N39 35.80' / W106 31.36'. Just to the right of the bulletin board, hike on what looks like an old wagon road. In a few feet the trail splits. Go right to Beaver Lake.

0.7   The trail joins a gravel road to the maintenance area. Near the water tank and the junction to Lost Buck Spur, continue straight ahead on Beaver Lake Trail.

1.5   Arrive at the junction with the Village to Village Trail. Continue straight ahead.

1.6   Cross a road after walking under a chairlift. Continue straight ahead. A little farther up, cross another road and continue straight ahead (follow the trail signs).

1.8   On your left is a nice place to sit close to the creek for a snack. GPS: N39 34.66' / W106 31.89'.

2.1   Turn left onto the hikers' trail and cross a nice bridge over Beaver Creek.

2.2   Turn left onto the road and head uphill.

2.4   The trail becomes a singletrack and mellows a bit before climbing steeply.

2.7   Arrive at the junction with Royal Elk Trail, which comes in from the left. Continue straight ahead. GPS: N39 34.20' / W106 32.04'. (*Option:* On the return, you can hike about 2 miles up Royal Elk Trail to Spruce Saddle and ride Chair 6 down to the base. Dogs are not allowed on the chairlift. Spruce Saddle also offers lunch and snacks. Contact the Beaver Creek Hiking Center for details before you start your hike.)

2.9   Come to the Holy Cross Wilderness boundary. You're almost there!

3.1   The trail splits three ways. Take the middle trail to Beaver Lake, and find a nice place to sit along the lakeshore. GPS: N39 33.89' / W106 32.08'. Elevation: 9,746 feet. Take some time to explore before returning the way you came.

6.2   Arrive back at the trailhead by the Beaver Creek Club.

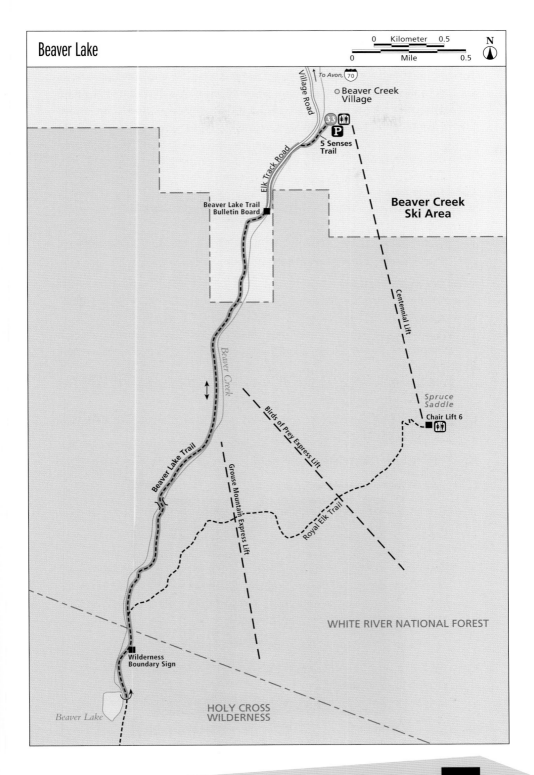

Beaver Lake

0 Kilometer 0.5
0 Mile 0.5

N

To Avon, 70

Beaver Creek Village

Village Road

33

P

5 Senses Trail

Elk Track Road

Beaver Creek Ski Area

Beaver Lake Trail Bulletin Board

Centennial Lift

Beaver Creek

Spruce Saddle

Chair Lift 6

Birds of Prey Express Lift

Beaver Lake Trail

Grouse Mountain Express Lift

Royal Elk Trail

WHITE RIVER NATIONAL FOREST

Wilderness Boundary Sign

HOLY CROSS WILDERNESS

Beaver Lake

Option

You can ride Chair 6 (Centennial Lift) up to Spruce Saddle and hike down Royal Elk Trail to the Beaver Lake Trail if you enjoy hiking downhill with a little uphill. From Spruce Saddle to Beaver Lake is 2.5 miles one way. Contact the Beaver Creek Hiking Center for details before you start your hike.

HIKE INFORMATION

Local Information

Vail Valley Partnership, 101 Fawcett Rd., Ste. 240, Avon; (970) 476-1000; www.visit vailvalley.com

Beaver Creek Resort Company, 26 Avondale Ln., Ste. 118C, Beaver Creek; (970) 845-5858; www.beavercreekresortcompany.com

Local Events/Attractions

Vilar Performing Arts Center, 68 Avondale Ln., Beaver Creek; (970) 845-8497; www.vilarpac.org

Wine & Spirits Festival, Beaver Creek; (800) 953-0844; www.beavercreek.com

Oktoberfest, Beaver Creek Hiking Center; (970) 754-5373; www.beavercreek .com

Colorado Ski and Snowboard Hall of Fame, 231 S. Frontage Rd. E., Vail; (970) 476-1876; www.skimuseum.net

Guided Hikes

Beaver Creek Hiking Center, Beaver Creek Village in the Summer Adventure Center; (970) 754-5373; www.beavercreek.com

Beaver Lake Trail

East Lake Creek Trail

The East Lake Creek Trail is a pleasant roller coaster through lush aspen forest with many types of vegetation, including thimbleberry and bracken ferns. The hike climbs about 230 feet, only to descend 300 feet to the sturdy bridge over East Lake Creek. What goes down to the creek must go back up to the parking lot. This trail is beautiful in autumn when the aspen leaves turn gold and the many bushes show off their red berries and red, orange, and yellow leaves.

Start: At the East Lake Creek Trail bulletin board
Distance: 4.6 miles out and back
Hiking time: 2 to 3.5 hours
Difficulty: Moderate due to a 530-foot elevation gain and constant undulations
Trail surface: Dirt trail
Best season: June through Oct
Other trail users: Equestrians
Canine compatibility: Dogs must be under control; uncontrolled dogs must be on leash in the Holy Cross Wilderness.
Land status: National forest and wilderness
Fees and permits: None required. Limit of 15 people per group in the Holy Cross Wilderness.
Maps: USGS Grouse Mountain; Nat Geo Trails Illustrated 121 Eagle/Avon; Latitude 40° Vail and Eagle Trails; USFS White River National Forest map
Trail contact: USDA Forest Service, Eagle-Holy Cross Ranger District, 24747 US 24, Minturn; (970) 827-5715; www.fs.usda.gov/whiteriver
Other: The last part of the hike is within the Holy Cross Wilderness. Please comply with wilderness regulations.
Special considerations: Bring water with you because only small seeps and creeks are along the trail until the bridge. Hunters may use this area during hunting season. The trail is neither marked nor maintained for winter use.

Finding the trailhead: From I-70 exit 163 (Edwards), head south into Edwards to US 6 and turn right. Drive for 0.7 mile and turn left by a church onto Lake Creek Road. In 1.9 miles, turn right onto West Lake Creek Road, which is easy to miss. A brown sign says "East Lake Trail #1880 4 miles." In another 1.6 miles the road turns to dirt. In another mile the road splits—go left. In 1.2 miles, turn left into the small parking lot just before the private property gate. No facilities are available at the trailhead. GPS: N39 35.14' / W106 35.74'.

THE HIKE

From the trailhead, East Lake Creek Trail meanders about 12.5 miles up a long valley in the Sawatch Range, but peters out a couple of miles before ending at Upper Camp Lake below 13,043-foot Eagle Peak. Along the way, high alpine lakes feed small creeks that tumble into the main creek.

East Lake Creek once appeared to be a promising mining area. Orin Packard mined his claims along East Lake Creek back in 1893. By 1899 various property owners envisioned a metropolis in the area and called it Althea. Officially it was the Mount Egley Mining District. Several companies hoped to recover profitable ore from numerous veins, some of which could be seen on the surface before dipping underground. By 1905 several companies had raised enough capital to work steadily to reach the veins of lead, gold, and silver.

The Miller Mining Company owned three claims named Little Annie. One sample of 10 tons of ore contained 70 percent lead, half an ounce of gold, and about 10 ounces of silver. In order to recover the ore, they planned to build a concentrating mill.

The East Lake Milling and Mining Company (ELMMC) was owned by several doctors and businessmen from Ohio. Their claims on the western slope of Mount Egley consisted of the Washington, Black Diamond, Lulu, Sunshine, and several others for a total of eighteen. The Washington vein, exposed for about 2,500 feet aboveground, was one of several on Mount Egley's west slope.

Trail leading to aspen forest

Miners hand-drilled the Ohio Tunnel attempting to reach the Washington as well as other veins. Hard rock challenged them, and in some months the tunnel progressed only 60 feet. By 1907 a waterfall near the Ohio Tunnel powered a 150-horsepower steam plant, which allowed miners to use machine drills. The Ohio Tunnel delved 925 feet into the mountain.

The Packard Power and Mining Company worked its claims across the valley from ELMMC. By late 1905 air compressors had enabled miners to drill about 375 feet into its claim, averaging 4 feet per day.

During the winter of 1906, equipment had been brought to the East Lake Creek mines over a snow road, and twenty men worked in the mines in two shifts. Men used compressors to run their drills and also to power a sawmill to cut logs for the mine supports, flumes, and buildings.

Although miners eventually reached the Washington lode and found adequate gold, little ore was shipped from the area. The mines usually closed in the winter and access was difficult. Today the ruins of many dreams lie silently along East Lake Creek.

You won't find mining remains along this hike, but the gold of the aspen are worth a fall walk! You'll notice that some clumps of aspen are red, some gold, and some still green. The "clump" of the same color is really a group of trees that grow from the same lateral root and have identical genes. An individual tree typically lives between 40 and 150 years in spite of numerous diseases that can infect it in addition to tent caterpillars and other insects that eat its leaves. The aspen forest along the trail is very lush, indicative of rich and moist soil. The decomposed aspen leaves provide nutrients, enabling many other plants to grow into a verdant garden. Bracken ferns grow thickly in places, enjoying the moisture. Thimbleberry with its large strawberry-like leaves, white flowers, and big fruits line the trail. Other types of berries and currants grow here, sporting bright red fruits. Bears eat the berries in the fall, trying to fatten up for the winter. If you're

Aspen

Aspen need sun to thrive, so as the forest grows and thickens, new shoots can't grow under the shady canopy. Instead conifers, such as spruce and fir seedlings that prefer shade, will gradually replace the aspen forest. As time marches on, if fire races through the conifer forest or another disturbance removes those trees, the newly opened sunny area creates an environment where aspen can once again sprout from their underground rhizomes. The roots can live for thousands of years, making some aspen colonies even older than bristlecone pines. Aspen can germinate from seed, but despite the thousand or more seeds produced by one tree, if conditions aren't right the short-lived seeds won't take root.

East Lake Creek Trail in autumn

hiking here in autumn, keep an eye, ear, and nose open for feeding bears. In addition to aspen, some Douglas fir, lodgepole pine, and spruce grow nearby.

Just before you reach the bridge, a meadow with large rocks and a little pond provide an openness not found in the thick forest. Find a nice rock to sit on and enjoy your lunch!

MILES AND DIRECTIONS

0.0 Start at the East Lake Creek Trail bulletin board. Elevation: 8,530 feet. The first 0.2 mile is on an easement through private property. Please stay on the trail.

0.9 Come to the junction on the right with Dead Dog Trail. Continue straight ahead. GPS: N39 34.75' / W106 35.23'.

East Lake Creek Trail

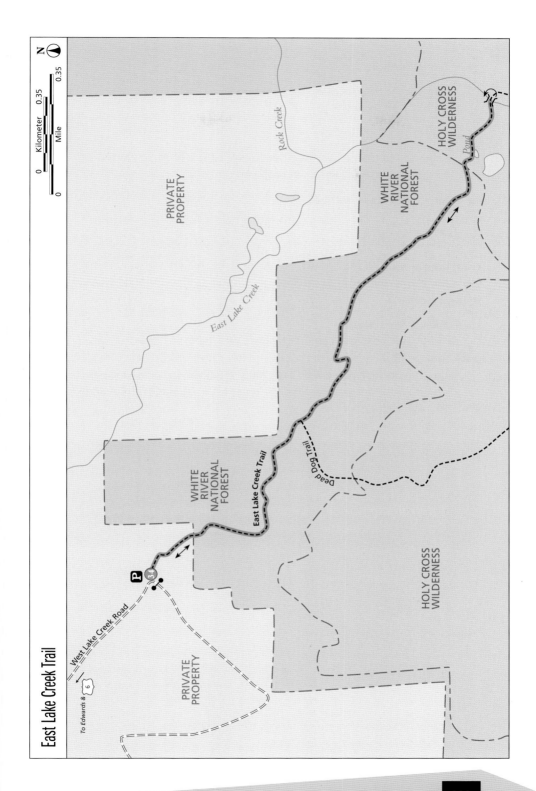

1.0 The trail switchbacks and starts to descend steadily.

1.9 Arrive at the Holy Cross Wilderness boundary.

2.1 The trail climbs up and over a little ridge. Where it appears to split, turn right.

2.3 Come to the bridge over East Lake Creek. GPS: N39 34.30′ / W106 34.15′. Elevation: 8,460 feet. Return the way you came.

4.6 Arrive back at the trailhead.

HIKE INFORMATION

Local Information
Vail Valley Partnership, 101 Fawcett Rd., Ste. 240, Avon; (970) 476-1000; www.visit vailvalley.com

Local Events/Attractions
Oktoberfest and Oktoberfest Shuffle, Beaver Creek; (800) 953-0844; www.beaver creek.com

Wine & Spirits Festival, Beaver Creek; (800) 953-0844; www.beavercreek.com

Colorado Ski and Snowboard Hall of Fame, 231 S. Frontage Rd. E., Vail; (970) 476-1876; www.skimuseum.net

> ### 🌿 Green Tip:
> *Carving initials or figures into soft aspen bark creates an opening for diseases and insects to infect the tree. Refraining from defacing the trees will allow them to survive longer and more successfully.*

Lake Charles

Lake Charles sits in a high basin beneath rocky peaks in the Sawatch Range. The beautiful setting makes a great destination for a day hike or an overnight backpack. Climbing past moss-draped boulders, through thick forest, occasionally near a sparkling creek, and through wildflower gardens, the trail steadily gains elevation. Water is plentiful in the area, and the resultant vegetation is thick and lush. Two steep climbs take you higher in the East Brush Creek valley. Several campsites can be found at appropriate distances (100 feet) from water and trails near Lake Charles. Enjoy the scenery during lunch or stay a night or two.

Start: At the Lake Charles/Iron Edge Trails trailhead bulletin board
Distance: 9.2 miles out and back
Hiking time: 5 to 6 hours
Difficulty: Difficult due to distance and a 1,635-foot elevation gain, plus various undulations
Trail surface: Dirt trail
Best season: July to early Oct (Access road closed by snow at road to Yeoman Park Campground in winter.)
Other trail users: Equestrians
Canine compatibility: Uncontrolled dogs must be on leash in the Holy Cross Wilderness; under control elsewhere
Land status: National forest and wilderness
Fees and permits: No fees required. Limit of 15 people per group. One person in each group of overnight users must carry a free self-issued wilderness use permit.
Maps: USGS Mount Jackson and Crooked Creek Pass; Nat Geo Trails Illustrated 126 Holy Cross/Ruedi Reservoir; Latitude 40° Vail and Eagle Trails; USFS White River National Forest map
Trail contact: USDA Forest Service, Eagle-Holy Cross Ranger District, 125 W. 5th St., Eagle; (970) 328-6388; www.fs.usda.gov/whiteriver
Other: The dirt access road may be bumpy with rocks and potholes. Most passenger cars can make the trip. Fulford Campground, which is near the trailhead, is a small but nice place to stay to get an early morning start. The trail is mainly within the Holy Cross Wilderness. Please comply with wilderness regulations.
Special considerations: Hunters may use this area during hunting season. Snowmobiles and cross-country skiers use the road from Yeoman Park to Fulford in winter. The Lake Charles Trail is neither marked nor maintained for winter use.

Finding the trailhead: From I-70 exit 147 (Eagle), head south about 0.3 mile to US 6 and turn right in the traffic circle onto US 6 West. Drive 1 mile, following the Sylvan Lake signs to a second traffic circle just past mile marker 149. You basically turn left via the traffic circle onto Sylvan Lakes Road. Continue 1.7 miles and turn right onto Brush Creek Road (Eagle CR 307). Drive about 8.8 miles to a fork in the road. Take the left branch, East Brush Creek Road (FR 415), a smooth dirt road. Drive another 6 miles to the junction with Yeoman Park Campground (winter parking), then drive straight ahead on FR 415 to Fulford Cave and Campground. The road narrows and becomes bumpier. In 1.2 miles, arrive at both the trailhead and the campground. The trailhead is to the left. GPS: N39 29.54′ / W106 39.50′.

THE HIKE

In the late 1920s Clyde and Adele Lloyd of Chicago obtained a special-use permit from the Forest Service and built six cabins on the north shore of Lake Charles. The cabins included one for the cook and a honeymoon cabin. A dock was built on the lake. Guests traveled to the resort on horseback from where the Fulford Campground is today. The cook and wranglers reportedly pampered the guests. The couple named their resort Skyland in the Rockies and renamed the lake to Lake Adele. Over time winter snows weathered the cabins beyond repair, and the Forest Service dismantled them in the 1940s.

The Lloyds became involved at Lake Charles when Ruggles and Lloyd, a Chicago mining company, leased the Martha Washington mine from Chicago investors. H. G. Gradwad and partners became owners of the mine in 1917. The Martha Washington was located on the western slope of the south shoulder of Fools Peak, which towers above Lake Charles. Assays from the mine ran from 1 to 35 ounces of gold per ton of rock. Transporting equipment to the mine and the ore to the railroad proved a challenge, although financing had been obtained. Miners originally accessed their claim from Lime Creek to the southwest. Workers waited until winter snows covered the trails to haul heavy equipment, which

Green Tip:
Campsites should be set up at least 100 feet from lakes, streams, and trails to protect water and allow for solitude for both campers and other visitors. One easy way to measure 100 feet is by walking approximately thirty-five adult paces. For more Leave No Trace camping techniques, check out www.LNT.org.

A rock that resembles a gnome's hat along the trail

moved more easily over packed snow. Progress in 1920 included building a good trail from Yeoman Park, bunk cabins for the miners, a blacksmith shop, and supply cellars. One cabin measured 18 feet by 29 feet. By August 1920 workers had completed all the startup work and had begun digging the development tunnel. Evidently the rich veins the owners and lessors expected were not intercepted, and the next August a mining engineer advised them to dig deeper into an earlier test shaft and abandon the 1920 development tunnel. By November 1922 two tunnels had been dug at the Martha Washington, but the mineral veins were too small to produce enough to pay for the work. Miners had dug one tunnel only 50 feet during the summer. Everyone hoped that as work progressed, better veins and ore would be found. Meanwhile the Lloyds built a summer home in 1921 and during the next summer added to it and built new cabins on the shore of Lake Charles. The resort operated successfully for 10 to 15 years—longer than

Boardwalk on the Lake Charles Trail

the Martha Washington. Mines in the Fulford area, including the Martha Washington, did not produce much profit, if any.

The trail climbs above East Brush Creek near the trailhead then levels off. One feature of this trail is the many huge granitic boulders along the trail. One is an upside-down cone shape—perhaps a bewitched wood gnome's hat. Some are covered with moss, with grouse whortleberry growing in the soft, green mat. The trail follows the creek in places then turns away for a while. Cascades fill the creek where the land is steeper, and in flatter areas the water flows along lazily. The first steep stretch climbs up along a humongous rock through a blanket of flowers. Numerous little creeks cross the trail. As you hike higher, the trees thin, more meadows interjected with rock slabs appear, and suddenly you're at Lake Charles! A 12,320-foot unnamed peak seems to rise out of the lake to the south, and neighboring Fools Peak emerges to the southeast. At the head of East Brush Creek you can see jagged Eagle Peak. Take a little time to explore Lake Charles and maybe hike up to Mystic Island Lake and take in the area's beauty.

MILES AND DIRECTIONS

0.0   Start at the Lake Charles/Iron Edge Trails trailhead bulletin board. Elevation: 9,445 feet. In about 240 feet is the junction with the Iron Edge Trail. Turn left onto the Lake Charles Trail.

1.6   Arrive at the Holy Cross Wilderness boundary. If you are backpacking and staying overnight, please fill out the free self-issued registration permit (one per party).

2.3   Cross a marshy section on a flat plank bridge.

3.0   The next 0.25 mile climbs pretty steeply, and you'll pass a huge boulder reminiscent of Big Rock Candy Mountain.

3.25   The trail appears to split. Continue hiking on the left branch.

3.7   Come to the top of another steep section.

4.3   Arrive at the northwest end of Lake Charles. A little trail leads to the right. The main trail continues straight ahead. GPS: N39 27.79' / W106 36.40'. Elevation: 11,060 feet. Several rock slabs make great lunch spots. (*Option:* You can return from here for an 8.6-mile out-and-back hike.) Continue another 0.3 mile to the southeast end of the lake.

Lake Charles

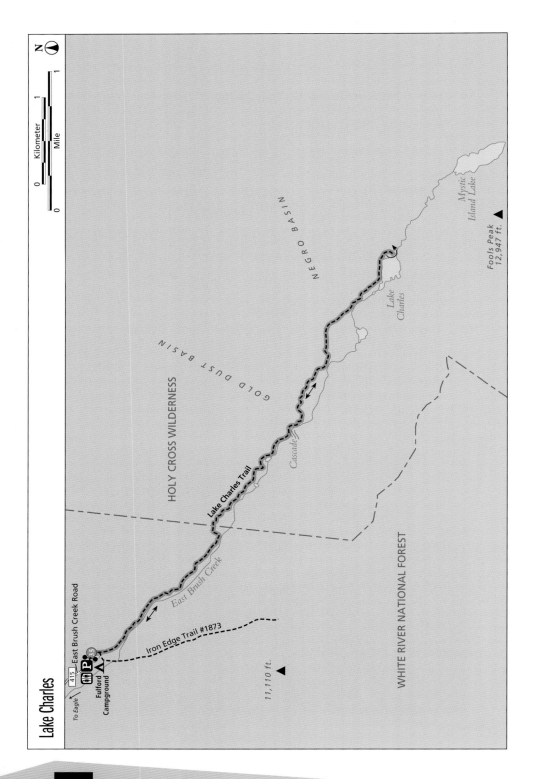

Lake Charles

To Eagle

East Brush Creek Road

Fulford Campground

Iron Edge Trail #1873

East Brush Creek

Lake Charles Trail

HOLY CROSS WILDERNESS

GOLD DUST BASIN

Cascade

NEGRO BASIN

Lake Charles

WHITE RIVER NATIONAL FOREST

11,110 ft.

Fools Peak 12,947 ft.

Mystic Island Lake

N

Kilometer

Mile

4.6 Near the top of the hill at the southeast end of the lake, look for a trail to the right that leads to a rock slab with a great view of Lake Charles and Fools Peak. GPS: N39 27.71' / W106 36.20'. Return the way you came.

7.6 What do you think the large boulder to the left of the trail looks like?

9.2 Arrive back at the trailhead.

Option
You can continue approximately 1 mile from the top of the hill (mile 4.6) to Mystic Island Lake, tucked beneath Eagle Peak, for an 11.2-mile out-and-back hike.

HIKE INFORMATION

Local Information
Eagle Valley Chamber of Commerce, Eagle; (970) 328-5220; www.eaglevalley.org

Local Events/Attractions
Sylvan Lake State Park, Eagle; (970) 328-2021; www.parks.state.co.us/parks/sylvanlake

Eagle County Historical Society's Visitor Center (museum), Eagle; (970) 328-6464

Clubs and Organizations
Colorado Mountain Club-Gore Range Group; www.cmc.org/groups/groups_gorerange.aspx

Fulford

From 1881 to 1882 Arthur Fulford had served as marshal of Redcliff. Fulford and his brothers later moved to the Eagle area and helped to settle a camp below the mines on the flanks of New York Mountain. The camp was called Nolan after an early settler whose rifle fired and severed his tongue while he crossed a log. He bled to death. Fulford died in an avalanche on New York Mountain on New Year's Day 1892, supposedly while trying to stake a new claim. The town was renamed Fulford in his honor and was the last mining camp to be developed during the gold rush.

Mount Thomas

The Mount Thomas summit, a bump on Red Table Mountain, offers a spectacular 360-degree panorama of the central Colorado Rockies. Overwhelming views stretch from the Maroon Bells and Elk Mountains in the southwest, circling northwest to the Flat Tops, then north toward I-70 and Eagle. The Gore Range rises in the northeast, with the Sawatch Mountains towering in the east and southeast. Beautiful alpine wildflowers decorate the upper ridges. The trail traverses an open ridge for about 1.6 miles, so be sure to make the summit and be heading down before thunderstorms hit.

Start: At the top of Crooked Creek Pass

Distance: 10.2 miles out and back

Hiking time: 4 to 7 hours

Difficulty: Difficult due to distance and a 2,382-foot gain and 200-foot loss

Trail surface: Dirt road and dirt trail with some steep sections and a boulder field

Best season: Late June to mid-Oct (Access road closed by snow just past Sylvan Lake State Park, 5.5 miles from trailhead.)

Other trail users: Equestrians

Canine compatibility: Dogs must be under control

Land status: National forest, proposed wilderness

Fees and permits: None required.

Maps: USGS Crooked Creek Pass; Nat Geo Trails Illustrated 126 Holy Cross/Ruedi Reservoir; Latitude 40° Vail and Eagle Trails; USFS White River National Forest map

Trail contacts: USDA Forest Service, Eagle-Holy Cross Ranger District, 125 W. 5th St., Eagle; (970) 328-6388; www.fs.usda.gov/white river; USDA Forest Service, Sopris Ranger District, Aspen; (970) 963-2266; www.fs.usda.gov/whiteriver

Special considerations: Bring water as none is available along the trail. Hunters may use this area during hunting season. The road is used by snowmobilers and cross-country skiers. The trail is neither maintained nor marked for winter use.

Finding the trailhead: From I-70 exit 147 (Eagle), head south about 0.3 mile to US 6 and turn right in the traffic circle. Drive 1 mile, following the Sylvan Lake signs to a second traffic circle just past mile marker 149. You basically turn left via the traffic circle onto Sylvan Lakes Road. Continue 1.7 miles and turn right onto Brush Creek Road (Eagle CR 307). Drive about 8.8 miles to a fork in the road. Take the right branch, the smooth dirt West Brush Creek road, again toward Sylvan Lake. Drive another 10 miles to the top of Crooked Creek Pass. The dirt road narrows and becomes FR 400 past Sylvan

Lake State Park. You have three parking options and starting points depending on road conditions and your vehicle. (1) You can park in the dirt area to the right at the top of the pass and start hiking there. GPS: N39 26.48' / W106 41.11'. (2) At the top of the pass, turn right onto an unmarked dirt road and drive 0.5 mile to the junction with FR 431. Park on the flat grassy area at the junction. GPS: N39 26.35' / W106 41.14'. (3) You can turn left onto FR 431 and drive 0.2 mile to the actual trailhead; park under the power lines. No facilities or water are available at the trailhead or pass. GPS: N39 26.18' / W106 41.03'.

THE HIKE

Mount Thomas (11,977 feet) was named after the head of the St. Louis & Colorado Smelting Company. Thomas (the rest of his name apparently lost to history) started a smelter along the Colorado Midland Railroad in the Fryingpan Valley around 1890. The town that grew nearby, Thomasville, also bears his name. He became involved in some mining ventures north of town in the Lime Creek drainage. He did not have much luck—the mines produced little ore and his unprofitable smelter closed in 1892. A little peak on the ridge between Lime and Brush Creeks commemorates his involvement in the area. The ridge itself is known as Red Table Mountain.

Mount Thomas Trail along the upper ridge

Grassy meadows provide good grazing for cattle in the Lime Creek drainage. When settlers arrived in Colorado in the late 1800s, cattle and sheep grazed freely on public lands. Ranchers and sheepherders ran as much stock as possible, damaging many acres across the West from overgrazing. The Taylor Grazing Act of 1934 created grazing districts to minimize the degradation of public lands. Today the USDA Forest Service grants grazing permits on the lands under its management. A rancher may hold several grazing allotments in an area. With guidance from the Forest Service, the rancher moves his herd at designated times, rotating cattle to different areas. Rotation has several benefits. The cattle continue to have fresh grass to eat, and the grass in any given area is not totally consumed and has time to recover and stay healthy. Fences help keep cattle in designated areas. The rancher holding the grazing allotments is responsible for maintaining the fences. The rancher also helps maintain the hiking and other trails, which his cattle use.

During the hike you may come across herds of cattle. They will not bother you and will just move up or off the trail as you approach. Please restrain dogs and do not harass the herd.

From the top of Crooked Creek Pass, the hike follows a narrow dirt road (sometimes requiring four-wheel drive) climbing steadily up to the trailhead located under some power lines. The turnoff to the trailhead is not marked, so follow the cues in the Miles and Directions carefully. A deep, thick spruce-fir forest surrounds the trail, creating a dark primeval atmosphere where the appearance of elves and gnomes would hardly be surprising. Slip past the forest spirits into an open meadow with an airy view of the Lime Creek drainage. The trail winds between small stands of conifers and open, flower-covered meadows.

Proposed Wilderness Designation Benefits Habitat, Solitude

Part of this area is currently being managed as a recommended wilderness area. In 2013 some members of Colorado's congressional delegation were working on legislation to include Red Table Mountain and surrounding areas in the National Wilderness Preservation System. Through many citizen and user group discussions, the original proposed boundaries were modified to allow continued use of a popular snowmobile area. The Colorado Army National Guard also uses part of this general area for high-altitude military helicopter training. One group has proposed 55,389 acres be designated as wilderness. The proposal includes land that ranges in elevation from 7,200 feet to 12,000 feet. Wildlife habitat and opportunities for solitude are two reasons given for wilderness status. Ecosystems represented included sagebrush, piñon-juniper, Gambel oak shrublands, lodgepole pine, spruce-fir, and alpine. For more information, check out www.whiteriverwild.org/p-red-table-22.html.

The trail continues up to a ridge and follows the north side. Below, the town of Eagle sits in the distance, with Sylvan Lake in the foreground. Catch a breather on a level area through the trees before negotiating an interesting skinny ridge. Red boulder fields drape the ridge to the north and south. The trail is tricky here, with a slippery climb up the next ridge. As the trail enters open meadow at treeline, the views are incredible. The Maroon Bells (Maroon Peak and North Maroon Peak), Pyramid, Snowmass, and Capitol Peaks rear their 14,000-foot heads to the southwest.

The trail traverses below the ridge on the south side. After attaining the ridge again, turn right and hike to the red rock Mount Thomas summit. The rocks are the Maroon Formation, the same rocks that comprise the famous Maroon Bells near Aspen. This formation eroded from the Ancestral Rockies in western Colorado. As streams buried the sediments, a rust-like stain formed from oxidized iron particles, creating the red color. There is no official trail to the top, but it's easy to find the way. Views in every direction include the Gore Range, the Flat Tops, Mount Sopris near Carbondale, the Holy Cross Wilderness, and the peaks mentioned above. Keep an eye out for thunderstorms. The ridge is no place to be if lightning is flashing or approaching. Enjoy a picnic lunch and return the way you came!

Mount Thomas summit cairn

MILES AND DIRECTIONS

0.0   Start at the top of Crooked Creek Pass. Elevation: 9,995 feet. Walk uphill on the dirt road to the left. When the road forks, stay to the right.

0.5   At the junction with FR 431 (optional parking place), turn left and walk uphill on FR 431.

0.7   A side road heads to the right by some power lines. Turn right here and walk uphill. Follow the road as it curves left (optional parking place). The Mount Thomas Trail trailhead is on the right. GPS: N39 26.18' / W106 41.03'.

1.1   The trail enters a meadow with beautiful views of the Lime Creek drainage.

1.8   The trail starts to switchback up the ridge.

2.5   The trail crosses some meadows. Cairns mark the route.

3.1   Pass a sign at the boundary of the proposed wilderness area. GPS: N39 25.51' / W106 42.88'. The trail climbs steeply up the ridge. Red boulder fields lie on both sides of the trail.

3.5   The trail is now above treeline. It is fairly easy to find and is marked by cairns.

3.7   The trail crosses a hump on Red Table Mountain and descends a little from here. Awesome views of the Maroon Bells are to the southwest.

Maroon Bells from Mount Thomas Trail

Mount Thomas

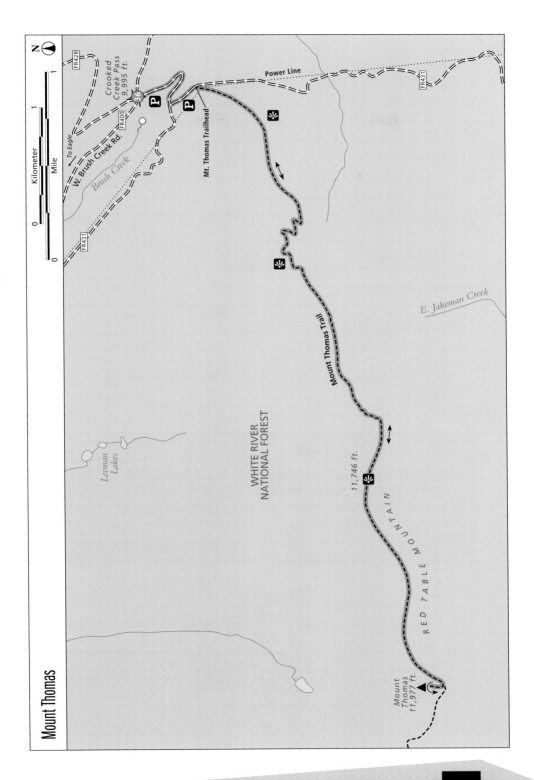

N

Kilometer
0   1   1

Mile
0   1   1

4.5   The trail leaves the ridge to traverse along the south side through a boulder field.

5.0   At a big cairn, turn right up the ridge to the summit of Mount Thomas. GPS: N39 25.11' / W106 44.63'. There's no trail, but there are some open areas between the krummholz (stunted trees) to walk on. Continue up a boulder field to the top.

5.1   Reach the Mount Thomas summit. GPS: N39 25.19' / W106 44.61'. Elevation: 11,977 feet. Return the way you came.

10.2 Arrive back at the trailhead.

HIKE INFORMATION

General Information
Eagle Valley Chamber of Commerce, Eagle; (970) 328-5220; www.eaglevalley.org

Local Events/Attractions
Sylvan Lake State Park, Eagle; (970) 328-2021; www.parks.state.co.us/parks/sylvanlake

Eagle County Historical Society's Visitor Center (museum), Eagle; (970) 328-6464

> **🌿 Green Tip:**
> *When backpacking bring a collapsible water jug to collect water from streams or lakes. Back at your campsite, pump water through your filter from the jug instead of at the water source. You'll spend less time at the water's edge, minimizing damage and lessening the effects of many footsteps in the riparian area.*

Honorable Mentions Eagle County

D. Julia's Deck

The trail to Julia's Deck is delightful and ADA accessible. Wonderful wildflowers line the gravel path, and it's easy to check out the various trees from wheelchair height or little legs. At the end of the 0.2-mile trail is an accessible wooden deck with a roof-covered bench on one end and three

benches in the middle. A gorgeous view of Mount of the Holy Cross rewards your journey. **Finding the trailhead:** From I-70 exit 190 (Shrine Pass Road/Redcliff), head toward the rest area, but then go straight onto the sometimes bumpy dirt road marked "Shrine Pass and Red Cliff (FR 709)." Drive 3.8 miles to the Mount Holy Cross Overlook sign and turn left into the little parking area with an ADA-accessible vault toilet. GPS: N39 33.59' / W106 15.39'. Elevation: 10,680 feet.

For more information, contact USDA Forest Service, Eagle-Holy Cross Ranger District, 24747 US 24, Minturn; (970) 827-5715; www.fs.usda.gov/whiteriver.

E. Gore Valley Trail

Starting by Bighorn Road at Vail's east entrance, this section of the paved Gore Valley Trail offers an easy walk along Gore Creek, past willows, aspens, lodgepole pines, and grassy meadows. Enjoy the scenery from benches and ADA-accessible picnic tables along the way. Three different turnaround points are suggested. At 0.65 mile a picnic table sits under a grove of aspen trees on the left. At 0.8 mile a little dirt, not-ADA-accessible trail heads to the right to a bench near a beaver pond. At 1.35 miles you'll arrive at a bench and a picnic table on the right. **Finding the trailhead:** From I-70 exit 180 (Vail East Entrance), drive on the south side of I-70 on Bighorn Road to the first left turn, which is trailhead parking. A bus stop

is 0.1 mile east on Bighorn Road. Walk across Bighorn Road to the paved recreation path. GPS: N39 38.58' / W106 18.42'. Elevation: 8,711 feet.

For more information, contact Town of Vail, 75 S. Frontage Rd., Vail; (970) 479-2100; www.vailgov.com.

F. Ridge Route

Ridge Route climbs steadily but easily up a ridge to Wildwood, one of Vail Ski Area's high points. Along the way you cross several ski runs filled with wildflowers underlining outstanding views of Mount of the Holy Cross and Mount Jackson. At Wildwood, enjoy the vista of the rugged Gore Range around the building's corner. Elevation: 10,982 feet. **Finding the trailhead:** From I-70 exit 176 (Vail), on the south side of I-70, turn right where the sign points to Lionshead Parking. Drive 0.3 mile to visitor parking and park. Restrooms are available on the upper level. At the southwest corner of the parking garage, walk down the stairs, cross the street, and head under the Eagle Bahn Shops arch. Turn left at the Arabelle arch.

Walk down the path and you'll see the gondola ahead. The gondola ticket office is to the left. Ride the gondola to Eagle's Nest (dogs not allowed). When you exit the gondola, turn right on the paved path and head toward the observation deck. Food and restrooms are available at Eagle's Nest. The Ridge Route trailhead is at the edge of the paved path and dirt road. Look a little to the left for the trail sign by a single-track trail—do not walk up the dirt road to the left. GPS: N39 37.06' / W106 23.19'. Elevation: 10,350 feet.

View of Mount of the Holy Cross and Mount Jackson from Ridge Route

For more information, contact Vail Mountain Information Center; (970) 754-8245; www.vail.com.

Glenwood Springs Area

Grizzly Creek and its namesake trail (hike 38)

Driving from Vail to Glenwood Springs takes you through scenic Glenwood Canyon, where I-70 was built with extreme care to protect this beautiful rock-lined passage along the Colorado River. Three tributaries have carved narrow and sometimes deep canyons into the north side. Three of the four hikes in this section explore these unique canyons.

One trail takes you up a steep, narrow canyon to the beautiful turquoise waters of Hanging Lake. Despite being a strenuous hike, climbing stone steps (complete with a handrail) up a cliff, this short trail is extremely popular. Bridal Veil Falls splash into the colorful little lake while water gushes from nearby Spouting Rock.

The hikes up Grizzly Creek and No Name Creek are sure to delight hikers, especially in spring and fall when temperatures are cooler. The endlessly cascading creeks produce a jungle of vegetation along their banks.

The fourth hike in this section takes you to an observation point across a gully from the steep slope where fourteen firefighters died when a wildfire blew up and overtook them as they tried to escape.

The Glenwood Springs area is a great place to start and end your hiking season. The lower elevations melt out sooner than the mountains around Vail and Breckenridge. They stay snow-free longer in fall as well, and with all the vegetation, the autumn colors are sure to please.

Falls, cliffs, and Hanging Lake (hike 37)

Hanging Lake

A must-see in the Glenwood Canyon area, turquoise-colored Hanging Lake nestles in a bowl amid limestone and sandstone cliffs. The trail is an extremely popular and steep climb up a narrow canyon, winding through thick vegetation and trees, passing mini-waterfalls and cascades. The final section takes you up big rock steps complete with metal handrails. A boardwalk on the south end of the lake helps to protect the fragile environment. Across the lake aptly named Bridal Veil Falls tumble down a cliff. Be sure to take a side trip to Spouting Rock, where water spouts from the side of the cliff.

Start: At the edge of the road in the Hanging Lake Rest Area near the restrooms

Distance: 3.2 miles out and back

Hiking time: 2.5 to 3 hours

Difficulty: Strenuous due to a 1,035-foot elevation gain in a short distance (over 16 percent gain from the recreation path)

Trail surface: Paved recreation path, rocky dirt trail, rock steps with handrails

Best season: May through early Oct

Other trail users: Hikers only

Canine compatibility: Dogs are prohibited

Land status: National forest and national natural landmark

Fees and permits: None required

Maps: USGS Shoshone; Nat Geo Trails Illustrated 123 Flat Tops SE/Glenwood Canyon; USFS White River National Forest map

Trail contact: USDA Forest Service, Eagle-Holy Cross Ranger District, 24747 US 24, Minturn; (970) 827-5715; www.fs.usda.gov/whiteriver

Other: Swimming, wading, soaking feet, and fishing in Hanging Lake are prohibited. Please do not walk out on the log that is in the lake! Oil from human bodies prevents deposition of travertine, which forms one edge of the lake.

Special considerations: Bring water and sturdy hiking boots. The trail is steep, rocky, and rooty. The creek is not always accessible. In summer, hike early or late to avoid the heat of mid-day. Due to the narrow canyon with steep rock walls, cell phones don't work and GPS coverage is intermittent. The trail is neither marked nor maintained for winter use. The trail is extremely icy and dangerous in the winter. Call first for trail conditions mid-Oct through Apr.

Finding the trailhead: You can only reach the Hanging Lake Rest Area from I-70 eastbound exit 125 (Hanging Lake). If you are traveling westbound on I-70, get off at exit 121 (Grizzly Creek), then get back on I-70 eastbound to exit 125. Drive 0.6 mile to the rest area parking lot (dead end). Park only in designated spaces. On busy summer days the parking lot may be full and you'll have to return another time. Illegally parked vehicles may be towed. Restrooms and water are available as well as picnic tables. GPS: N39 35.36' / W107 11.41'.

Parking is a bear in the summer. Your best bet to find a parking space is to arrive before 10 a.m. or after 4 p.m. Starting before 10 a.m. also means you'll hike during a cooler time of day, because the canyon can get hot! To avoid most parking and heat issues, hike this trail in spring before Memorial Day and in fall after Labor Day.

THE HIKE

On June 15, 2011, Secretary of the Interior Ken Salazar designated Hanging Lake as a national natural landmark. The press release stated: "The site is an outstanding example of a lake formed by travertine deposition. The lake and associated falls support a rare wetland ecosystem, including hanging gardens."

Fed by Bridal Veil Falls, Hanging Lake is a unique and beautiful turquoise color.

Hanging Lake

You could ride a bike about 3.5 miles downhill from the Bair Ranch Rest Area (exit 129) to the Hanging Lake trailhead, or uphill from either the Grizzly Creek Rest Area (exit 121) or the No Name Rest Area (exit 119).

About 340 million years ago, a shallow sea covered Colorado. As marine shellfish died, their shells fell to the bottom, were later covered by sediments, and turned into a formation called Leadville Limestone. Fast forward to 57 million years ago, when the White River Plateau was slowly uplifted. The Colorado River started carving Glenwood Canyon while its tributaries created canyons such as where you are now hiking. When a geologic fault broke, the little shelf where Hanging Lake now "hangs" dropped down from the valley above. As time marched on, calcite from the limestone formations above the lake dissolved at its edge, creating a natural dam of travertine (similar to the rims on the terraces in Mammoth Hot Springs in Yellowstone National Park). Hanging Lake exists due to the fragile travertine, so please stay on the boardwalk to prevent damaging the "dam."

As you walk along the paved Glenwood Canyon Recreation Path, think back to the 1970s when vehicles drove here on what was twisty two-lane US 6. Construction on I-70 began in 1980 and was completed in 1992. The Shoshone Power Plant and its dam, downstream of the trailhead, were built in 1906, creating the small reservoir along which you are walking. When you arrive at the start of the Hanging Lake Trail, envision Thomas F. Bailey and his family homesteading the land back in the early 1900s. In 1924 the City of Glenwood Springs purchased his land and about 760 acres of public lands including Hanging Lake. In the 1930s

Stairs on the trail below Hanging Lake

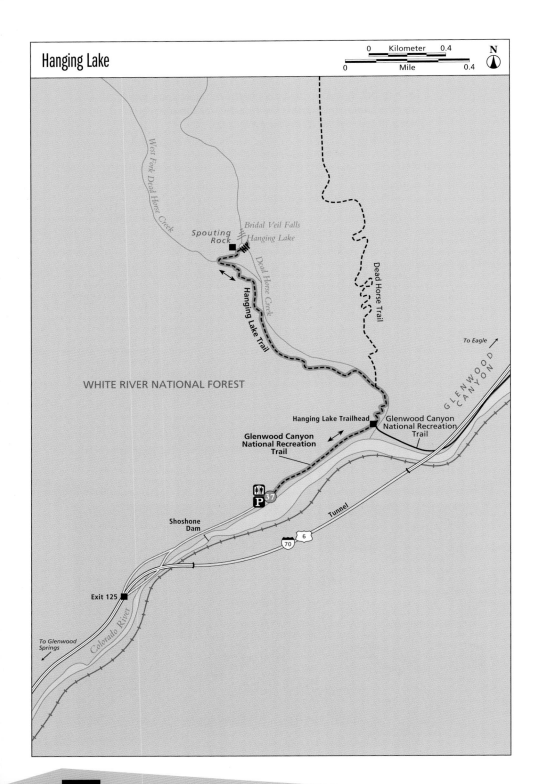

Hanging Lake

0 Kilometer 0.4
0 Mile 0.4
N

West Fork Dead Horse Creek

Bridal Veil Falls
Hanging Lake
Spouting Rock

Dead Horse Creek

Hanging Lake Trail

Dead Horse Trail

To Eagle

WHITE RIVER NATIONAL FOREST

GLENWOOD CANYON

Hanging Lake Trailhead
Glenwood Canyon National Recreation Trail

Glenwood Canyon National Recreation Trail

P 37

Shoshone Dam

Tunnel

70 6

Exit 125

To Glenwood Springs

Colorado River

> *The water gushing out of Spouting Rock comes from a spring that has worn a hole in the limestone cliff. Over the millennia, water has dissolved some of the limestone in the Glenwood Springs area, creating features such as Spouting Rock and caves. Glenwood Caverns/Fairy Caves in Glenwood Caverns Adventure Park are open to the public for tours.*

the Civilian Conservation Corps worked on the Hanging Lake Trail, building the stone shelter about 1 mile up and the seven bridges. The Hanging Lake Resort, complete with eight rental cabins, a cafe, gas station, and horses, stood near where the trail now starts. For $3, people could rent a horse and ride to the stone shelter, tether the horse, then hike the rest of the way to the lake.

At the beginning of the singletrack trail, you're walking past Precambrian bedrock (metamorphic and igneous rocks). Once you pass the 0.5-mile marker, you're hiking next to the sandstone that started as sandy beaches 500 million years ago. In between, about 1 billion years of rocks are missing! Those rocks eroded away, leaving no record.

A great variety of vegetation grows along Dead Horse Creek. The cream-colored flowers of the serviceberry bushes bloom in spring. Chokecherry, gooseberry, and golden currants grow among the Gambel oak. Tall Douglas fir and blue spruce tower above. Ferns enjoy moisture from the creek and shade from the tall cliffs. Take time to catch your breath while enjoying the little waterfalls and cascades that dance next to the trail.

After crossing bridge 7, the trail traverses along the base of a cliff and then climbs up the escarpment on big stone steps with a metal handrail at strategic places. At one turn on a stairway landing is a beautiful view down the canyon. In no time at all, you'll find yourself on the boardwalk along the edge of the beautiful Hanging Lake. Benches provide a great place for lunch with incredible views. Please follow regulations: No fishing, no swimming, no wading, no walking on the log in the lake—and please don't feed the cute ground squirrels, for they become real pests. Take a few minutes to walk up to Spouting Rock, where water literally spouts from the side of the cliff!

MILES AND DIRECTIONS

0.0 Start at the edge of the Hanging Lake Rest Area road near the restrooms. Elevation: 6,140 feet. Walk past the restrooms and head to the right to the Glenwood Canyon National Recreation Trail, then curve left.

0.4 Arrive at the Hanging Lake Trail bulletin board and picnic tables. Turn left off the recreation trail onto the dirt trail and head uphill. The mile markers start at 0.0 mile here. GPS: N39 35.56' / W107 11.05'.

0.6 Come to the junction with Dead Horse Trail (to the right). Continue straight ahead and up on the Hanging Lake Trail.

0.9 Cross bridge 3 and find the 0.5 mile marker. You're over halfway there!

1.2 Cross bridge 6 to the west side of the creek. The trail mellows a little here. A little farther is a rock shelter with benches.

1.4 Bridge 7 takes you to the east side of the creek. You'll soon come to big rock steps complete with metal handrails as you "climb" the side of the canyon to the lake.

1.6 Arrive at the junction with the trail to Spouting Rock; just ahead is Hanging Lake. GPS: N39 36.075' / W107 11.49'. Elevation: 7,175 feet. Take time to enjoy the beautiful lake and waterfalls. Return the way you came. (**Option:** On the way back, take the side trail to Spouting Rock, about 0.2 mile out and back.)

3.2 Arrive back at the trailhead.

HIKE INFORMATION

Local Information
Glenwood Springs Chamber Resort Association Visitor Center, 802 Grand Ave., Glenwood Springs; (970) 945-6589; www.glenwoodchamber.com or www.visit glenwood.com

Hanging Lake information: www.visitglenwood.com/hanging-lake

Local Events/Attractions
Strawberry Days Festival, Glenwood Springs; (970) 945-6589; www.strawberry days.com

Hot Springs Pool, 415 E. 6th St., Glenwood Springs; (970) 947-2955; www .hotspringspool.com

Glenwood Caverns Adventure Park, 51000 Two Rivers Plaza Rd., Glenwood Springs; (800) 530-1635; www.glenwoodcaverns.com

Yampah Spa (hot springs vapor caves), 709 E. 6th St., Glenwood Springs; (970) 945-0667; www.yampahspa.com

Organizations
Roaring Fork Outdoor Volunteers, 214 Midland Ave., Basalt; (970) 927-8241; www.rfov.org

The Forest Conservancy, 1012 Brookie Dr., Carbondale; (970) 963-8071; forest conservancy.com

Grizzly Creek Trail

Grizzly Creek tumbles and cascades merrily through a thick forest filled with wild-flowers and berry bushes. You can hike as far as you like while enjoying this beautiful little canyon with its limestone cliffs. The hike description takes you down to the creek across from an aqueduct that carries water from Grizzly Creek to No Name Creek and on to Glenwood Springs for drinking water.

Start: At the Grizzly Creek Trail bulletin board
Distance: 7.4 miles out and back
Hiking time: 3.5 to 5 hours
Difficulty: Difficult due to distance and a 1,820-foot elevation gain
Trail surface: Rocky dirt trail
Best season: May through early Oct
Other trail users: Equestrians
Canine compatibility: Dogs must be under control
Land status: National forest
Fees and permits: None required
Maps: USGS Glenwood Springs; Nat Geo Trails Illustrated 123 Flat Tops SE/Glenwood Canyon; USFS White River National Forest map

Trail contact: USDA Forest Service, Eagle-Holy Cross Ranger District, 125 W. 5th St., Eagle; (970) 328-6388; www.fs.usda.gov/whiteriver
Other: The canyon is narrow in places and GPSs can lose satellite connection. Cell phones don't always work.
Special considerations: Bring water because the creek is not always accessible. Berry bushes are plentiful so keep an eye out in autumn for black bears feeding to fatten up for winter. Hunters may use this area during hunting season. In summer, hike early or late to avoid the heat of mid-day.

Finding the trailhead: From I-70 exit 121 (Grizzly Creek), look for the road that crosses under I-70 to the north and is east of Grizzly Creek. A sign indicates "No Vehicles Over 21 Feet." It's straight north of the little parking lot by the boat launch. Turn north here and park. The trailhead is on the east side of Grizzly Creek just below the parking lot. GPS: N39 33.68' / W107 14.98'.

THE HIKE

Back in 1881 a wealthy game hunter reportedly shot the largest grizzly bear in western Colorado in the upper end of this canyon—hence the name Grizzly Creek. Although grizzlies lived for years in the western part of Colorado, their

Grizzly Creek

population declined dramatically after 1900. A hunting guide killed a grizzly in Colorado in 1979 in the San Juan Mountains. Today they are no longer found in the state to the best of anyone's knowledge.

In the late 1800s a little settlement called Grizzly Creek started at the mouth of the canyon. Houses, summer cottages, a gas station, and apple trees filled the little town. When construction on I-70 started back in 1980, the new highway destroyed the town, replacing it with the rest area, boat launch, and Grizzly Creek Trail parking lot.

The first part of the trail is very flat and wide, with little trails heading off to the creek. Several picnic tables provide a scenic place for a picnic. Wheelchairs can probably navigate the first 0.25 mile to enjoy a picnic by the frothy creek. Gambel oaks, rabbitbrush, Woods' roses, spruces, and big cottonwoods line the trail. A limestone cliff towers above the creek on the west side. By 0.5 mile the trail starts to climb through a landscape filled with Douglas fir, blue spruce, ponderosa pine, a variety of deciduous trees and bushes, blue violas, red columbines, alders, ferns, blue harebells, and more. The trail sometimes wanders close to the creek, but is often high above it. Raspberry plants, currant bushes, scarlet gilia, strawberries, thimbleberry bushes, white geraniums, and white pussytoes brighten your way. The trail crosses several boulder fields. During spring, at around 1.2 miles you may feel some cool air coming from rocks to the right of the trail. Ice may linger here under the rocks, and a bit of air conditioning results to cool your journey. In some places you may wish for a machete to find the trail under the thick growth of bushes. After mile 2.5 the trail climbs very steeply for 0.25 mile. After coming close to the creek, the trail starts climbing steeply again. The creek drops just as steeply, with nonstop cascades defining the term "white water."

At about 3.7 miles the trail curves left to the creek. Turn here and head to the creek. A big boulder makes a nice lunch seat and table.

With Gambel oaks, currants, and berry bushes plentiful here, keep an eye open in autumn for black bears, who madly munch as many as 20,000 calories a day to fatten up for their winter sleep. Black bears are Colorado's largest carnivores, with males weighing at least 275 pounds (and up to 450 pounds) and females about 175 pounds, and standing about 3 feet tall when on all four legs. They can be black, brown, honey-colored, cinnamon, or blond. Bears love berries and nuts, with the acorns from Gambel oaks being a staple. Bears also enjoy various grasses, insects, beetle larvae, even ants! They may kill rodents and rabbits to add some meat to their diets.

Near the beginning of Grizzly Creek Trail

38

Bears mate before denning for the winter. In midwinter a litter of one to three cubs is born in the den after two to three months gestation. They each weigh less than 1 pound and are blind and toothless, covered with very fine hair. Bears typically emerge from their dens in early to mid-May, at which time the cubs weigh around 12 pounds. Keep an eye open for mother bear with her cubs and give them wide berth. Like most mothers, bears are very protective of their young. Bears usually avoid humans and will walk or run away. If you see a bear, blow a whistle, clap your hands, or make other loud noises.

The canyon can get hot during the summer, so start early to avoid the midday heat. Enjoy your hike up a beautiful, lush canyon along a sparkling, cascading creek.

MILES AND DIRECTIONS

(*Note:* The mileage may be a little off due to loss of satellite coverage in several places along the trail.)

0.0 Start at the Grizzly Creek Trail bulletin board. Elevation: 5,900 feet.

1.1 A bench sits near the creek, which is easy to access.

2.2 Notice the interesting cribbing made of planed trees with knots still in them along the trail. GPS: N39 35.41' / W107 15.62'.

2.9 Walk through a boulder field along a level stretch of trail.

3.7 The trail curves left and heads down to Grizzly Creek. Some rocks provide a nice lunch spot. GPS: N39 36.41' / W107 16.33'. Elevation: 7,720 feet. Take time to enjoy sparkling Grizzly Creek with a view of the aqueduct. (*Note:* The trail crosses the creek here, climbs the ridge, and drops down to the Jess Weaver Trail along No Name Creek.) Return the way you came.

7.4 Arrive back at the trailhead.

HIKE INFORMATION

Local Information
Glenwood Springs Chamber Resort Association Visitor Center, 802 Grand Ave., Glenwood Springs; (970) 945-6589; www.glenwoodchamber.com or www.visit glenwood.com

Hanging Lake information: www.visitglenwood.com/hanging-lake

Local Events/Attractions
Strawberry Days Festival, Glenwood Springs; (970) 945-6589; www.strawberry days.com

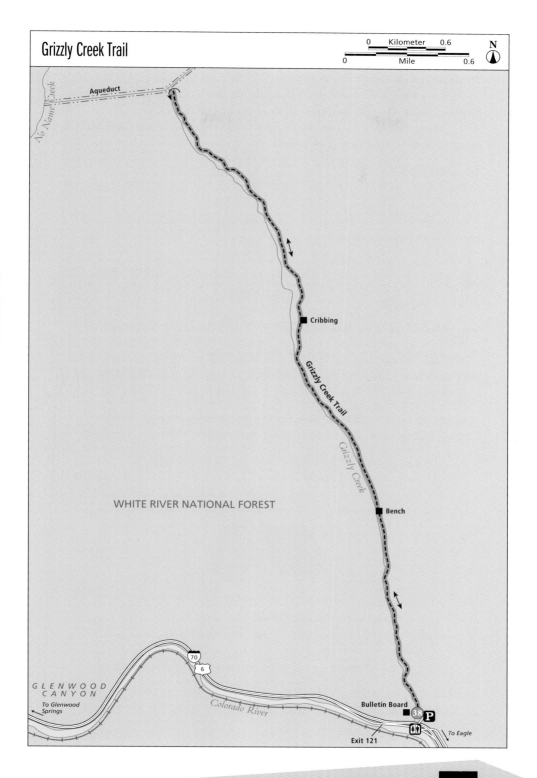

Grizzly Creek Trail

0 Kilometer 0.6
0 Mile 0.6

N

No Name Creek

Aqueduct

Cribbing

Grizzly Creek Trail

Grizzly Creek

WHITE RIVER NATIONAL FOREST

Bench

70
6

GLENWOOD
CANYON

To Glenwood
Springs

Colorado River

Bulletin Board
38
P

Exit 121

To Eagle

Hot Springs Pool, 415 E. 6th St., Glenwood Springs; (970) 947-2955; www .hotspringspool.com

Glenwood Caverns Adventure Park, 51000 Two Rivers Plaza Rd., Glenwood Springs; (800) 530-1635; www.glenwoodcaverns.com

Yampah Spa (hot springs vapor caves), 709 E. 6th St., Glenwood Springs; (970) 945-0667; www.yampahspa.com

Organizations

Roaring Fork Outdoor Volunteers, 214 Midland Ave., Basalt; (970) 927-8241; www.rfov.org

The Forest Conservancy, 1012 Brookie Dr., Carbondale; (970) 963-8071; www.forestconservancy.com

Gambel Oaks

Gambel oaks grow between 6,000 and 9,000 feet elevation in western Colorado. They also grow south of Denver along the Front Range. Other plants growing in the same ecosystem include serviceberry, snowberry, mountain mahogany, and chokecherry. Oakbrush also grows near aspen in places, and near ponderosa pine in others. In the fall the oaks produce yellow-brown acorns, which are eaten by bears, mule deer, and wild turkeys. Gambel oaks burn easily, but regrow quickly after a fire. Rarely reproducing from acorns, the oaks sprout from a deep, widespread root system. While often growing as a bush, some oakbrush can grow up to 20 feet in height. American Indians collected the acorns to make mush and thicken soups and stews.

Jess Weaver Trail

The Jess Weaver Trail follows No Name Creek through lush forest, past boulder fields beneath ancient cliffs, and along a sparkling, cascading creek. The pretty trail sometimes wanders gently along the creek and at other times climbs steeply above it. Ferns flourish in damper areas. This hike ends at the bridge that crosses No Name Creek about 3 miles up—although the trail continues. Some places may be impassable during high runoff in spring. The many deciduous trees turn gold and red in autumn, making this trail a delightful hike.

Start: At the bulletin board at the north end of the parking lot
Distance: 6.2 miles out and back
Hiking time: 3 to 4.5 hours
Difficulty: Difficult due to a 1,720-foot elevation gain and rough trail in spots
Trail surface: Dirt trail with some rocky sections
Best season: May through early Oct
Other trail users: Hikers only
Canine compatibility: Dogs must be under voice control
Land status: National forest
Fees and permits: None required
Maps: USGS Glenwood Springs; Nat Geo Trails Illustrated 123 Flat Tops SE/Glenwood Canyon; USFS White River National Forest map

Trail contact: USDA Forest Service, Rifle Ranger District, 0094 CR 244, Rifle; (970) 625-2371; www.fs.usda.gov/whiteriver
Other: The canyon is narrow in places and GPSs can lose satellite connection. Cell phones don't always work. Because No Name Creek is Glenwood Springs' water supply, no camping is allowed along the first 5 miles.
Special considerations: Berry bushes are plentiful along the trail so keep an eye out especially in autumn for black bears feeding to fatten up for winter. Hunters may use this area during hunting season. The trail is neither marked nor maintained for winter use. In summer, hike early or late to avoid the heat of mid-day.

Finding the trailhead: From I-70 exit 119 (No Name), drive north on No Name Lane for 0.5 mile to the parking lot on the left. The parking lot is very small. Please respect owners' access rights and do not block the road or their driveways. No facilities are available at the trailhead. GPS: N39 34.02' / W107 17.61'.

THE HIKE

The hike up No Name Creek on the Jess Weaver Trail offers a little of everything. The first part heads up the service road to the No Name Creek intake for Glenwood Springs' drinking water. Water flows from Grizzly Creek (in the next drainage to the east) via aqueduct to No Name Creek and then via another aqueduct, eventually reaching the water treatment plant. While you're walking up the road, look to the left for the remains of Glenwood's old wooden water flume. After the intake the trail narrows to singletrack. Gambel oak, blue spruce, cottonwood trees, Rocky Mountain juniper, thimbleberry bushes, Douglas fir, various deciduous bushes and trees, along with wildflowers, a tangle of willows, and some ferns line the trail—a canyon-style jungle.

The trail climbs gently, with occasional rocks to step over or up, and crosses several little creeks flowing down from the cliffs above (look for the waterfall near one). After the 1-mile marker (a post), the trail switchbacks up above the creek, contouring along the hillside. After the second mile the trail climbs steeply for about a quarter mile along a boulder field, followed not long after by another boulder field. The trail comes close to the creek, with a million little waterfalls splashing down the rocks. This stretch may be impassable in high water and is a bit of an obstacle course. Continue past a two-story-high boulder and through a grove of oakbrush to the bridge with handrails. On the other side you can find some good lunch spots. The creek is really pretty here, cascading down among the boulders in mini-waterfalls. The trail continues farther and intersects a trail that crosses the ridge over to the Grizzly Creek Trail to the east.

No Name Creek and Jess Weaver Trail

Jess Weaver, for whom the trail was named, lived in No Name and traveled often to his summer horse camp 10 miles up No Name Creek. He raised horses for the US Cavalry and was a champion horse-breaker. In 1978 he and his mare were swept away during high runoff while crossing the creek as he led a herd of mares to his camp. His family built a bridge at the crossing where he died.

While hiking up the trail, occasionally you get a glimpse of lighter- and darker-colored cliffs in the distance. Five hundred million years ago, Colorado straddled the equator, covered by a shallow sea. The sandy shore was compressed over millennia into sandstone, which you see stacked like thin layers in a cake in the canyon walls in parts of Glenwood Canyon. About 340 million years ago, a shallow sea again covered Colorado. As marine shellfish died, their shells fell to the bottom, were later covered by sediments, and turned into a formation called Leadville Limestone. These light-colored cliffs form the upper heights of the canyon. About 300 million years ago, as the Ancestral Rockies began to rise, marine sediments collected in basins between ranges and later turned to sandstone on top of the Leadville Limestone. Fast forward to 57 million years ago, when forces started to slowly uplift the White River Plateau. The Colorado River, already flowing along what would become the plateau's edge, started carving Glenwood Canyon while its tributaries created canyons such as No Name Creek. About 5 million years ago much of the Colorado region was uplifted 5,000 feet. Three periods of glaciation buried the high peaks in snow and glaciers. As the climate warmed and the snow and ice melted, huge floods roared down the Colorado River, eroding deeper into the canyon with the help of the uplifting land. As the Colorado eroded deeper into millennia of layers, it reached bedrock composed of Precambrian granite, formed deep in the earth by volcanic forces over 1.7 billion years ago. The hard, black rock lies in the core of the canyon.

The Jess Weaver Trail is less crowded than the Hanging Lake Trail, so enjoy the cascading creek, ancient geology, and lush vegetation in this little piece of paradise.

MILES AND DIRECTIONS

0.0 Start at the bulletin board at the north end of the parking lot. Elevation: 6,000 feet. Walk up the road to the gate and turn right onto the singletrack.

0.4 Come to a diversion dam and building. The trail turns into a singletrack here.

1.1 Come to the 1-mile marker. The trail starts to switchback soon.

2.0 Cross a nice creek near the 2-mile marker.

2.4 The trail passes between a boulder field and lush vegetation next to the creek. The trail closest to the creek is easier walking.

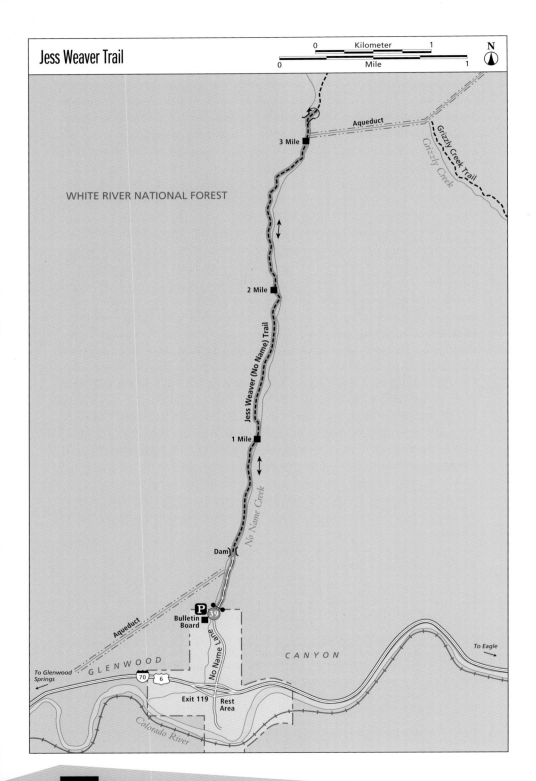

Jess Weaver Trail

2.9 The trail is very rocky and close to the creek with its many little waterfalls.

3.0 Pass the 3-mile marker.

3.1 Arrive at the bridge over No Name Creek. Enjoy your lunch and the cascading creek. GPS: N39 36.42' / W107 17.04'. Elevation: 7,720 feet. Return the way you came.

6.2 Arrive back at the trailhead.

HIKE INFORMATION

Local Information
Glenwood Springs Chamber Resort Association Visitor Center, 802 Grand Ave., Glenwood Springs; (970) 945-6589; www.glenwoodchamber.com or www.visit glenwood.com

Hanging Lake information: www.visitglenwood.com/hanging-lake

Local Events/Attractions
Strawberry Days Festival, Glenwood Springs; (970) 945-6589; www.strawberry days.com

Hot Springs Pool, 415 E. 6th St., Glenwood Springs; (970) 947-2955; www .hotspringspool.com

Glenwood Caverns Adventure Park, 51000 Two Rivers Plaza Rd., Glenwood Springs; (800) 530-1635; www.glenwoodcaverns.com

Yampah Spa (hot springs vapor caves), 709 E. 6th St., Glenwood Springs; (970) 945-0667; www.yampahspa.com

Organizations
Roaring Fork Outdoor Volunteers, 214 Midland Ave., Basalt; (970) 927-8241; www.rfov.org

The Forest Conservancy, 1012 Brookie Dr., Carbondale; (970) 963-8071; www.forestconservancy.com

> *A little town started at the mouth of what is now called No Name Creek in the early 1880s. Residents couldn't decide what to call their little town when they filled out a state form for the town site name. They entered "no name" on the form. The state officially named the town No Name and the creek became No Name Creek.*

Storm King Memorial Trail

This trail, built by volunteers, is a memorial to fourteen firefighters who lost their lives in a wildfire on Storm King Mountain in July 1994. Interpretive signs explain wild-land firefighting and this unfortunate disaster. At the observation point you can look across to the ridge where the firefighters died. The trail is a journey into a once burned land, now recovering. You'll gain a brief insight into and feeling for the work of the men and women who fight wildland fires.

Start: At the Storm King Memorial Trail trailhead
Distance: 2.0 miles out and back
Hiking time: 1.5 to 2 hours
Difficulty: Difficult due to a 680-foot elevation gain in 1 mile
Trail surface: Dirt trail mainly on south- and southwest-facing slopes
Best season: Apr to Nov
Other trail users: Hikers only
Canine compatibility: Dogs must be on leash
Land status: Bureau of Land Management
Fees and permits: None required

Maps: USGS Storm King Mountain; Nat Geo Trails Illustrated 123 Flat Tops SE/Glenwood Canyon; BLM Colorado Glenwood Springs map
Trail contact: Bureau of Land Management, Colorado River Valley Field Office, 2300 River Frontage Rd., Silt; (970) 876-9000; www .blm.gov/co/st/en/fo/crvfo.html
Special considerations: Bring water with you, as none is available along the trail. Hunters may use this area in season. Call first for trail conditions Dec through Mar. In summer, hike early or late to avoid the heat of mid-day.

Finding the trailhead: Take I-70 west to exit 109 (Canyon Creek). Turn right then immediately right again onto the frontage road. Drive back east past Canyon Creek Estates 1 mile to a dead end with a parking lot. The trail starts by several interpretive signs at the east end of the lot. A portable toilet is available at the trailhead, but no water. GPS: N39 34.43' / W107 26.07'.

THE HIKE

On July 2, 1994, a very natural event occurred. A lightning strike started a small fire in a piñon-juniper-Gambel oak forest on Storm King Mountain (8,793 feet). Several large wildland fires were already burning across Colorado, strapping fire-fighting resources. The small fire received low priority. By July 5, the fire covered 5 acres, and crews arrived to build fire lines. But Mother Nature had other plans. The fire grew to 50 acres and crossed one fire line. By mid-afternoon on July 6,

View of Observation Point and the fire line

fifty firefighters were trying to control the blaze. A dry cold front passed through the region causing very strong winds, which fanned the fire into a roaring inferno traveling much faster than any human could run, especially uphill. The fire soon consumed over 2,100 acres. Fourteen firefighters could not escape the 100-foot-high flames racing toward them. Thirty-six others escaped either by hunkering down in their fire shelters or by slipping down an eastern gully to the highway.

Although forest fire is a natural and important process, a fire on Storm King Mountain could endanger homes and businesses in West Glenwood to the east

Primitive trail to the memorial sites

Two Rivers Park

Two Rivers Park in Glenwood Springs contains a memorial to the fourteen firefighters who died on Storm King Mountain. A bronze sculpture depicting three wildland firefighters is surrounded by a garden, pictures, and information about each of the fourteen firefighters.

To reach Two Rivers Park from Storm King Memorial Trail, take I-70 eastbound. Exit at West Glenwood and turn left under the highway, then turn right onto US 6 eastbound. Go 1.8 miles to Devereux Drive and turn right. Drive 0.3 mile, crossing over I-70, and look for the park on the left. Turn left into the park. The memorial garden is straight ahead.

John N. McLean captured the story of the Storm King Mountain Fire (mistakenly reported as being in South Canyon) in the book Fire on the Mountain, *published by William Morrow and Company, Inc. in 1999. The History Channel produced a documentary,* Fire on the Mountain, *in 2002.*

or Canyon Creek Estates to the west. The trees on Storm King also provided essential erosion control. Storm King and surrounding mountains are a combination of red sandstone and shale, called the Maroon Formation, deposited over millennia by inland seas. When shale gets wet, mudslides often result. With I-70 downslope, a mudslide could cause a major travel and supply line disruption.

Volunteers built this trail in 1995 to honor wildland firefighters nationwide and to provide an insight into their experiences. The trail begins with several interpretive signs about the July 1994 fire. They invite you to imagine being a firefighter, hiking up steep slopes, and carrying 30 to 60 pounds of equipment.

The trail climbs steeply along the south side of a ridge, through rabbitbrush, wild roses, Mormon tea, and cheatgrass, with numerous log steps to hike up. Where the trail turns to follow the west side of a ridge, a small sign relates the camaraderie of firefighters and gives you a chance to take a few deep breaths. The Colorado River roars below, as does the traffic on I-70. The trail continues to climb through piñon-juniper forest. The steepness of the trail is tiring even with a light pack. About 0.25 mile up, a sign announces entry into lands managed by the Bureau of Land Management (BLM). Switchbacks take you steadily uphill. A bench provides a handy place to check out the western view and catch your breath again. Down in the valley, I-70 twists like a serpent, following the river's contours. The Grand Hogback and Coal Ridge form the horizon to the south.

At 0.6 mile the trail reaches a ridge at 6,280 feet. Storm King Mountain with scorched sticks and green Gambel oak comes into view. You can see how the fire raced up gullies to different ridges. The trees to the right of the trail are blackened snags of their former selves. To the left, most trees are green and alive. Narrow-leaved penstemon and blue flax flowers grow among the ghostly trunks. Across the gully, Gambel oak once again covers the slopes, although junipers and piñon pines may take forty to one hundred years to reestablish themselves.

The trail follows a mostly flat ridge 0.4 mile to the observation point. Three large interpretive signs explain the events of that fateful July day. You can see the slope that twelve firefighters scrambled up trying to reach safety. Nine members of the Prineville (Oregon) Hotshot crew and three smokejumpers died there when quickly moving flames engulfed them. With a pair of binoculars, look closely for the pair of crossed skis marking one memorial site. Farther to the left

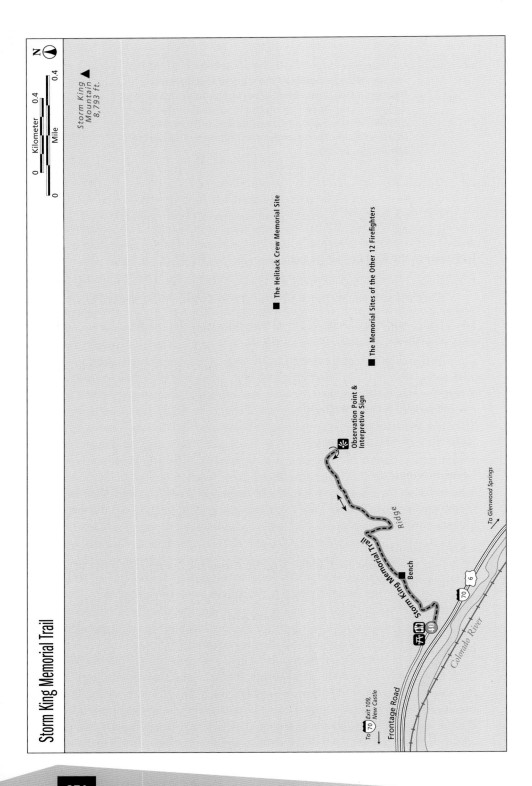

Storm King Memorial Trail

N

0   Kilometer   0.4

0   Mile   0.4

Storm King Mountain ▲
8,793 ft.

■ The Helitack Crew Memorial Site

■ The Memorial Sites of the Other 12 Firefighters

Observation Point &
Interpretive Sign

Ridge

Storm King Memorial Trail

Bench

To Glenwood Springs

70 6

Colorado River

*To Exit 109,
New Castle*

Frontage Road

near a rock outcropping is the site where two helitack crewmembers died. Look around, see and feel the steepness of the slopes. Imagine what it would be like to have a fire chasing you up that hill. Be thankful for the people who gave their lives to protect the lives and property of others.

40

MILES AND DIRECTIONS

0.0 Start at the trailhead east of Canyon Creek Estates. Elevation: 5,680 feet. Take a few minutes to read the interpretive signs. (**Note:** The first part of the trail crosses private property on an easement. Please respect the owners' property.)

0.25 Reach the BLM boundary sign.

0.3 Reach a bench and interpretive sign on the right side of the trail, a good place to catch your breath and enjoy the view down the Colorado River.

0.6 Gain a ridge with views of Storm King Mountain and the area that burned in 1994. GPS: N39 34.52' / W107 25.68'.

1.0 Arrive at the observation point with interpretive signs. GPS: N39 34.68' / W107 25.38'. Elevation: 6,360 feet. Return the way you came.

2.0 Arrive back at the trailhead.

HIKE INFORMATION

Local Information
Glenwood Springs Chamber Resort Association Visitor Center, 802 Grand Ave., Glenwood Springs; (970) 945-6589; www.glenwoodchamber.com or www.visit glenwood.com

Local Events/Attractions
Glenwood Hot Springs Pool, 401 N. River St., Glenwood Springs; (970) 947-2955; www.hotspringspool.com

Glenwood Caverns Adventure Park, 51000 Two Rivers Plaza Rd., Glenwood Springs; (800) 530-1635; www.glenwoodcaverns.com

Strawberry Days Festival, Glenwood Springs; (970) 945-6589; www.straw berrydays.com

Appendix A: Clubs and Trail Groups

CLUBS

Colorado Mountain Club, State Office, 710 10th St., #200, Golden; (303) 279-3080; www.cmc.org

Gore Range Group (serves Summit County and Vail area); www.cmc.org/About/CMCGroups/GoreRange.aspx

TRAIL GROUPS (EDUCATION, TRAIL MAINTENANCE, ADVOCACY)

Colorado Fourteeners Initiative, 1600 Jackson St., Ste. 352, Golden; (303) 278-7650; www.14ers.org

Colorado Trail Foundation, 710 10th St., #210, Golden; (303) 384-3729; www.coloradotrail.org

The Forest Conservancy, 1012 Brookie Dr., Carbondale; (970) 963-8071; www.forestconservancy.com

Friends of the Dillon Ranger District, PO Box 1648, Silverthorne 80498; (970) 262-3449; www.fdrd.org

Friends of the Eagles Nest Wilderness, PO Box 4504, Frisco 80443; contact Dillon Ranger District at (970) 468-5400 for the current contact.

Roaring Fork Outdoor Volunteers, PO Box 1341, Basalt 81623; (970) 927-8241; www.rfov.org

Volunteers for Outdoor Colorado, 600 S. Marion Pkwy., Denver; (303) 715-1010; www.voc.org

Appendix B: Further Reading

COLORADO HISTORIC NEWSPAPER COLLECTION

For very interesting reading, check out Colorado's Historic Newspaper Collection online at www.coloradohistoricnewspapers.org. Newspapers published in various Colorado towns and cities between about 1859 and 1923 have been scanned. You can search on a topic, pick an appropriate newspaper(s), and see the world through the writer's eyes in the actual format of yesteryear. Information from old newspapers was obtained from this collection for this hiking guide.

History

Aldrich, John K. *Ghosts of Summit County: A Guide to the Ghost Towns and Mining Camps of Summit County, Colorado.* Denver, CO: Columbine Ink, LLC, 2009.

Burnett, Bill. *Minturn, A Memoir.* Gypsum, CO: The Old Bypsum Printer, Inc./Wings Publishing, 2007.

Clarke, Charlotte. *The Mines of Frisco: A Self-Guided Tour.* Self-published, 2004.

Clawson, Janet Marie. *Echoes of the Past: Copper Mountain, Colorado.* Denver, CO: Waldo Litho, 1986.

Fiester, Mark. *Blasted Beloved Breckenridge.* Boulder, CO: Pruett Publishing Co., 1973.

Fountain, Bill, and Sandra F. Mather PhD. *Chasing the Dream: The Search for Gold in French Gulch Breckenridge, Colorado.* Breckenridge, CO: Breckenridge Heritage Alliance, 2012.

———. *Breckenridge: 150 Years of Golden History.* Silverthorne, CO: Alpenrose Press, 2009.

———. *Frisco! A Colorful Colorado Community.* Silverthorne, CO: Alpenrose Press, 1984.

Gilliland, Mary Ellen. *Summit: A Gold Rush History of Summit County, Colorado, 25th Anniversary Edition.* Silverthorne, CO: Alpenrose Press, 2006.

Knight, MacDonald B, and Leonard Hammock. *Early Days on the Eagle.* Publisher unknown, 1953.

Marx, Seth H. *Mountain Vision: The Making of Beaver Creek.* Publisher: Beaver Creek Resort Company, Peter Cummins and Jean Dennison. Printer: Knudsen Printing, year unknown.

Mather, Sandra F., PhD, and the Frisco Historic Park & Museum. *Frisco and the Ten Mile Canyon.* Charleston, SC: Arcadia Publishing, 2011.

Mather, Sandra F., PhD, and the Summit Historical Society. *Images of America: Summit County.* Charleston, SC: Arcadia Publishing, 2008.

McGregor, Heather. *A Guide to Glenwood Canyon.* Glenwood Springs, CO: Pika Publishing Co., 1993.

McLean, John N. *Fire on the Mountain.* New York, NY: Harper Perennial (reprint edition), 2009.

Pritchard, Sandra F. *Dillon—Denver and the Dam.* Dillon, CO: Summit Historical Society, 1994.

———. *Roadside Summit: Part I, The Natural Landscape.* Dillon, CO: Summit Historical Society, 1988.

———. *Roadside Summit: Part II, The Human Landscape.* Dillon, CO: Summit Historical Society, 1992.

Roberts, Jack. *The Amazing Adventures of Lord Gore: A True Saga from the Old West.* Silverton, CO: Sundance, 1977.

Simonton, June B. *Beaver Creek: The First One Hundred Years.* Publisher unknown, 1984.

Welch, Shirley, and the Eagle County Historical Society. *Images of America: The Eagle River Valley.* Charleston, SC: Arcadia Publishing, 2008.

Natural History

Gellhorn, Joyce G. *Song of the Alpine: The Rocky Mountain Tundra through the Seasons.* Boulder, CO: Johnson Books, 2002.

Guennel, G. K. *Guide to Colorado Wildflowers, Volume 2: Mountains.* Englewood, CO: Westcliffe Publishers, 2004.

Hopkins, Ralph Lee, and Lindy Birkel. *Hiking Colorado's Geology.* Seattle, WA: The Mountaineers, 2000.

Matthews, Vincent, PhD, Katie Keller Lynn, and Betty Fox, eds. *Messages in Stone: Colorado's Colorful Geology.* Denver, CO: Colorado Department of Natural Resources: Colorado Geological Society, 2003. Printed in Canada.

Nelson, Mike. *The Colorado Weather Almanac.* Boulder, CO: Johnson Books, 2007.

Zwinger, Ann H., and Beatrice E. Willard. *Land Above the Trees: A Guide to the American Alpine Tundra.* Boulder, CO: Johnson Books, 1996.

About the Author

A native of Colorado, Maryann Gaug was born in Denver and spent much of her youth dreaming about living in the mountains. While working on a BS degree in mathematics at Gonzaga University in Spokane, Washington, she started backpacking and downhill skiing. Missing the mountains of Colorado, Maryann returned and earned an MS in computer science at the University of Colorado Boulder. The Boulder Group of the Colorado Mountain Club and their mountaineering school provided new friends and a great education on enjoying Colorado's mountains. Between the Colorado Mountain Club and the Rocky Flats Mountaineering

Maryann Gaug

Group, Maryann continued to hike, backpack, backcountry ski, and otherwise love doing mountain-oriented activities.

After twenty years at Rocky Flats, Maryann took a voluntary separation plan and moved to Silverthorne, Colorado. Her initial mountain life included working as a cross-country ski instructor at Copper Mountain Resort, completing a Wilderness Studies Certificate at Colorado Mountain College and becoming a master of Leave No Trace. Maryann also started following another dream: to write about the mountains and canyons that she loves. Her articles—ranging from her outdoor adventures to natural history—have been published in several Summit County newspapers and the e-zine *Cyberwest*. Writing *Best Hikes Near Breckenridge and Vail* is her latest adventure. Her other books include *Hiking Colorado, Best Hikes Near Denver and Boulder, Best Easy Day Hikes Vail*, and *Hiking Colorado's Summit County Area*. For more information and updates, check out www.facebook.com/HikingColoradoGuides and www.falcon.com/author/maryann-gaug.

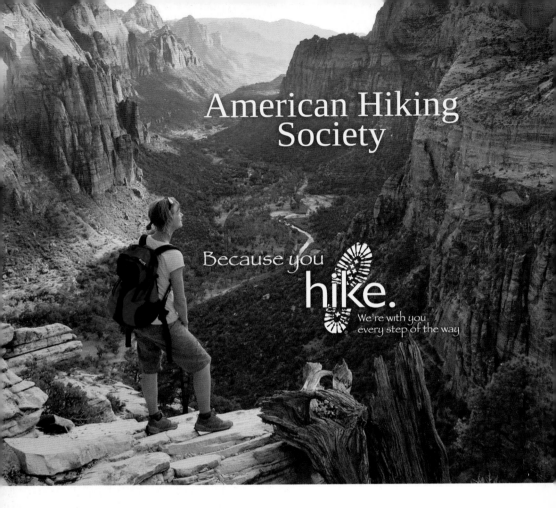

American Hiking Society

Because you
hike.
We're with you
every step of the way

As a national voice for hikers, **American Hiking Society** works every day:

- Building and maintaining hiking trails
- Educating and supporting hikers by providing information and resources
- Supporting hiking and trail organizations nationwide
- Speaking for hikers in the halls of Congress and with federal land managers

Whether you're a casual hiker or a seasoned backpacker, become a member of American Hiking Society and join the national hiking community! You'll enjoy great member benefits and help preserve the nation's hiking trails, so tomorrow's hike is even better than today's. We invite you to join us now!

American Hiking Society